reel
arguments

Related Reading from Westview Press

The Naked and the Undead
By Cynthia Freeland

Unlikely Couples
By Thomas Wartenberg

More Than a Movie
By F. Miguel Valenti, Foreword by Peter Bogdanovich

Visions of Virtue in Popular Film
By Joseph Kupfer

What Is Non-Fiction Cinema?
By Trevor Ponech

Screening the Sacred
By Joel W. Martin and Conrad E. Ostwalt, Jr.

reel
arguments

Film,

Philosophy,

and

Social

Criticism

ANDREW LIGHT

Westview
PRESS

A Member of the Perseus Books Group

Copyright © 2003 by Westview Press, A Member of the Perseus Books Group

Westview Press books are available at special discounts for bulk purchases in the United States by corporations, institutions, and otherorganizations. For more information, please contact the Special Markets Department at the Perseus Books Group, 11 Cambridge Center, Cambridge MA 02142, or call (617) 252–5298 or (800)255-1514 or e-mail j.mccrary@perseusbooks.com.

Published in 2003 in the United States of America by Westview Press, 5500 Central Avenue, Boulder, Colorado 80301–2877

Find us on the World Wide Web at www.westviewpress.com

Library of Congress Cataloging-in-Publication Data
Light, Andrew, 1966-
    Reel arguments : film, philosophy, and social criticism / Andrew Light.
       p. cm.-- (Thinking through cinema)
    Includes bibliographical reference and index.
    ISBN 0-8133-6573-2 (pbk. : alk. paper); (0-8133-6486-4 (hc)
    1. Motion pictures--Social aspects. 2. Motion pictures--Moral and ethical aspects. I. Title. II. Series.
PN1995.9.S6 L54 2002
302.23"43--dc21

                                                                          2002015343

The paper used in this publication meets the requirements of the American National Standard for Permanence of Paper for Printed Library Materials Z39.48–1984.

10   9   8   7   6   5   4   3   2   1

For Eric, Susan, Emma, Ani, and Jonah
La mia seconda famiglia

Contents

Acknowledgments

I am very grateful to numerous friends and colleagues who have provided critical comments on earlier versions of these chapters, in particular, Amelia Amon, Yoko Arisaka, Davis Baird, Murray Baumgarten, Michael Bennett, Albert Borgmann, Allen Carlson, Melissa Clarke, Avner de-Shalit, Ed Dimendberg, Andrew Feenberg, Larry Hickman, Doug Kellner, Michael Kohler, Bill Lawson, Bernd Magnus, Jonathan Maskit, Patrick Maynard, Carl Mitcham, Carole Pateman, Joe Pitt, David Rothenberg, Jim Sheppard, Jonathan Smith, Lisa Stefanoff, Bob Stone and David Strauss, Julia Voss, Bob Stone and Camille Watts. I would also like to thank my Spring 1999 film and philosophy students at SUNY Binghamton, several anonymous readers who originally refereed some of these chapters as journal articles, and those who reviewed the proposal for this collection. Katherine Streckfus, my copy editor, provided many suggestions that improved the manuscript.

Several audiences heard earlier versions of these chapters, and I learned much from every response to those presentations. I am particularly indebted to Michael O'Rourke, Daniel Bukvich, Rick Fehrenbacher, and other faculty participating in the May 2000 McCall, Idaho, workshop on humanities and technology sponsored by the University of Idaho's Humanities Fellows Program, and the subsequent "Tools Symposium," held a year later at the University of Idaho in Moscow. The invitation to work with this group was invaluable in helping me to rethink many of the core concepts in the first part of the book.

At NYU I have the good fortune to be housed in a school and a department that is supportive of departures from my normal topics in applied philosophy. My thanks to all of my colleagues in the Department of Humanities and Social Sciences in the Professions in the Steinhardt School of Education, and others in the Department of Culture and Communication and in the Department of Philosophy, for encouraging me as I was preparing this manuscript, especially Rene Arcilla, Richard Arum, Joy

Boyum, Tom Hilde, Tom James, Helen Nissenbaum, John Richardson, Bill Ruddick, Charles Sprague, Jon Zimmerman, and in particular dear friends Jonathan Burston, Sue Murray, and Aurora Wallace, who in very different ways somehow got me through the final stretch.

Finally, I especially wish to thank Nöel Carroll for providing guiding inspiration in this field and for personally encouraging me to continue with this work; my editor at Westview Press, Sarah Warner, for her excellent advice on every part of the manuscript, and especially for her supererogatory patience; and Dorit Naaman and Tom Wartenberg, who, more than anyone else, sharpened my take on these topics, prodded me to continue, served as role models as keen film critics themselves, and offered warm and friendly advice. Though these two colleagues and friends are certainly not responsible for the many flaws that may remain in this book, it would not exist without either of them.

I have dedicated this book to the Barbash-Katz family, Eric, Susan, Emma, Ani, and Jonah. My own parents, grandmother, brother, and sister have never failed in their unwavering support for me, no matter what strange pathways and far-flung roads I have taken. I am twice as fortunate though as those with one loving family to have a second as well, composed of these dearest friends, along with their parents and extended families, who have been there for me during some of the most important moments of my adult life. I am not always certain what I bring to their lives, but to me they make humanity more admirable, and the world more beautiful.

A few of these chapters have been adapted from previously published material, though substantially revised and expanded so that the most work in this book appears here for the first time. Nonetheless, the following chapters originated in earlier papers: Chapter 3, from "Wim Wenders and the Everyday Aesthetics of Technology and Space," *Journal of Aesthetics and Art Criticism* 55, no. 2 (Spring 1997), pp. 215–229; Chapter 4, from "Boyz in the Woods: Urban Wilderness in American Cinema," in Michael Bennett and David Teague, eds., *The Nature of Cities: Ecocriticism and Urban Environments* (Tucson: University of Arizona Press, 1999), pp. 137–156; and Chapter 6, which includes material from both "Media, Identity, and Politics: A Critique of Kellner," *Research in Philosophy and Technology* 17 (1998), pp. 187–200, and "What Is an Ecological Identity?" *Environmental Politics* 9, no. 4 (2000), pp. 59–81, Andrew Light, New York City, August 2002.

1
Introduction:
Film as Social Philosophy

As is true of many philosophers, my relationship with my discipline has often taken the form of a love affair, and as with many such relationships, it hasn't always been a good one.

For me, the first true heartbreak occurred during my second year in graduate school when I was struggling through a paper on Kant's *Critique of Pure Reason*. I'll never forget the feeling I had, sweating out a Riverside, California, springtime in a friend's unair-conditioned bungalow, trying to make sense of Kant's often impenetrable text. More than once I thought that the best way to get through this assignment would have just been to quit school. As my mind wandered to other career paths I hit upon the next move—I'd become a filmmaker! Perhaps it was the heat, but I knew that if anything could tempt me away from philosophy, it had to be film. Although certainly not the most practical career path, film had always been the most moving of art forms for me, and a romantic dream of becoming an artist of some kind often tempts a young mind despite limited artistic talents. Besides, I thought, if I wanted to go to film school, I wouldn't have to move too far away.

But I persisted with philosophy and never seriously pursued the study of film, either in its theory or practice. What did not occur to me then, but which is in some sense the theme of all of the chapters in this volume, is that film and philosophy, while surely two different career paths, are more closely related than one might think. In the episode just related, film stood as an escape for me, an exotic fling as it were, away from philosophical reflection. But the potential of film is so much more than escape. Film may also be a medium that introduces us to several important topics in philosophy, and we can actively watch films through the framework of philosophical interests.[1] This is not to say that the importance of film is reducible to its relation to philosophy, but more accurately, that the analysis of many philosophical topics is considerably helped along by looking at the films and filmmakers who have produced substantial works on these same themes.

Some readers may find such a point so obvious as not to be worth mentioning. But I expect that others will be skeptical, and in part the purpose of this book is to try to mitigate such doubts by offering several examples of the substantive relationship between philosophy and film. To be certain, some films appear to be explicitly philosophical at face value, such as Louis Malle's *My Dinner with Andre* (1981), Bernt Amadeus Capra's *Mindwalk* (1990), and Derek Jarman's *Wittgenstein* (1993). But many philosophers might view such films as either not really being philosophical, and actually belonging to some other species of intellectual exercise, or else might find the philosophy that is in them very bad—some of it no doubt is. But the vast majority of films do not offer themselves as interlocutors on philosophical topics in an obvious way. I find the process of discovering the philosophical potential in films to be much more challenging and enriching when the films are ostensibly about something other than philosophy.

For the past eight years I have been working steadily in three areas of philosophy: environmental ethics, social and political philosophy, andphilosophy of technology. But because of the connections I see between philosophy, film, and social issues (which I will briefly relay in this chapter), I have produced a number of papers on film. For this book, I decided to overhaul them completely and write several new chapters. As a result of working on this project, I am even more convinced than I was before that many films offer a unique view on a variety of philosophical topics. This approach to film and philosophy is not only interesting in and of itself but also highly useful in the classroom for helping to stimulate discussions of philosophy.

What follows then in this volume is not intended as a book-length argument. Each of these chapters may stand alone, though I have thoroughly revised all of them, previously published or not, so as to draw their conclusions closer together. I have added a good deal of new material, so that the vast majority of this work appears here for the first time. The reader will find, however, a great deal of variety in the style, scope, and detail of these essays, and in their balance between attention to film and philosophy. In addition, some chapters focus on multiple films, others on one, and one mostly on a handful of scenes. Still, despite this variety, I believe that the result, as a whole, is a set of philosophical distinctions and readings of various films that are unique and that may inspire others to think about both film and philosophy in new ways. In what follows in this chapter I will make one case for the skeptical reader of the utility of bringing philosophy and film closer together. Those not worried about such things may wish to skip directly to the substantive discussions of particular films in the chapters themselves.

Why Philosophy and Film?

Even if the charitable reader finds my arguments in these chapters valuable it is certainly true that I am not the first philosopher to see that film has substantial and useful philosophical content. I come to this conclusion relatively late in the game of philosophical reflection on film, and I have been inspired by those who have already explained those connections in both theory and interpretation, including Stanley Cavell, Nöel Carroll, and Thomas Wartenberg. Increasingly, philosophers from a broad range of backgrounds are turning to film in their professional work. They are using it to inspire classroom discussions, have formed professional societies and conferences highlighting film and philosophy as interconnected fields, and have begun to publish professional journals on the topic, such as *Film and Philosophy*. This Westview Press series, "Thinking Through Cinema," has already published several works that look at the philosophical underpinnings of film. This interest is also encouraging more philosophers to follow the professional activities and journals of film theorists (such as *Cinema Journal*) than in the past.

But even observing all of this activity, this last observation about the broader community of film theorists raises one of the persistent questions I've had since I started writing on film: What does it mean for a philosopher to work on film? Are we just doing film studies in philosophy departments or is there something else to it of value? Philosophers have long developed areas of "applied philosophy," extending philosophical tools to the understanding of a variety of problems in the world, and there are particular subfields of philosophy devoted to such specific endeavors as economics, archaeology, biology, and chemistry. Often there is at least a minimal relationship between philosophy and these fields of inquiry that goes something like this: Philosophers set out to understand what is going on in another field of inquiry and then argue that there are particular problems that arise in that field that a philosophical analysis is in a uniquely good position to comment upon. It might be, for example, that archaeologists are not in as good a position as philosophers to recognize intrinsic ethical and methodological questions that arise in connection with the practice of archaeology. If that case can be made, then we can take the position that the conversation over resolving those questions ought not to happen without the contribution of a philosopher.

But is the same true of the relationship between film and philosophy? I believe that it is not; rather, the field of philosophy and film is more like the related field of philosophy and literature. Many philosophers writing in this area would deny that it is their job to read tomes of literary criticism about some author in order to bring out the connections between a literary text and philosophical questions. They may think that literary texts are already sufficiently philosophical that a philosopher can engage in such analyses without the mediation of literary criticism (I take it that this is part of Richard Rorty's approach). Others might say that regardless of the merits of responding to the work of literary critics, a philosopher can nevertheless respond to the text directly, thus spending the time necessary to bring out philosophical lessons that literary criticism misses (I take this as part of Martha Nussbaum's approach).[2] The interaction between philosophers and literary critics can come in at times during the interpretation of a text but is something that more likely will happen after the philosophical work has been done. Then, the different interpretations, where they are found to be necessarily incommensurable, can clash with each other.

So, while it could be argued that the best philosophers of literature are those that devote themselves to understanding and interacting with their colleagues in other departments looking at the same texts, it surprises no one that philosophy departments offer courses on literature or that philosophers write on these same texts without always interacting with their colleagues across campus. Perhaps they should, but they don't have to in every case because there is so much more to these texts than any one field can lay claim to by itself. In other words, the texts can inspire numerous kinds of intellectual insights. The same may be true for philosophers teaching and writing about film.[3]

But the question then remains as to what philosophy brings to the understanding of film that other academic fields do not? Is it just that films are a convenient way to stimulate philosophical discussions, in the same way that some of them could be used to stimulate questions in sociology, evolutionary biology, or quantum mechanics? Certainly, the work of particular philosophers on film must justify itself. The leaders of this small field may well be those who interact with film theorists the most, though that cannot be a hard and fast rule. After all, many others in the academy who wind up writing on substantive philosophical topics also borrow ideas for a time to be applied to another field of inquiry without interacting fully with the critical literature on that topic. The reason is usually that one hopes to make a contribution to another end; the application of the ideas occurs with the realization that almost every idea and every text worth talking about is being actively debated and discussed by a larger audience. This amounts to a justified excuse in the limits of what we all do with each other's work.

Still, others who have made a substantial contribution to the connection between philosophy and film have offered reasons why philosophers should develop their own path toward understanding film that is separate from the techniques developed by many film theorists. Thanks to Carroll's work, for example, I understand that I take a cognitive, as opposed to a psychoanalytic, approach to philosophy and film. Carroll takes psychoanalytic criticism to be the dominant paradigm for understanding film among film theorists; the contribution of philosophers to this field of inquiry is to work with film theorists to provide an alternative to psychoanalytic approaches.[4] But cognitive film theorists and philosophers do not conform to a single methodology. Cognitivists range from a variety of empiricists, including those interested in the actual application of the lessons of cognitive science to the understanding of, for example, visual narratology, to those interested more in the development of rational reconstructions of the philosophical importance of films.

I do not develop my own cognitive theory in this book, though my interest in cognitive approaches informs these essays. Someday I would like to write more directly on such matters and defend the claim that some films can be interpreted as visual arguments (as those arguments are discussed in the literature on informal logic and practical reasoning), which are both like and not like other visual arguments, such as paintings and editorial cartoons, an account defended by philosophers such as Leo Groarke.[5] This might be a better answer to the question of what philosophers could bring to an understanding of film, but it would take a book to prosecute such an approach and I don't do it here, nor do I rely on such a view in any of these chapters. For while throughout this book, like Carroll, I will often discuss the "claims" and "arguments" of films, in this instance I'm using those terms in a more ordinary, everyday sense.[6]

My answer for now about the larger question of what philosophy brings to film is therefore that some films already have a substantial enough philosophical content to independently justify what philosophers have been doing in this area. It is the job of the philosopher, along with other readers of film, to bring out these connections. The easiest way to find out if those connections exist is to try to do just that, and I hope that is what I have accomplished in this book. Still, there are some general things to be said about why we should look to film for philosophical inspiration.

Film and Social Philosophy

At the start I said we can come to philosophy through film just as we can approach film through the orientation of philosophy. The reason is that one of the characteristics of many films is that they must represent people in a way that weighs in on some of the fundamental questions of social philosophy. But what are those questions?

Jan Narveson has argued that social philosophy, broadly speaking, is the "philosophy of society," including the main components of a philosophy of social science but also the conceptual study of society more generally. It is that part of moral philosophy that "concerns social action and individual involvement with society in general." We could add to that description many areas of political philosophy as well as the social dimensions of more narrowly defined philosophical subfields, such as the philosophy of technology, environmental philosophy, and other areas of applied ethics.[7] According to Narveson, one of the major methodological questions in social philosophy is between some version of "holism" and "individualism." The former holds that some "social groups may be studied as units, irreducible to their members," while the latter "denies that societies are 'organisms,' and holds that we can understand society only in that way."[8]

Narveson was quick to point out, however, that most work in this area is a combination of holism and individualism. I certainly agree. I started my philosophical career more enamored with some version of holism, later drifted closer to individualism, and now hold a modified view somewhere in between the two poles depending on the particular subject that I'm addressing. Those considerations aside, it seems to me that regardless of which account of the study of society is closer to the truth of the matter, it would be odd to only try to understand social groups by the individual behavior of those who claim to be members of those groups or to take such groups as always fundamental. One reason is that, whether we like it or not, many people believe that they act regardless of the claims of social groups on them, or even of the claims of the interests of others at all. Other people take the groups they belong to—everything from affinity organizations and identifications with families, peoples, or nations to membership in formal or informal political groupings around personal identity or particular concerns (feminists, environmentalists, and so on)—to be fundamental to the question of who they claim to be and sufficient as providing good reasons for how they act in the world toward others. I don't mean to suggest that we need to assume the existence of these various relations between individuals and social groups because people act this way. We don't have to accept either of these broad categories of self-description at face value. But before criticizing them it helps to understand how people see themselves.

One first task then for any adequate social philosophy is to try to understand the various approaches that people have to the relationship between individuals and societies, appreciate them, and then go on to assert a view about which way of thinking is right. I do not mean to suggest that philosophers need to become empirical social scientists, giving people surveys to try to figure out how they relate to the world. This is information they should pay attention to, but social scientists are better equipped to gather it. Instead, what I mean is that a complete understanding of how people ought to think of themselves in relation to their fellows and the larger world entails more than simply sitting down and coming up with hypothetical examples of how they should do this. Most social philosophers would not disagree. Though I would hesitate to describe all of what we do as "interdisciplinary," most philosophers interested in larger social questions are also interested in the outward manifestations of how individuals and groups represent themselves to the world and put forward a vision of their own place in it. Our theories of society are always both in conversation with these representations and in some sense meant to influence them. And in the end, many social philosophers believe that the best way to organize a larger society is not to force a particular conception of how one should see one's self in relation to that society or in relation to different social groups, but instead to figure out the best principles for organizing a society that must inevitably negotiate between these competing notions of individuals and groups.

All films—documentaries, fiction films, even avant garde films (though I could be dissuaded of this last point)—are about something. And what they are about can be trivial and merely entertaining or profound. No matter what our reasons are for watching films, though, they are better, at least today, than most of the other arts at grabbing our attention and holding onto it for a significant period of time. Part of the reason is simply that they are more popular than other visual arts, especially in more affluent parts of the world, and thus we have easier access to them, at least to the big-budget Hollywood variety. Looking at paintings or sculpture and appreciating them requires discipline, as does reading poetry and literature. The same is true of music, dance, theater, and other performance arts. To critically appreciate a film requires much discipline as well, and eventually, if it is to be done right, at least a passing familiarity with the techniques of the medium. Like all the arts, films run the gambit from the very difficult to watch, understand, and interpret to the seemingly simple. But the ubiquity and varieties of films also belie their power, and once we enter the theater (and I do believe there is a difference between watching films in a theater and watching them at home), we are taken into the world of a film in a way that is often difficult to escape for its duration. To be sure, we can find ourselves unable to turn away from a painting or put down a book, or become riveted by a concert, but more of us today find ourselves captivated by film.

One thing that most films have in common is that they drop us into a set of relationships between people that we have to be able to understand immediately, or at least eventually on reflection, in such a way that we are entertained by them or become concerned about what the people in these relationships are concerned about. In this way, films engage in one of the first tasks of social philosophy described above: They necessarily must work quickly to show us complex portrayals of how people see themselves and interact with each other on whatever subject, real or imagined, that they are about. They do not do this by simply holding up a mirror of the world as it is; they assume certain things—some people are islands unto themselves, while others run with a pack—and then construct a narrative that we can understand and in which we recognize others as like ourselves or come to appreciate that other people can live in very different ways than we do and still be people like us. When films do this they represent and then investigate the variety of ways that people understand themselves and relate to both social groups and the larger society and so begin a process that is the fundamental stuff of social philosophy. It should be no surprise, then, that, after some work, we can discern fundamental questions of social philosophy and social criticism in many films (some do it more immediately and directly for us than others) and, in turn, build a body of social criticism both about film and through film.

If films do not do this work then we may find them incoherent. Films do not always fall on either side of the holist-individualist divide, but they must be able to represent some range within that divide in order to show us a picture either of beings like ourselves, or of our world, that will make sense to us. The same is true of the most outlandish science-fiction, horror, and fantasy films. If a science-fiction film builds dramatic tension with a character, then we need to be able to feel that tension for the scene to be effective. We must be able to understand, at least to some degree, who that character is and why he or she is reacting to the stimuli in particular ways.[9]

I will leave the examples of how this works to the chapters which follow, as I think it is better that we discuss films in relation to particular moral, political, and social questions rather than in the broad terms I have been painting here. One last point, though, which may seem obvious to many people: Films do not merely represent individuals and groups but also help to actually create understandings of who we think we are, how we regard others, and how members of groups identify and understand their group membership and their obligations to that group. We empathize with the characters we see on screen; with popular films we may even idealize the movie stars who play them. We try to be cool like one character, chic like another, tough, sexy, and so fourth. But more than this, we can come to accept the picture that a film offers of some bit of the world as true and then come to react to those inhabiting that world as a unified whole. It is astonishingly difficult to appreciate every individual as an individual, and films encourage us, sometimes for good and sometimes not, to group people together as part of a larger category that we can more easily understand. So powerful is this connection that modern dictators have looked to film to help shape a population's understanding of themselves as a unified "people" and direct their obedience to the state—the clear case is Leni Riefenstahl's *Triumph of the Will* (1934).[10] Even if some may disagree with my contention that films, like social philosophers, must represent the varieties of ways of living in the world with others, then at the very least critical philosophers must admit that they should pay attention to film because of its power to shape how we think about who we are, especially when this power is used for pernicious purposes.

That said, I would not want someone reading this section to come away with the idea that films are only about that slice of life that they most straightforwardly represent themselves as being about. In most of the chapters that follow I end up arguing that a film suggests one thing even though one can imagine that it was intended to suggest another. So, the power of films is not just to represent the different ways that we live with each other, and how we see ourselves in relation to the larger society, but also to stimulate a response in us without us always knowing it. I will try to illustrate this point with a personal example.

Depending on what is going on with us at any given time, some films can be difficult, even impossible, to watch. The same, again, is true with any art form, and also with any interaction one might have with another person. But still, we may find ourselves taken aback or troubled to find that we cannot watch a film. We might rent a film to try to escape from our everyday problems and find that it is too banal in comparison to the emotional turmoil that we are going through to be any help. Or we may find that a film sparks too many emotions in us that have an uncomfortable association with other events in our lives. For someone experiencing an almost overwhelming emotional trauma, films may make things better, by bringing out the tears when one needs to cry, but may also seem overwhelming, bringing us too close to the pain that we need to eventually put in some kind of perspective.

Upon reflection, what is interesting about such times is that the films that so affect us are often not directly about what we are going through. They can be about all manner of things, most of which are far removed from our own troubles and involve relationships with others in situations that have nothing directly to do with what we are going through. Still, they can have a power over us that works more through association than through representation. This is just another way of putting another obvious point, that underneath every film text are a variety of subtexts. The images can speak to us even if the situations and characters seem very foreign.

But this same problem that we may experience watching films when we are down has another side, and that is the remarkable and surprising way that films can help to heal us by connecting us with others despite the distances of time, place, memory, or differences in how we see the world. As I will relay in the next chapter, I live in New York City and witnessed the events of September 11, 2001. There are many stories I could tell from that time, but the one that is most illustrative here is an experience I had on September 30 at the movies.

Lukas Moodysson's *Together* (2000, original title *Tillsammans*) had been playing in my neighborhood, Greenwich Village, prior to the 11th. I knew it was about a Swedish commune in the 1970s and that it was a small, independent film that had done very well in its home country. I had read a review about it but couldn't recall much of the content. I put it on my list of films to see, but not so high that I couldn't just rent it later. As with most New Yorkers, and many people in other parts of the world, I was still in shock, deeply traumatized by the events that had happened. I was fortunate not to lose anyone myself, but the realization that others were going through even more intense emotions was palpable. Pain was in the air, and hope seemed difficult to get access to during most days.

On the 30th, I went to see *Together* with a friend. I didn't exactly know what to expect, but the billowing cloud from the fires burning at the World Trade Center site could be seen clearly as we walked the four blocks to the theater, casting a shadow on my expectations. I knew this much going into the film: *Together* is not about a tragedy like the 11th, it isn't about terrorism, it isn't about finding out that loved ones have died and knowing that there is nothing you could have done to prevent it, it isn't about a community as large as a city going through a major disaster. Because the film is set in a communal house, a place far from my own experience, I didn't expect that it would take me back to the safety of my own home, either as a child or today. In short, I wasn't sure that this movie would help much other than to distract me for a couple of hours.

But *Together* did so much more than that. I won't summarize the plot here other than to say that the title is apt. Most simply put, this film is about people trying to live together and then finding themselves pulled in very different directions. The result, for me, in that place, and for many other New Yorkers at the time, was that it gave us some of that hope we were so desperate for, something that grand proclamations about going to war against the enemy could never give us. Perhaps the power of the film was just that, in the end, it portrayed a close community of people who became reconciled to each other's needs, though not without recognition of the problems awaiting them in the future.

I'm sure this film did different things for different people. Still, another friend across town who had seen it around the same time said that her audience stood up and cheered afterward, overwhelmed at how a simple, clear story could speak to them. Neither of us experienced the film as merely an escape; instead it gave us a chance to participate in a portrayal of hope with others trying to find solace in a community. Such a community is what we all so desperately wanted to believe that New York could be in that moment, and this strange film, about people so different from ourselves, helped us to believe in that hope, at least for a while.

Perhaps I have strayed a bit now from my topic of the connection between film and social philosophy. If so, then maybe this last example just gives us another reason why we can turn to films, not just to find the philosophy in them, but as part of the fabric of our lives during the good times and the bad. That fabric is the subject of the philosophy that I care about most, so I suppose it is no surprise that I see philosophy in film. For in the end, I am attracted to philosophy because it gives me a chance to express myself about things that I care deeply about in the world. The same must be true of why I have written about film: It, too, as with most artistic expressions, offers a chance to share a vision of what we ought to care about in the world in which we find ourselves.

Contents of the Volume

As I have already mentioned, this book is a collection of independent chapters that, though revised to work better together as a coherent whole, can and should be read independently of each other. I have not updated the theoretical literature discussed in the essays, nor have I attempted to focus on films that are more recent than the ones I chose when the essays were originally conceived and written. I have added several footnotes that do make reference to later films, in the case of some specific directors, and to more recent books, in the case of some philosophers and critics. I have little doubt that readers will make connections to more recent texts than those I have discussed here. Still, none of these chapters aim to discuss a film genre as such, or a director's entire body of work. Nevertheless, with those caveats, anyone who might have seen one of these chapters in an earlier form will find it here thoroughly revised in almost every other aspect of its argument.

The three chapters in Part 1 investigate either a filmmaker or a group of films that make a substantial contribution to ongoing debates in the philosophy of technology and environmental philosophy as viewed through the lens of the social dimensions of ethics, politics, or aesthetics. While the first two chapters focus explicitly on issues in the philosophy of technology, as opposed to the third chapter, which works with themes in environmental philosophy, all three have in common an analysis of how the films they investigate articulate a critical issue in our understanding of built space, a medium that is comprised of natural and technological elements.

Chapter 2 is oriented around the fundamental question that inspired the field of philosophy of technology: Do technological artifacts have socially normative dimensions inherent in them that are separate from the uses to which such artifacts are put? The particular set of artifacts in this case are the technologies of electronic surveillance. My central claim is that this fundamental philosophical question is investigated on screen in a variety of films, and that if we look at them together, against the broad background of the philosophical debate over this topic, we will see that those films extend and develop the positions on that debate in some novel and important ways. While I do not take the extreme position that the moral and social potential of technologies is completely divorced from their designers or users, I think that some films take the opposite extreme position that these technologies are "neutral," except for how they are used. Such films may not only fail to take on the philosophical and political complexities of this issue but may do some damage as well. This is especially true in a society, such as ours, that is increasingly reliant on these technologies and confused about how they should be regulated.

The three films analyzed here are *Enemy of the State*, *The Conversation*, and *The End of Violence* (I give details on the year and director of each film I discuss in the body of the chapters). My argument is that *Enemy of the State* presents electronic surveillance technologies as morally neutral, but we may not see this immediately because the film is dressed in the sophisticated clothing of a comparison with the earlier film, *The Conversation*. Those familiar with both films will see an ingenious set of intertextual references in *Enemy* to *The Conversation*. But compared to *Enemy*, *The Conversation* is much more philosophically important, arguing that electronic surveillance corrupts the user by creating a culture of paranoia. In contrast to both, Wim Wenders's film *The End of Violence* explores the depths of a society controlled by electronic surveillance, one in which new forms of violence are perpetuated by the very technologies designed to suppress it.

In chapter 3 I argue that one of Wim Wenders's earlier films, *Alice in the Cities*, offers a unique set of insights on another key debate in the philosophy of technology: If we assume that technological artifacts can be normatively significant, can the normative implications of a technology be changed? In other words, if artifacts have politics, are those politics necessarily determined by the kind of thing that they are, or can the ends that they serve be transformed to some other moral, political, or social purpose?

After briefly reviewing two answers in the philosophical literature on this issue, I argue that *Alice in the Cities* provides an interesting aesthetic argument about this question when we move from looking at particular technological objects to the larger built spaces that they help to create. Wenders's film is not just interesting because it helps to answer this philosophical debate but because it offers an aesthetics of everyday life that in many ways is superior to the standard treatments of this issue. As such, the film tempts us to go back and rethink the terms of the philosophical debate. Finally, I take a look in this chapter at how Wenders's work also provides an occasion to consider the important topic of the relationship between film as an art form and its technological form of reproduction. Importantly, the same theoretical debate that the narrative speaks to helps us to understand Wenders's challenge to the increasingly received relationship between the viewer and the film.

In chapter 4 I turn to themes in environmental philosophy, though again, as they are tied to questions of built space rather than the traditional domain of that field in natural resource conservation, preservation, and restoration. This chapter furthers earlier arguments I have made cautioning against use of the metaphor of "urban wilderness" to describe inner cities. Contemporary versions of such descriptions feed the desire to separate these places from other areas and often vilify their inhabitants. This argument, as I point out in the opening of the chapter, was inspired by my experience of the Rodney King riots in Los Angeles in 1992.

Here, however, after summarizing my understanding of the distinctions that geographers have made concerning different views of wilderness, I track the imagery of an urban wilderness in several recent American films. As I also point out in chapter 2, the power of film as a medium, especially popular films, to shape public opinion makes it important to call attention to its questionable themes. In this vein, first I offer a sustained examination of the film *Falling Down*, which portrays Los Angeles as an urban wilderness. Our acceptance of the breakdown of the antihero at the heart of the film, an unemployed defense worker, is parasitic on a depiction of Los Angeles as this kind of wilderness. Second, and more hopeful, are the appeals to an urban wilderness in portrayals of the inner city by African-American filmmakers such as John Singleton and the Hughes brothers. The chapter concludes with a very brief look at another film, John Sayles's *City of Hope*, as both a positive antidote to *Falling Down* and an alternative to the films of Singleton and the Hughes brothers, which continue the metaphor of urban wilderness for different reasons than we find in *Falling Down*.

This theme of race and identity in chapter 4 serves as a helpful transition for Part 2, which focuses on the representation of group interest and political identity in film. The contents of this section also more directly speak to the basic philosophical themes I see in many films such as those discussed above. The two chapters in this section look at political interests and identity as they show up in films about racial formation, identification with particular causes, and economic classes. Again, as with Part 1, this focus puts films and filmmakers in conversation with arguments in the philosophical literature. In what I hope is a helpful connection, just as chapters 2 and 3 both look at the work of one common filmmaker (Wenders), chapter 5 looks at the work of John Sayles.

Chapter 5 focuses on the problem of the representation of class interests, against other political identities, in Sayles's film *Matewan*. This is a historical film about the coalfield wars in 1920s West Virginia. Though Sayles is often thought to be one of the most sophisticated political filmmakers working today, this film is open to criticisms that it presents an overly romantic view of the role of class interest in political struggle, reducing all social complexity of group identity (race, gender, and so on) to questions of class politics.

The goal of the chapter is to defend what I take to be Sayles's position on this cluster of issues against such criticisms. My central claim is that part of what makes this film a very helpful representation of working-class history and politics is its sustained pursuit of a representation of class as the glue of interest that can reconcile different political priorities formed around personal identity, especially racial identities, without necessarily reducing them all to the same kind of interest. But again, the argument for this thesis comes out of this film when read in conjunction with texts in certain philosophical debates and also against other films. My foil in this chapter involves a brief look at Richard Linklater's *Slacker*, which I argue contains at least one scene that would dismiss class interests in the same way that some may accuse Sayles of dismissing racial interests.

Understanding the politics of political identity is tricky, and something that I once spent a lot more time thinking about than I do now. Though I have many reservations about the excessive focus on the politics of race, class, gender, sexual orientation, and the like exhibited in some parts of the academy, I still hold the position (defended in part in chapter 5) that no serious philosopher who wants to make a practical contribution to the resolution of actual political problems can hope to ignore it. Chapter 6 starts with an overview of this issue and goes on to offer a distinction between different kinds of political identity, so as to make room for both traditional topics, such as the nature and implications of feminism, and those identities formed around particular interests, such as the protection of the environment. But these political identities are never uniform, and they never absolutely determine the views of those who embrace those identities. They are always in some state of flux and under some amount of direct and indirect discussion over their meaning and implications. Out of this distinction I raise the issue of how we can understand the representation of political identity so as to appreciate that these political positions are always evolving. Is it possible to represent the process by which these identities are always struggling with what they mean to their individual members, both in conversation with each other and in conversation with a past community that has also shared in that identity? The representations I am concerned about here are in film, a medium known for its stereotypical representations of feminists and other communities of interest and identity.

Therefore, the next part of this chapter takes up the critique of Spike Lee's *Do the Right Thing* offered by philosopher Douglas Kellner over just this issue. Kellner has argued that despite their virtues, Lee's films can promote a divisive identity politics of race reducible to a thin cultural identity connected more to commodity choice than substantive politics. I defend Lee against these criticisms. Lee's films are arguably directed at both the African-American community, offering an opportunity for the members of that community to understand the complexities of what it means to be black in America (without reducing the answers to simple slogans), and to those outside of that community, offering a window through which to appreciate how the community is evolving and to understand the questions over which it is struggling.

Given the different kinds of politics of identity distinguished earlier in the chapter, the question is raised though whether it is better or worse to misrepresent the politics of groups like those with a race-based identity or those formed around political interests such as the environment. In the last part of chapter 6 I explore that question with special attention to *The Burning Season,* a film depicting the life of Chico Mendes, a leader of the Brazilian rubber tappers union, who was murdered for his work trying to protect the Amazon rainforest for the welfare of the community in which he was a part. I use as a foil here a quick look at the Steven Seagal film *Fire Down Below,* which does a particularly bad job, in my view, of representing the political interests and identity of an environmentalist. Not a huge surprise, of course, but still an illuminating and entertaining comparison.

A couple of final caveats on this book before continuing with the particular chapters. First, many may find my choice of films, and perhaps even of philosophical topics, haphazard. In the case of film they are correct, and in defense I plead only that film is not my main area of research. But in each case I think I can make a strong connection between what I have chosen to write about, the films that either illustrate or inspired that choice, and other interests that I have. As with most of my work, there are also personal reasons why I have decided to write on what I have written about, and I'm not shy in these chapters about giving those reasons where I think it appropriate. But again, this is just part of my view that there is nothing wrong with doing philosophy out of personal interest, even passion. If I thought otherwise I would probably do something else or do philosophy as a nine-to-five job.

In terms of my choice of philosophical topics, every issue discussed here is something that I also care about. While I believe that the topics are important enough to justify their attention, I do not do very much work in these chapters to defend the grounds of the philosophical debates at issue, and so these essays cannot be taken by themselves as complete justifications of their subject matter. For example, I take for granted that the question of whether technology does or does not have inherent social dimensions to be something that is adequately defended in other publications either by me or by other philosophers. In order to have enough space here to get into the criticisms of specific films, I must assume some degree of sympathy by the reader for these topics. In the footnotes I have tried to indicate where a more thorough defense of those issues can be found. I trust that the balance, given the purpose of this book, is acceptable.

Second, some may not like my critiques of popular films such as *Enemy of the State* or *Fire Down Below* and find them unfair. I address such concerns throughout several of the chapters and try to make a specific case for the films I am criticizing. Still, I wouldn't be surprised if a reader came away from this book thinking that I'm an art house snob who only condescends to see films marketed toward mass audiences in order to trash them. This is simply not true. I think that some of the most profound moments in film history actually come from popular movies, despite many of the inherent limitations of the system that now produces them. Even when such films don't offer profound moments, I still love to go to them and usually thoroughly enjoy myself, as we all should. Despite evidence to the contrary, academic criticism ought not be just about learning to dislike everything corporate or popular in a sophisticated manner. I also have many critical things to say about the pretentiousness of much independent cinema, especially that recently produced in the United States, which seems to require a postmodern gimmick to go into production and has too often abandoned good storytelling.

This is all to simply conclude that there are many reasons to watch a vast variety of films. I trust that some readers have experienced my sense of profound awe at the movies and have seen their connection to important philosophical topics, important because they help us to live our lives better, or at least with more understanding of each other. For those who have not, I hope this book will encourage them to share in that kind of experience. But I would not want anyone to think that all films need to be understood through the lens of philosophy all the time. There is just too much that we get out of them to come to such a conclusion.

PART ONE

Film, Technology, and Built Space

2

Enemies of the State?
Electronic Surveillance and
the Neutrality of Technology

The academy is often slow to pick up on issues of social importance. Philosophers are no exception to this general rule. Indeed, they are often rightly accused of being late to the game concerning commentary on pressing issues of the day. Although many of my colleagues do not see any problem with this—a familiar refrain is that it is not the job of philosophers to solve the problems of the world—many others have made a point of doing something about it. In the early 1970s, several ethicists and social and political philosophers started what was then called the "practical ethics movement," especially around the journal *Philosophy and Public Affairs*. Figures such as Thomas Nagel, Peter Singer, Judith Jarvis Thompson, and Michael Walzer weighed in on contemporary social issues from abortion rights to famine relief to just war theory.[1] Since then, we have seen the rise of a variety of areas of applied philosophy focused on particular areas of professional life, including biomedical ethics, environmental ethics, information technology ethics, business ethics, engineering ethics, philosophy of technology, and other specialized areas connected to philosophy and public life. Philosophers drawn to these areas have come from a range of backgrounds, including Anglo-American "analytic" approaches, German and French inspired "continental" philosophy, and pragmatism.

But even with all of this activity, there are still some notable gaps. For example, relatively little has appeared by philosophers about electronic surveillance technology, arguably one of the most influential transformations shaping contemporary society in the last half of the twentieth century and with increasing relevance in the present day. A striking amount, however, has been written on this topic by academics in other fields. Sociologists, geographers, anthropologists, and many others have had a great deal to say about technologies of surveillance and how they are impacting our day-to-day lives.[2] These theorists did not come late to the game at all but were there all along, often anticipating new developments in surveillance technology and policy and warning us to beware before such innovations hit the streets.

One irony, though, from the perspective of a philosopher, is that much of this work was inspired by the French philosopher Michel Foucault's meditations on technologies of surveillance, which itself was a response to the ideas of the eighteenth-century British philosopher and social reformer, Jeremy Bentham, who pioneered what he called a "Panopticon" penitentiary design in 1791. David Lyons has summarized Bentham's design:

> Essentially, it was for a building on a semi-circular pattern with an "inspection lodge" at the center and cells around the perimeter. Prisoners, who in the original plan would be in individual cells, were open to the gaze of the guards, or "inspectors," but the same was not true of the view the other way. By a carefully contrived system of lighting and the use of wooden blinds, officials would be invisible to inmates. Control was to be maintained by the constant sense that prisoners were watched by unseen eyes. There was nowhere to hide, nowhere to be private. Not knowing whether or not they were watched, but obliged to assume that they were, obedience was the prisoner's only rational option.[3]

Bentham was not successful in getting the British government to invest in this idea, but his innovations were enormously influential in later variations of prison reform—and, some would argue, in the development of other forms of surveillance outside of the penitentiary walls.

Not too long ago, I toured the ruins of a nineteenth-century model prison that is part of the old British prison colony at Port Arthur, Tasmania. There I saw a vestige of the Bentham plan that actually did get built. The model prison was designed to isolate problem prisoners from the rest of the colony. The complex prison designs and rules insured that they would never come into contact with another prisoner, even in public spaces such as the prison chapel. Prisoners entered the chapel with blinders affixed to their heads so that they couldn't see to their right or left.

Once they were settled into their places in specially designed pews, doors would shut on either side of them, making it impossible to see anyone but the minister at the front of the room. With this method of restraint, the individual prisoners not only couldn't see others around them, but, following Bentham's model, couldn't see who was watching them, or indeed when they were being watched. As Lyons put it, "uncertainty" about whether one was being watched was "a means of subordination."

Foucault took Bentham's idea as paradigmatic of a form of control that would become ubiquitous in many other spheres of daily life. To live in a world where we do not know whether we are being watched, but still know that it is a possibility that we are, Foucault reasoned, produces a disciplined society and disciplined persons. We would no longer need excessive forms of violent control, such as public torture, in a "panoptic" society, but could order the world in a cleaner and more rational way. Foucault took Bentham's ideas to much more interesting and expansive conclusions than will be discussed here. Debate continues about whether this understanding of Bentham's Panopticon really is helpful for understanding the world of electronic surveillance, which uses similar techniques to shape the human landscape outside of the prison. But what is interesting for me now is that such debates are going on primarily outside of the philosophical community.

Of course, it wouldn't be the first time that the concern of a philosopher would stimulate more inquiries by nonphilosophers than by his or her colleagues. The history of ideas is littered with such examples, and in this case probably has more to do with the admirable evolution of philosophy into a more disciplined profession than it has been in the past, focusing on more discrete problems. Still, as a result, philosophers have unfortunately ceded whole areas of inquiry to other areas of scholarship, creating in essence an interdisciplinary conversation in which they do not participate. So, too, when philosophers return to such areas of work after a long time away, they find the terrain transformed into one too far afield from anything they can recognize as traditional forms of philosophical argumentation with which they could grapple, or else that the questions that have risen to the fore on such issues are ones to be answered by empirical methodologies rather than philosophical analysis. In the case of work on, first, surveillance technology, and second, electronic surveillance, the evolution of the lessons brought forward initially by Foucault's analysis of Bentham have gone well beyond practical considerations into general debates about the nature of "modernity" and "postmodernity"—ground which often feels uncomfortably broad for the skills of philosophers more adept at trying to answer more specific questions.

But I believe that, outside of a few noteworthy exceptions, philosophers have been remiss to entirely give up the topic of surveillance technology to the rest of the academy. For surveillance, especially in its new electronic forms bolstered by rapid advances in computers, optics, cameras, and satellites, has evolved from a system we use to best watch over those who have already violated the law, as Bentham saw it, to one where the state exercises power over us to insure compliance before any law is broken, and even more troubling, to keep tabs on us while we exercise those rights which the state has given to us, such as our right to privacy in our homes. State use of electronic surveillance is not the end of the story, of course. Private corporations make ample use of such tools for a variety of purposes. On all fronts this use seems to be ever expanding. And in the United States in the aftermath of the events of September 11, as we see the creation of a new cabinet-level federal authority with the mandate to bring more security through closer scrutiny, we can only expect that whatever concerns we now have about electronic surveillance will only increase. As Alison Mitchell put it in the *New York Times,* George W. Bush's plan to collapse twenty-two agencies and thousands of federal employees into a new Department of Homeland Security, justified by an open-ended war, threatens a permanent erosion of civil liberties justified by the necessity of domestic spying. Creating such a department, according to Tom Ridge, the current director of homeland security, is not the end of this trend but instead only "the beginning."[4]

Perhaps such a cautionary remark comes across as overly caustic, if not downright foolish. When terrorists are prepared to use any means necessary to kill us for reasons that strike us as wholly unjustifiable, why not use all means at our disposal to stop them? The tools of electronic surveillance are just that, tools. Using them is no better or worse than using any other tool; it is the intentions of the users that matter. But even though they have said little about surveillance technology as such, philosophers focusing on questions concerning technology have disputed such an overly simple assessment of the social meaning and moral implications of technology writ large or individual technologies in particular. Applied to this case we can wonder whether technologies of surveillance really are technologically neutral. While they are not wholly sinister, to be sure, we would be hard pressed to say they are value free. Such considerations warrant closer scrutiny by philosophers as they speak to the fundamental issue of whether a form of social order or a moral imperative is necessarily built into the design of a thing, and hence into the thing itself, and as a consequence into the fabric of our daily lives.

I will leave to others the task of a more thorough engagement with the literature on surveillance technology as such. My goal here is more modest. Consistent with the overall theme of the essays in this book, I turn to film as a resource for helping us to formulate some of our first philosophical intuitions on this topic, in particular the question of whether these new tools are value free. Fortunately, many filmmakers have had much to say of substance about the social implications of surveillance technology. In this chapter I will try to tease out what some films have been saying about electronic surveillance. I do this not simply because I think that filmmakers are at the forefront of philosophical discussion of this technology, but because whatever they have to say about it will reach a much wider audience, and influence many more people, than anything that will most likely be written by a sociologist or geographer, let alone a philosopher. Films have often shaped debates of national importance even as they simultaneously reflect them (consider the rise of concern around genetic manipulation technologies that helped drive the making of the film *Gataca* (1997), which in turn raised questions to be debated by a variety of commentators and pundits in the media).

But the point of this chapter is not simply to praise the responsible presentation of electronic surveillance in film, but also to show how some films may take up this important topic in a manner that shoves important social and moral issues under the rug, so to speak. Pointing out such lapses is a good role for the philosopher, consistent with the resources of our discipline. After trying to clarify what I take to be one of the fundamental questions about the social importance of surveillance technology, I will look at three films that arguably have something to offer on this topic. These films do not necessarily give us an accurate representation of the world we will make through this technology but should be seen as guides, some better than others, to help us understand the questions we ought to ask about the world we are making.

Surveillance Society

That we live in a surveillance society should be no surprise to us. Even prior to recent debates about homeland security, it was something that we experienced on a daily basis. To give just one example: In 1999 I was

working in a research center at New York University, housed just south of
Washington Square Park in New York City, the eight-acre historic center
of Greenwich Village. Surrounded now by the downtown campus buildings of NYU, Washington Square serves as a kind of campus quad. But
unlike most university common areas, this one is a public park, drawing
residents and visitors from the neighborhood for all manner of activity,
from musical performances (some officially sponsored but most not), to
speed chess games (as featured in the film *Searching for Bobby Fischer*,
1993), to sunbathing, dog walking, political protest, and debate, as well as
just hanging out in general. Washington Square is our version of a town
commons. It is where we come together as a community to make our life
together. This being New York, it is also our backyard, as only a small fraction of apartments in the area have access to their own bit of green space.

One of my fellow office mates at the center that year was someone who
had lived in the neighborhood fifteen years previous and had just moved
back after living abroad. One day we had a conversation about how much
the neighborhood had changed since he had lived there before: the
restaurants that had come and gone, the way the university had torn
down many old buildings to make way for expansion, how much more
expensive rents were in the neighborhood, that sort of thing. But for him
the biggest indicator of change was one thing—the availability of drugs
in the park. You can't buy drugs easily in Washington Square Park anymore. The reason is pretty obvious for anyone strolling by. Just across the
street from the building we were both housed in sits a large baby blue
New York Police Department mobile command center, really sort of a
glorified trailer. Like many units in trailer parks all across the country, it's
not really designed to go anywhere. Instead it has become a permanent
feature of the park. If you were to go there and look closely at the top of
the trailer, you would see a number of cables coming out of it that reach
across to a network of surveillance cameras. The network has the park
under twenty-four-hour surveillance. Like a classic panoptic system, one
doesn't know when one is being watched from any particular part of the
park, nor indeed if anyone is in the command center watching at any
given moment. Illegal activity still goes on in the park, to be sure, but the
savviest drug dealers, and their most cautious clients, have moved down
the street to the West 4th subway entrance, further away from the ever-
present electronic eye of the state.

As with the office of homeland security, the intention here is not just to
discipline the populace using the park, but also to make it safer.

Colleagues in my department at NYU have told me several times how much safer they feel in the park than in the days prior to the arrival of the NYPD surveillance center. To be sure, these steps toward increasing security in the park, and in public spaces across the city, help to explain why people are visiting the city now in greater numbers than they were fifteen years ago, though arguably the upturn in the economy in the 1990s had more to do with reducing crime than anything else. In cities throughout North America, we have become accustomed to such intrusions in our lives, partly because we all want to feel safer. But police network surveillance systems like this one are just the tip of the iceberg. Think of the numerous cameras that capture your image every day at ATM machines, supermarkets, and just about every other business or institution one walks into. Consider as well how many times your driver's license, work or student ID card, passport, or bank card is scanned, leaving a trace of a permanent record of you wherever you go. Consider the tracking devices on our cars, such as the EZ Pass system in New York, which tracks the movement of commuters in and out of the city by recording automatic payments at toll bridges and tunnels, thus insuring that friends, foes, and the merely curious can know when and where we have left or entered a place on any given day. We don't even need examples from the Internet to quickly recognize that we are always being watched.[5]

Such casual observations lead me to the conclusion that our urban and suburban infrastructures are becoming dependent upon surveillance just as they are already dependent on the automobile. In most cities, we must have a car to get from place to place. So, too, in many cities we rely on the tools of surveillance to manage the scale of the city. As cities and suburbs become more diffuse, there is more anonymity between persons. We either see too many people to know many of them by sight, or else never see our neighbors, because our only contact with them is mediated by cars, and so we need some way of keeping track of each other. This is the magic of the centralized databases that record our comings and goings. They trace our movements so that our neighbors don't need to know who we are. The scale of our reliance on surveillance is larger, however, than individual communities. Increasingly, our sense of personal and national security is defined by our dependency on surveillance. But the worry is that such structural dependencies may mean that we are deprived of a lifestyle choice, namely, one where we are not constantly surveyed. And since many of us justifiably feel an erosion of privacy because of this surveillance, those who would consider privacy a right may see the erosion of lifestyles that do not include surveillance as an erosion of an important right.

What is to be done? If we can't escape the eye of the camera, should we head for the hills or just accept this situation and transform it into some wondrous celebration of the new technologically mediated species we have become? Perhaps the appropriate attitude toward being under constant surveillance is to relish the thought that we are constantly being watched! However we decide to respond to the surveillance society that we have created for ourselves, or that has been created for us, we need to think more critically about the issues involved in surveillance than either one of these two responses seem to do. I don't think the question is whether the level of surveillance today is disturbing, but how deep our disturbance should go, and how we should shape and frame our political and social discussions of the effect of surveillance on our lives and on the masses of people that will be called upon to work in the industry of surveillance.

But there is at least one very significant hurdle to jump in order to deepen the discussion of surveillance technology: The tools of surveillance are increasingly being described, especially in representations of them in film and other media in popular culture, as morally and socially neutral. Many of these representations, as we will shortly see, describe the advancements in computer technology that make surveillance possible as good or bad only in the context of the intentions of those who are using these tools. If the NYPD or the Department of Homeland Security is a benign agency full of well-meaning officials interested only in protecting us, then we should no more worry about the surveillance techniques they are using than worry about their fingerprint powder and handcuffs. These are just tools of the trade. But if one of those agencies were to become corrupted by the megalomania of an individual director, such as arguably was the case during J. Edgar Hoover's tenure as FBI director, and used to further that person's private agenda on security and order, then we would have something to fear. Such tools would only magnify corrupt power. But even under this last scenario, the tools themselves are not the problem, only the persons using them.

This lack of discussion about the possible deeper implications of surveillance duplicates other discussions in our society of the moral, political, and social neutrality of tools. The same attitude, for example, helps to shape the public debate on handguns. The ongoing discussion over the regulation of handguns in the United States has been heavily influenced by what I will call the "Hestonite" view of this technology (following from

Charlton Heston's leadership position in the National Rifle Association). The NRA, as we all know, claims that "guns don't kill people, *people kill people.*" There is nothing about the distribution of guns in and of itself that increases the propensity toward violence, even of the most tragic sort, such as the highly publicized school shooting cases over the past few years. Guns are not to blame for these horrors, but the people pulling the trigger, or their parents, or other societal forces. The regulation of guns shouldn't hinge then on their use in such incidents. And especially where we have a constitutionally protected public good at stake (the right to bear arms), the correlation of the use of guns in violent crimes should not be understood as a causal relation justifying any increase in their regulation.

In the case of electronic surveillance, there is a similar line, though often it is masked by sophisticated presentations of the technology in popular culture. According to these presentations, surveillance is bad only if the information is used by the wrong people or if the information gathered winds up in the wrong hands. The technology itself is not a problem. I expect that as debates over surveillance increase in the United States, we will see this line of reasoning become more and more pronounced. We have a clear public good that must be protected: maintenance of security in the face of a serious threat. Any abuse of the tools of surveillance in the provision of that good should not raise any red flags about the tools themselves, only their administration. In short, there is nothing inherently wrong with any given technology, and our only worries should be over the use to which it is put.

There is a tradition in the small circle of philosophers who study technology of calling such a line of reasoning the "neutrality thesis." Primarily after the technologically enhanced devastations of World War II, thinkers such as the French sociologist Jaques Ellul and the German philosopher Martin Heidegger attacked the neutrality thesis by claiming that technologies are not neutral but in some sense even autonomous from human intentions.[6] Technologies, or perhaps designs, contain an inherent moral or political dimension, and to these early thinkers this dimension is corrupting of human character and even devastating for the possibility of humans living sustainably with the rest of nature. Technologies, in Heidegger's words, "frame" the Earth as only a resource to be manipulated and inevitably lead to an almost unstoppable drive toward domination and destruction of the planet.

From our contemporary perspective, there is a tendency to see these early attempts to formulate a philosophy of technology as fairly crude. For example, Ellul claims that all of modern technology (which he calls "*technique*") shares an overarching normative dimension, one that is too often harmful to humans. But considering the period in which these views were expressed, such one-sided criticism of technology is understandable. After all, the prevailing view against which such accounts were directed was an instrumental description of technology along the lines of the neutrality thesis. By claiming that technology is normatively substantive, even autonomous, thinkers such as Ellul and Heidegger made a case for something other than the overly simple instrumental view of technologies that were changing the world, such as the newly developed tools of nuclear warfare. How could we possibly see the development of a technology capable of destroying the planet as socially neutral—just a tool like any other tool of warfare or diplomacy? In the field's natal stages a strong but defensible normative thesis was needed to counter the dominant view that technology had no substantive content outside of its forms of production. If Ellul and Heidegger did nothing else, they established that technology was a philosophical issue worthy of careful attention. Following others I will call views like theirs, which explicitly deny the neutrality thesis, the "substantive" view of the meaning or implications of technology.

Of course, substantive theses about the moral, social, or political dimensions of technology are not only found in the philosophical literature. Though more subtle, the shades of Luddism going back to the popular movements to smash the machines of industrial production are a precursor, and that conversation has progressed to influence other infamous thinkers (and I suppose activists) of the twentieth century, such as Ted Kazinski, the Unabomber. But perhaps one reason that philosophers of technology have not come to the same conclusions as Kazinski is that our conversations about substantive alternatives to the neutrality thesis have become more nuanced since the early pronouncements of Ellul and Heidegger. A variety of modified substantive views in philosophy of technology can be found in the myriad works available today, inspired by pragmatism, critical theories of various sorts, phenomenology, and analytic philosophy.[7]

On many of these accounts, technology does not have an ambiguous and somewhat occult power over us but instead can serve as the repository of particular intentions by particular persons or elements in a society. Hearteningly, such views have been influential in shaping the discussions of some scholars who have been looking at these topics. The Australian planner Jean Hillier started off a brief mediation on the municipal surveillance system in Perth, Western Australia, with the following modified substantivist observation: "Electronic surveillance technologies are certainly not value free or technologically neutral. They largely reflect the power relations and structures of society in which those with power exploit surveillance systems to protect the status quo, to organize and normalize others, so that they can be seen, known and controlled."[8] Whether this broadside is correct or not, it does reflect the philosophical discussion that has been going on for some time on this issue.

But while philosophers may rest a bit easier that our views are potentially influential on our fellow academics, it is highly doubtful that the finer distinctions that we have brought out, which open up far more interesting positions between the extreme poles of the neutrality and substantive theses, have had much effect on the popular discussions of technology. One bit of evidence for such a conclusion is the ubiquitous presence of the neutral Hestonite view in discussions by pundits and policymakers alike. As we will see, there are more powerful venues for the neutrality thesis at work in our culture.

Surveillance Technology Goes to the Movies: *Enemy of the State* vs. *The Conversation*

If philosophers aren't shaping the public understanding of the possible perils or lack thereof of surveillance technology, who is? In addition to the other scholars mentioned at the start, it is arguably true that filmmakers have been stimulating much more interesting and influential discussions of these tools. I will discuss three important films that focus on issues concerning surveillance technology and offer a critique of the limitations of one of them.

The films are the 1998 holiday blockbuster *Enemy of the State*, directed by Tony Scott, the classic 1974 film by Francis Ford Coppola, *The Conversation*, and the 1997 film by German director Wim Wenders, *The End of Violence*. *Enemy* is important if for no other reason than that it was the most successful of the three at the box office. Along with Brian DePalma's *Blow Out* (1981), *The Conversation* is a classic in this vein and one of the most interesting, evocative, and indeed beautiful films ever made about surveillance technology, even though it is limited by its portrayal of what we would consider today to be very crude technologies, such as bugging devices and still photographs. I will argue though that *Enemy of the State*

tries to gain a kind of parasitic respectability as an equally compelling presentation of the dangers of surveillance technology by its intertextual
references to *The Conversation*, down to replaying scenes from the earlier
film. But *Enemy* does not move very far from the neutrality thesis as applied to surveillance technology, even though it has grander pretensions.
Films like *Enemy* fail as substantive accounts of the technology if they du-
plicate the neutrality thesis, intentionally or not. As such, the comparable
depth of a film like *The Conversation* comes through its portrayal of the
effects of these technologies on the moral character of the users of these
tools (this is in part how it resists the neutrality thesis). I'll finally argue
that the technological limitations of the portrayal of technology found in
The Conversation are made up for in Wenders's *The End of Violence*, which
provides just as nuanced a discussion of the problems of surveillance technology as *The Conversation* while updating the portrayal of technology for
a contemporary audience.

Enemy of the State is a pop thriller starring Will Smith and Gene
Hackman. The plot is fairly simple, involving the mistaken identity of
an unsuspecting everyman who winds up being a hero of national pro-
portions in the end, taking on suspect corners of the U.S. government,
à la *North by Northwest* (1959). This time, however, the plot is driven by
a scheme involving a corrupt undersecretary of the National Security
Agency (NSA), played by Jon Voight of *Midnight Cowboy* fame, who
we find out at the beginning of the film is responsible for a political assassination plot against an upstate New York congressman (played by
Jason Robards). Robards is standing in the way of an executive
branch–sponsored "security act" authorizing domestic spying, perhaps
going well beyond the current Homeland Security Act (though the extent to which it goes beyond this act is a matter only of speculation). We
are told that this new set of laws will wind up seriously threatening the
privacy of ordinary Americans by making it easier for the government to
use sophisticated electronic surveillance devices for domestic spying in
the name of national security. Voight is using the proposed security act
as a vehicle for a climb to supreme power in the intelligence community.
After Robards is assassinated by Voight's henchman, while the latter
looks on, it is discovered that the dastardly deed was accidentally taped
by a nearby video camera.

The camera, however, was unmanned and had been placed in a nearby
"hide" (a small camouflaged box with a window in it, making it possible
for the camera to start automatically filming when activated by a motion

detector). The hide had been set up by a do-gooder environmentalist, Daniel Leon Zavitz (played by Jason Lee, one of the stock actors in Kevin Smith's films, such as *Mallrats, Chasing Amy,* and *Dogma*). Lee, as Zavitz, had set up the hide in a project to track the migration habits of Canada geese. When the congressman was attacked, the motion detector started the camera, and as a consequence the assassination, including the identity of the NSA director responsible for it, was all captured on tape. Before Voight learns of the presence of the hide and the camera, Lee collects the tape, and upon returning home, realizes that he has an incredibly valuable piece of footage. He downloads a copy of it onto a high-density computer disk and hides it in a handheld video game, planning to take it to a friend who publishes a far left magazine.

But before he can deliver the disk, the evil NSA director learns of the existence of the tape and orders his men to go after the environmentalist. FBI approval to engage in a training operation is forged, releasing a small private army of "techno-geeks" (my term), operatives of the NSA adept at the newest and latest techniques of electronic surveillance, and "ex-military cutouts," essentially gun thugs who were kicked out of the U.S. Marine Corps for attacking their officers. The chase ensues. Using what is represented as the full arsenal of surveillance technology at the U.S. government's disposal, in the first twenty minutes of the film the NSA operatives track Lee down via satellite technology, helicopters, which appear to be the infamous "black helicopters", access to street-level public surveillance cameras, and the security cameras in private businesses.

The film is highly effective at representing these technologies, using well-edited succession of jump cuts. We move rapidly from computer-generated images of satellites, pulling into orbit over the scene of the chase and sending direct images to the techno-geeks below, to on-the-ground footage of a hapless Lee, running across rooftops and through a succession of stores with the gun thugs hard on his heels. The pursuers receive continuous instructions from the electronic surveyors. Every time the "target," as Lee is labeled by the techno-geeks, makes a move out of sight of the men he sees chasing him, they are redirected by those he does not see. By the end of the chase, Lee is killed. But before the culmination of the scene he runs into an old college buddy, played by Will Smith, who is innocently shopping for a Christmas present of lingerie for his wife. With no end to the pursuit in sight, Lee dumps the videogame containing the disk into one of Smith's shopping bags, without the latter knowing it, and then rushes out the door to his death.

After some investigation, the NSA operatives begin to guess that Smith has the disk copy of the tape (the scene where they figure this out is fascinating, as it involves not simply the footage from the security cameras from the lingerie store, but also a hypothetical computer-generated analysis of the shifting dimensions of Smith's shopping bag before and after the video game containing the disk was dropped into it). Smith becomes the new target of their electronic pursuit. Unbeknownst to Smith, the NSA places tracking devices in his cell phone, pager, fountain pen, watch, shoes, and even pants; taps his phones, and those of everyone he might possibly call; and begins systematically taking apart his life on the assumption that Smith knows he has the evidence incriminating Voight and plans to use it. Using more traditional scare tactics, the operatives plant fake newspaper articles that Smith, a progressive Washington, D.C. labor lawyer, is actually in bed with the mob, and that he is involved in an affair with a beautiful young researcher, played by Lisa Bonet, whom he had used previously as an intermediary to hire a private investigator specializing in, of course, electronic surveillance espionage. Smith quickly loses his job, or is put in a position where he has no choice but to quit, his bank accounts are seized, and his credit cards canceled. Photos of Smith and Bonet are secretly taken (in a scene to be discussed shortly) and sent to his wife, which she uses as justification to kick him out of the house.

As Smith's life is completely destroyed in a matter of days, our desperate hero tries to contact the private investigator whom he had hired through Bonet. Smith has never met or seen this investigator and knows him only by his code name of "Brill" (the character is played by Gene Hackman). At this point in the narrative, Smith has no idea who is ruining his life. Based on an earlier set of establishment scenes, Smith reasonably infers that it is the mob who is doing the hatchet job on him. Planting fake newspaper stories does not seem beyond their powers. It is only after Smith finally meets Brill, through an extraordinarily complicated set of arrangements, which the NSA tries to foil in part by sending a fake Brill to meet him, that Smith finally begins to see who is really after him.

The scene where Smith meets Hackman is revelatory. It takes place with ominous chase music in the background and the NSA agents hard on his trail trying to intercept his meeting with the mysterious Brill. Hackman takes Smith into a hotel elevator, stops between floors, and holds him down at gunpoint. Then, as the techno-geeks in the NSA vans try to figure out where Smith is, we see Brill methodically rip the tracking devices out of Smith's shoes, pager, cell phone, and other accessories—the pants will come later, and then only because Brill realizes that the reason the NSA helicopters are still bearing down on them is because there must still be a tracking device hidden on him somewhere. Throughout the ordeal in the elevator, Smith has no idea what is happening to him or why Brill is holding him at gunpoint. A disjointed conversation ensues where it becomes clear to Brill that Smith has no idea who is after him or why. Revealing his own secretive side, he screams at Smith, "Who are you working for? Is this about me? Am I a target here? Do they know me?!" Smith replies that he has no idea what Brill is talking about and Hackman retorts, "You're either very smart or incredibly stupid."

Smith learns a lot from this encounter, especially that it can't be the mob that has access to the technology that's been planted on him. Such tracking devices are only available, according to Brill, to the NSA. And while a bewildered Smith listens to Brill lecture him about the pulsing rates of the satellite trackers planted on his body, Smith slowly becomes aware that he is at the mercy of the most powerful surveillance infrastructure on the planet. Realizing the danger, Brill abandons Smith on the roof of the hotel, not wanting to become a target of the NSA as well. Later we will learn that Brill's obsessions with privacy are the result of his own work with the NSA years previous. Now, in private life, he has done everything possible to create a secure cocoon of anonymity around himself, going so far as to live in an electronically hardened bunker in an abandoned warehouse, unconnected to any outside phone or cable lines.

But what Smith still does not know, even after meeting Brill, is why he is a target. If surveillance produces subordination through uncertainty, then the reversal here is that when it is known, even while its motivation remains a mystery, surveillance produces fear, panic, and a desire to flee the grasp of the state, to in essence become an enemy of the state even when no crime has been committed. From here the plot unfolds, with Hackman eventually joining Smith in his fight against the NSA, first by finding the disk that had been planted on him by Jason Lee, and then by turning the tables on the corrupt NSA director by using his own technology against him, bugging Voight's house and cleverly planting the GPS tracking devices in a congressman's hotel room so that they will be discovered by other NSA operatives not working for Voight. The surveyor becomes the surveyed—a theme we will pick up on again below.

As mentioned above, the narrative power of *Enemy of the State* as an argument about the dangers of surveillance technology comes most powerfully from its intertextual references to the earlier film, *The Conversation*. The most striking, and indeed the most telling, of these references is that Gene Hackman not only plays Brill in *Enemy* but also the main character of *The Conversation*, who is also a PI specializing in electronic surveillance. And since the lives of both characters are portrayed as highly secretive, and much time passes between the time frame of both films, there is even an implied suggestion that it might be the same character, not just the same actor, showing up in both films. One warning, however, before launching into comparisons between the two films in more detail: Such observations do not mean that one has to have seen *The Conversation* to appreciate *Enemy* as a film critical of surveillance technology. In the filmic discussion of surveillance technology spanning a number of films, however, *Enemy* is inescapably linked, and most likely intentionally so, to *The Conversation* for the critical viewer. For many film buffs, the enjoyment of *Enemy* came principally from its connection with *The Conversation* through the very similar characters both played by Hackman.[9] Even though we don't know for sure that the two characters are identical, the shared identities and occupations of the characters invite the comparison.

But *Enemy*, I will maintain, is a very crude film when compared with *The Conversation*, because it never considers the possible problems inherent in surveillance technology. Instead, *Enemy* appears to be more interested in showing off the sophistication of its computer-driven surveillance equipment than in understanding the implications of the use of such technologies. In contrast, *The Conversation* arguably makes the case that the use of surveillance technologies corrupts its users and, at least in that sense, is substantive rather than neutral. Even when the users have the best of intentions, as Hackman's character does in *The Conversation*, the technology is still corrupting. While the NSA director in *Enemy* is portrayed as corrupt, there is no similar problem with our heroes, Hackman (as Brill) and Smith, when they employ the same technologies against the NSA. Charlton Heston may as well have written this one: The message of the film appears to be that surveillance technology doesn't hurt people, people hurt people. This aspect of the film comes out most openly in the ending of *Enemy*, which I will return to below.

The plot of *The Conversation*, though not as flashy, is much more interesting than that of *Enemy*. In it, a younger Hackman plays Harry Caul, a PI specializing primarily in electronic audio surveillance. Caul has been hired by a wealthy business client to tape a conversation between the client's wife and a male employee. This is a tricky job for Caul because the conversation between the two, which opens the film, takes place outside on a noisy afternoon in San Francisco's Union Square. Caul has to assemble a special team using hidden and directional microphones to target the couple as they walk through the square. Their conversation therefore has to be pieced together from various sections of tape picked up by different sources. When Caul returns to his shop to edit the tape, he has to employ homemade filtering devices to decrease the ambient sound that drowns out much of what the original recordings were trying to capture. The results, however, are quite surprising.

But before getting into the interesting twist that *The Conversation* puts on the social act of electronic surveillance and the implications of this technology on the moral life of its users, let's go back to *Enemy*. For in addition to casting Gene Hackman in both films, the opening scene of *The Conversation* just briefly described is duplicated almost exactly in *Enemy of the State*. In *Enemy*, however, it is the NSA's techno-geeks trying to tape a conversation outside between Smith and Lisa Bonet around Baltimore's Mount Vernon Square.

The Mount Vernon Square scene in *Enemy* occurs prior to the meeting of Brill and Smith. In this scene, Smith calls Lisa Bonet for a meeting in what he thinks will be a location where they will not be noticed. The purpose of the meeting is to try to get her to tell him how to contact Brill. Smith has just lost his job and is trying to find out who is behind the fake newspaper stories implicating him in shady dealings with the Mafia. Because Smith had used Brill, through Bonet, to gather secret tapes of mob bosses colluding on the rigging of a union election, Smith thinks that Brill may be able to confirm that the mob is now out to get him, or even that Brill may somehow be involved in his public evisceration. Because the NSA has tapped Smith's phones, they know where and when he will meet with Bonet, and they set up their operation accordingly.

As the scene opens, we see Smith and Bonet from above, from the perspective of one of the surveyors. The NSA has set up a team around the square coordinated by a command unit in a nearby van. The first shot of one of the team members shows an agent standing on a concealed ledge overlooking the square with both a directional microphone, which looks like a small handheld satellite dish, and a camera with an extremely large telescopic lens. Still frames from the camera pointed at Smith and Bonet are frozen onto the screen so that we see them through the camera viewfinder of the surveyors. The importance of these first few shots in the scene should be noted because they are strikingly similar to shots of an almost identical agent working for Harry Caul, using similar equipment and working from a nearly identical vantage point, opening the parallel scene in *The Conversation*.

As Smith and Bonet walk around the square, the camera follows them. But instead of staying with them, we get shots of the other NSA agents working the job. One sits on a park bench with a microphone hidden in a newspaper; another is disguised as a homeless person with a mike hidden in a garbage bag. The voices we hear in the scene alternate between those of Smith and Bonet as they would hear themselves talking to each other, and the recording of their conversation as it is picked up by the NSA agents, slightly garbled with overtones of electronic filtering. At times what they say is clear to us, at times it is not. When the couple walks under some trees, our vantage point shifts to the agent overhead using the satellite dish mike and we are unable either to see them or to make out what they are saying.

For anyone who has seen *The Conversation*, the reference in this scene in *Enemy* to the opening of the earlier film is obvious. We watch in *The Conversation* as a couple walks through Union Square, again beginning from the same high camera angle. Just as the first few shots of the parallel scene in *Enemy* are mixed in with photos superimposing a still camera lens over the frame of the film, the first few shots of the scene in *The Conversation* are through the telescopic lens of Caul's high-perched agent, so that we actually view them as if we are looking through the same scope—the couple appears as a target viewed through a hunting rifle. When the camera moves to the level of the square itself, we see the couple come into and out of the frame. Sometimes the shot focuses on them, and sometimes it pulls away to show us an unidentified figure wearing a raincoat, seemingly disconnected from the couple, as well as a few other figures with small earplugs, evidently agents, just as in *Enemy*, trying to blend in with the crowd in the square while helping to record their conversation. We only discover later that the figure in the raincoat is Caul.

Also as in *Enemy*, what we mostly hear during this scene is the sound of the couple's voices filtered through the listening devices of Caul's crew, rather than only hearing them as they would sound to each other. Unlike *Enemy*, though, most of the conversation between the couple in Union Square is inaudible and garbled by a very strange electronic wobbling sound. Until the scene finishes, we don't even know for sure that what we've been hearing is the sound of the conversation as it is being recorded.

It just sounds like something is wrong with the soundtrack of the film. In part, the power and superior aesthetic quality of this scene over its companion in *Enemy* are due to the fact that we only slowly discover what is going on in the scene. We don't have the same point of view as the agents recording the couple's conversation, since it's not apparent what point of view we're being afforded in the film as it begins. The flashier jump cuts in *Enemy* are in part only made possible by the foreknowledge provided to the viewer by the script.

But in addition to the similarities between these two scenes, there is one critical difference: At the end of the scene in *The Conversation,* the camera follows the younger Hackman character back to the control van (similar to the one coordinating the parallel scene in *Enemy*), rather than staying with the couple under surveillance. We don't actually see much more of them, other than in flashbacks throughout the film, whereas the target of the recording operations in *Enemy,* Will Smith, is the main character of that film. Already we know that *The Conversation* will focus on a very different set of problems and issues about surveillance technology. Some might even say that the focus of the film is too different for a useful comparison. *Enemy* is a spy thriller, and *The Conversation* is a psychological drama about a tortured surveillance agent. I will turn to this issue in more detail at the end of this section. While undeniably true, both films still have the same ostensible focus: the use and abuse of surveillance technology. But the similar focus in *Enemy* does not grant the film a similar depth on the issue.

What then is more interesting about *The Conversation*? From this opening scene we learn that Hackman's Harry Caul has a long and distinguished history in the business of private eavesdropping—people almost fall over him as a legendary figure at a bugging trade show that he attends midway through the film. But we also learn some even more unusual things about Caul over the course of the film. His past is dark, and he feels responsible for deaths that may have resulted from information that he obtained for previous clients. Caul is trying to assuage his guilty conscience through a constant argument with himself that there is a strong separation that he can draw between his work life and his private life. In an early scene, Caul's assistant, played by John Cazale (later Fredo Corleone in the *Godfather* films), starts to press Caul about the topic of the conversation they have just recorded. Hackman refuses to answer, and when he gets irritated at Cazale, asking him why he wants to know, Cazale retorts that it's simple curiosity, just "goddamn human nature." Caul then lectures him, saying that if there is one thing he's learned in this occupation, it is that, "I don't know anything about human nature. I don't know anything about curiosity. That's not part of what I do." And then, finally tripping over his own words, "This is my business." A disgusted Cazale gets up and leaves.

But almost immediately we learn that this separation between work and private life is not something that Caul can pull off. After Cazale's exit, Caul works with increasing fervor on the tapes of the conversation in Union Square, carefully filtering out background music obscuring the voices. What he hears surprises him. Caul begins to suspect that the couple that he has taped is in grave danger and that the person that paid him to record their conversation is planning on killing one or both of them, presumably because they are having an affair.

As this knowledge presses more and more on him, we get a stronger sense that Caul is no longer at ease with his profession and the tools of his own trade. At one point he goes to a Catholic priest for confession and, after divulging some very minor sins, hesitatingly unburdens himself, stammering, "I've been involved in some work that I think will be used to hurt two young people." But before the priest can respond, Caul, audibly wrestling with himself, blurts out that he is "not really responsible" for what might happen to the couple and ends the confession. Finally, Caul tries to intervene in what he thinks will be the couple's murder. (The ending to this film, however, presents a dramatic reversal that I don't need to divulge here.) Caul is left shattered by his experiences involving the couple, and no amount of good intentions on his part, like those later motivating Smith and Brill to use the tools of surveillance against the NSA, changes the damage done by the technology.

When we compare Caul's internal struggles with the techno-geeks' attitude toward their work in *Enemy*, we get an even stronger contrast. These characters (played, for example, by cool twenty-somethings such as Jack Black) seem to blithely and gleefully go about their business without much by way of self-reflection and nothing by way of self-doubt. Although we could understand the importance of not showing any second guessing on the part of the evil NSA director (after all, that would diminish his spectacularly one-dimensional character development), there is no explanation for why there is no regret expressed by the techno-minions around him. Even if we appeal to the tendency for minor characters like these to rarely get any development in big-budget Hollywood films, there is something more going on here.

The techno-geeks of *Enemy* represent people so thoroughly imbued in computer culture, one might even want to say that they are drawn to be indistinguishable from average mid-1990s dot-com programmers, that they become a distraction from any worries we may have about the invasiveness of this kind of technology. The problem is not so much the portrayal of the neutrality of the technology here but the "gee-whiz" enthusiasm of its users who, I suppose like many of us, just consume any shiny electronic object that is sent down the pipeline. In scene after scene, they make fun of the gun thugs who don't understand the technology they are employing to track down Smith and Brill. When following their targets, they easily make jocular comments about the women they see through their view scopes (the Jack Black character evidently is attracted to Will Smith's middle-aged Hispanic maid). These are not so much evil users as they are banal users, which we might expect to be somewhat more accurate as a portrayal of users of most harmful tools than someone like Jon Voight. They are like SUV drivers who never give a thought about the increased production of greenhouse gases coming from their tailpipes. Similarly, the techno-geeks in *Enemy* are comfortably unaware of the damage they are creating around them. They could be any of us, and so might even be the characters we can most empathize with.[10]

What is the damage though that Caul has done, or that the film helps us to recognize, which is not present in *Enemy*? Not so much a harm he has perpetrated on others, though that is surely there, but a kind of harm to himself. Caul's profession provokes a crisis of conscience in him that makes it impossible for him to distinguish between private and professional life. As that profession is defined through the technology he is using, it plays a necessary and unique role in producing this crisis of conscience. This is not to say that working with the tools of surveillance technology necessarily corrupts the user—such a conclusion would only be justifiable using a strong autonomy thesis about technology, which I do not endorse—but that the mediated distance that the technology offers between the surveyor and the surveyed poses a danger to the surveyor himself, who ends up objectifying his or her targets—becoming so disconnected from them that ordinary human empathy, or even "curiosity," is cut short for the purposes of completing a task. As suggested above, I have no doubt that surveillance technology can produce needed security, especially in times of crisis. But to live in a world imbued with surveillance is to live in a world that places technological hurdles on everyday acts of empathy. Even if one objects to this reading of the possible dangers of this technology, then at least it is the case that such an issue is worth investigating in an adequate discussion of it. To simply overlook such questions and rest comfortably with the Hestonite line is to be too naïve as to the possible dangers of the widespread use of this kind of technology. *Enemy* makes it easy for us to forego such discussions in the name of entertainment; *The Conversation* invites us into these discussions, an important activity whether we wind up agreeing with the neutrality thesis or not.

Another thing we learn about Caul that is interesting, and which takes *The Conversation* in very different directions from *Enemy*, is that Caul, like Brill, is obsessed with maintaining his own privacy. For Caul, however, this obsession, intrinsically tied to his technologically defined profession, has had an almost overwhelming debilitating effect on him. In contrast, Brill's obsession with his own privacy is used mostly in *Enemy* as a curiosity, a foil for Smith's jokes at Hackman's expense. Caul, like Brill, fears the technology that he uses because he has intimate knowledge of its power. But Caul is palpably plagued by such worries. Through a series of establishment scenes we learn, for instance, that he refuses to give out his phone number, or even tell people that he owns a phone. He is visibly disturbed when anyone shows any knowledge of him, such as when, in an early scene in the film, he is upset to learn that a casual girlfriend (played by Teri Garr) knows his birthday. Caul's obsession with privacy stunts his development as a person who can enjoy what we would assume is the normal range of human contact. Surely one of the things that makes human relationships pleasurable, at least for most people, is when a friend or lover knows something about us and takes an interest in what they believe is important to us. Caul is in a position, however, where he can enjoy none of that: Every instance of recognition is instead for him an exercise in anxiety and fear.

The most striking instance of this problem is at the end of the film when Caul realizes that he in fact has been the subject of surveillance himself. The closing scene of *The Conversation* opens with Caul sitting in his apartment after he has experienced the tragedy involving the couple that closes the story of the film. He has a jazz record going and he is playing along with it on a saxophone. Suddenly his phone rings (the one that he obsessively keeps hidden from everyone around him). The voice on the other end is that of Harrison Ford, who plays the assistant to the client who hired Caul to record the conversation between the couple in Union Square. Ford says, "We know that you know Mr. Caul. For your own sake, don't get involved any further. We'll be listening to you." After Ford hangs up, Caul hears the sound of a reel-to-reel tape recorder rewinding and then being played. The sound on the other end of the line is that of Caul playing along on his saxophone to the jazz record he was just listening to. Instantly, he knows that his apartment, his zone of privacy, has been bugged.

The last few minutes of the film see Caul falling apart. Haunting piano music plays in the background as he wanders around the apartment wondering where the bug might be. He begins going over every inch of the place with a bug-detecting device; finding nothing, he starts unscrewing electricity sockets, ripping down curtains and blinds, and examining every knickknack on his shelves. Light fixtures, the telephone itself, a heating element—everything is taken apart to try to find the bug. As the apartment is slowly dismantled, we see that he has left standing a small plastic statue of the Virgin Mary, which he was hoping to avoid desecrating. Desperate, he finally picks it up, beats it with his fist, and rips open the back, and still he finds nothing. An increasingly desperate Caul tears apart his wallpaper and even begins ripping out his wooden floorboards with a crowbar. Still nothing. In the final shot of the film, which may be one of the most sublime in American cinema, we start with a pan shot from the right side of Caul's living room, moving slowly across to the left, revealing a completely and utterly destroyed apartment. It is as if the apartment had been condemned decades before and vandals had removed everything that might have been left in it. The camera, still moving left, passes by Caul sitting in a corner of his ruined home playing a mournful tune on his saxophone, and then briefly pans back right to rest on him as the final shot of the film. Caul has been ruined. Whether he will be harmed by Harrison Ford and the people he works for is unimportant. The inner life created by Caul's "business," as he put it to his assistant, has destroyed him.

In this light, the ending of *Enemy* can be seen as a bizarre reversal of the powerful ending of *The Conversation* and more proof that the film embraces a neutrality thesis with respect to surveillance technology. *Enemy* leaves us with a happy ending for the same character, namely, Hackman, in his portrayal of Brill. In that closing scene we see Will Smith now sitting again at home watching TV with his wife and son. The evil Jon Voight has been vanquished, and Smith, at least, has become a hero. Brill has used the opportunity of the confusion ending the main story of the film to finally slip away and get the privacy he now wants. After Smith's wife and son leave the room, he starts to flip through the TV channels with a remote control. Static starts to cloud the picture, and Smith finds that the remote control no longer works. Finally, the TV settles on one picture only; it is Smith himself, sitting on his couch, watching TV. He looks up and realizes that Brill has left a tiny camera in a smoke detector in Smith's living room so that he can keep watch on him. Then the images on the TV screen change and we get a series of shots of a sailing ship at sea, a person (off camera) playing with a cat on a beach, words written in the sand saying "Wish You Were Here," and finally, a shot of some very pale legs. Smith laughs in amazement, realizing it is Brill sending him a message that he is all right. We end with Smith saying to the legs on the TV, "You're gonna have to get a tan on those things."

Comparing these two closing scenes crystallizes the difference between these two films, at least on the issue of what this kind of technology may do to its users. In *The Conversation* the technology harms Caul greatly; it has no comparable effect on Smith or Hackman in *Enemy*. Again, the message in the latter seems to be that so long as the technology is in the right hands, one doesn't have to worry. At the close of *Enemy*, Smith receives a message magically beamed in over his television from Hackman. While Hackman has hacked into Smith's private space to get him this message, the intrusion this time is not an unwelcome, even devastating invasion of privacy but a communication as innocuous as a piece of e-mail. And significantly, this technology has apparently done nothing to harm Brill himself, only made it easier for him to retire early and keep in contact with his old friends.

One thing more before moving to our next film. As I said above, one might object that these two films are so different that it is unfair to compare them. *Enemy* is a thriller and we are remiss to blame it for being shallow; *The Conversation* is a sophisticated art film about a tortured surveillance expert. Or *Enemy* is about the dangers inherent in state control of surveillance technology and *The Conversation* is about the dangers posed to users by this technology, and because the focus is different, they are not comparable. Such a response, though, would be missing the critical similarities of these two films. Three points here. First, this view reduces the strong intertextual references between the two films to mere incidental window dressing. As every surveyor eventually becomes surveyed in both of these films, the differences in their respective plots may not matter that much. Second, while surely both of these films are about lots of things—*Enemy*, for example, may be about racial prejudice as much as it is about anything—the predominant focus of both films is some set of arguments about the general dangers of surveillance technology. Both point to dangers about these tools, and, I want to argue, both have an answer to the fundamental philosophical question concerning this technology, and many others, with which I started off this chapter: Are these just neutral tools or not? My claim is that what *The Conversation* goes on to say about surveillance technology is much more substantive than what *Enemy* says. As a consequence, we can criticize *Enemy*, and if asked to think further about filmic portrayals of surveillance technology, can use this criticism to find other films about surveillance that don't have the same problem (which I will do next). I would maintain though that *Enemy* could have given us the same story without presenting a Hestonite interpretation of these technologies as neutral. It needn't have come to the same conclusion about the possible dangers of these technologies on their users as *The Conversation* has in order to take a more substantive line.

Finally, whether *Enemy* should get a free pass because it was produced as a holiday blockbuster is beside the point from the perspective of the crucial discussion that we must have about the use, abuse, and extent of our surveillance society. For surely it is almost trivial to say that surveillance technology represents an intrusion on our privacy. But as part of the public debate that we must have about surveillance technology, *Enemy* actually does more harm than good by reducing the implications of technology to nothing much more interesting than Charlton Heston's pronouncements about the dangers of handguns. To argue that this critique is unfair or out of bounds would put us in an uncomfortable position with respect to other films on other important topics. Do we really want to say that films that unreflectively glorify war and the military, such as *Top Gun*, also directed by Tony Scott (1986), can't be criticized because, after all, they are just fun shoot-'em-up star vehicles? Would we really want to give up on the possibility of articulating the comparative virtues of a film like *Saving Private Ryan* (1989), because, at least in its famous opening sequence of the Battle of Normandy, it shows us more realistically that war is hell? Both films arguably propose that military service is not only honorable but something to be praised and appreciated, and that Americans have done, or can do, much that is brave in the defense of their country. But the virtues of *Saving Private Ryan*, in showing how truly difficult, horrific, and multidimensional warfare can be, despite what I think are some serious flaws of that film, are in part noteworthy because of the comparison we can make to films that, less responsibly, reduce military service to a two-hour recruitment commercial.[11]

Updating the Conversation:
The End of Violence

Wim Wenders's film *The End of Violence* serves both as a good counterpoint to *Enemy* and as an extension of the critique of surveillance technology offered by *The Conversation*. This is important because, as mentioned above, one limitation of the argument of *The Conversation* concerning surveillance technology is that the technology represented in it seems antiquated to today's viewers. Because *Enemy* does such a superior job of representing this technology to us, its ridiculously happy ending may be quite seductive. We might be tempted to conclude that the worries voiced by the earlier film are just as antiquated as the technology it represents. The technology represented in *The End of Violence*, however, is more up to date, and in many ways the limitations presented by its lower budget in the portrayal of this technology is made up for by a kind of realism in its suggestion that these technologies are works in progress rather than finished products.[12]

The plot of *The End of Violence* is fairly complicated and I will not try to summarize it now. Suffice to say that it is a mystery involving an investigation carried out jointly by a Hollywood producer, Mike Max, played by Bill Pullman, and another surveillance expert named Ray Bering, this time played by Gabriel Byrne.[13] Byrne plays a former NASA scientist who has been hired by an unnamed government agency to complete an elaborate electronic surveillance network in Los Angeles, seemingly bigger than the surveillance network described earlier in Washington Square Park only in scale. As far as Byrne knows, the network will be used for standard police surveillance. But as the plot unfolds, he becomes aware that the network may actually be used for enforcement as well as surveillance. We learn that high-powered, long-range guns may be attached to these cameras, so that if the police, or whatever government agency is running the network, can see a criminal, they can also execute them on the spot. Focusing, however, only on the comparison of Byrne to the two Hackman characters and the techno-geeks, we find a more substantive treatment of technology in this film than in *Enemy*.

When we first meet Byrne's character, he is walking up to Los Angeles's Griffith Observatory, high over the city on the southern slope of Mt. Hollywood. Entering his workspace in the observatory, we see a large domed room crowded with television monitors, most of them haphazardly piled on top of each other with yellow stickers affixed to them scrawled with numbers or small notes. (The irony of the setting of the hub of the surveillance system in an old observatory should not be lost on us—where once we located such structures to look upward and outward in a process of discovery, we now use them here to focus down on a space to be controlled.) Byrne sits at a simple keyboard amid the apparent chaos and begins talking to a techie in another room, whom we see only through a monitor. The techie informs him of the night's work, which involved setting up more of what sounds like surveillance cameras all over the city. He then teases Ray about his habit of walking up the mountain to the observatory rather than driving. Ray quips, "Truth is, I try to avoid modern technology whenever I can."

A couple of things in this first introduction to Byrne's character strike us, especially in comparison to the other two films already discussed. First is the unfinished state of the surveillance project. This setting may help to empower the concerned viewer that there is still room to discuss the use of this technology before it is fully enabled, a point I will return to below. Second, and perhaps more important, are the very human qualities exhibited by Byrne while he is going about his tasks of setting up the network. It is clear that his character is more like Harry Caul than Brill, and even further removed from the techno-geeks of *Enemy*. But he is in a similar position to the techno-geeks of *Enemy*. Like them, Ray works for the government, rather than as a private surveillance expert like Brill or Caul.

As Byrne gets on with what we can assume is a fairly typical work day, he starts checking the installation of the new cameras in the system. Much of this work appears to be mundane—not at all the glamorous, streamlined tasks of the techno-geeks, though still more complicated, in many ways, than the audio surveillance that Caul does. But in checking the status of the new cameras, Byrne is also clearly not a cold professional. Shots move back and forth from the street scenes captured by the surveillance cameras to the expression on Byrne's face as he takes in these views. In one of the most dramatic and touching contrasts, Byrne moves from assessing the intended features of the surveillance network—helping police chase down suspected criminals by allowing them a bird's-eye view of fleeing suspects—to long pauses where he realizes that the new camera angles allow him access into people's private lives.

On one monitor we see a suspicious-looking man on a street corner, apparently looking around to see if he is being watched. Another focuses in on a woman sitting in a window, apparently having an argument with someone whom we can't make out in the background. Perhaps it is a lover's quarrel. As Byrne's eyes move back and forth between the two scenes, he becomes less interested in the suspicious man on the corner, and instead, captivated by the blonde in the window. The person she was arguing with has left the room and she's sitting, staring off into space, visibly upset. But rather than just showing us a scene of the surveyor as voyeur, something we also saw in *Enemy*, the shots of Byrne's face watching this scene reveal someone who has become both attracted to and repelled by the power he now wields through these cameras. The watcher hesitates and cannot decide, as perhaps most people wouldn't be able to decide, between the official use of the technology and its almost casual invasive consequences. It is as if Byrne is realizing in the scene that he has created a system that makes it possible to intrude on the most intimate moments of people's lives. Byrne's gaze over the woman crying in the apartment is not so much malicious as awed, and even embarrassed.

In terms of our earlier analysis of the effects of this technology on Harry Caul in *The Conversation*, here we again have a picture of the surveyor as deeply affected by the technology that has come to define a large portion of his life. We can surely imagine similar moments of self-reflection by people in other professions, but in this film it is important that this technology has an effect on the user that is intimately tied to the purpose of the technology. In this scene, and in many more explicit ones that follow as the plot of the film gradually unfolds, Byrne struggles with the potential for this technology to create a moral distance between himself and others, very close to the issue at the heart of *The Conversation*. At this early stage in the development of this particular system, we can imagine that Byrne has the space to be more self-reflective about what is being created while at the same time being concerned about its future. Would those taking over the system after he is finished set aside similar qualms and simply indulge the invasive tendencies of the technology as they become more and more numb to the privacy of those they are watching? We can imagine that those later users of the system might be more like the techno-geeks of *Enemy*. Even before Byrne finds out about the dangerous extension of the network to include a stronger enforcement potential, he worries about its possible abuse. And in contrast to Caul (and also Brill), Byrne's Ray is not presented as someone obsessed with privacy. The particular worries that he has about the surveillance network can't be explained away as an overactive sense of paranoia that could or could not be caused by the technologies he works with on a day-to-day basis. Ray is instead a person with a past, even a limited family, who has become aware of the possible inherent dangers of the system he is creating.

Another commendable aspect of this portrayal of the technology is that the system is not perfected. In *Enemy*, it was only other technology or technological knowledge that could interfere with the power of the surveillance tools—Smith can't fight the system alone, he needs the help of an expert. But in addition to the representation of the technology as unfinished, in *The End of Violence* we also see that natural objects, like clouds, cause problems for it. In a later scene, Byrne, again working in his observatory office, tries to focus in on recorded satellite imagery of a suspected kidnapping and assassination, which is at the center of the plot of the film. He is foiled, however, by an overcast sky, which prevents him from having access to the exact time index he is trying to locate. Surveillance technology does not grant him all-seeing power over the world at any time and any place, a picture of these tools that is surely closer to the truth. The satellite imagery also looks more primitive, in contrast to its portrayal in *Enemy*; people appear as bright blobs on the landscape rather than figures that we can distinguish from one another. In contrast, when Brill first meets Smith, he is able to keep his identity from the NSA satellites only by first putting himself in proximity to TV satellite dishes, which he hopes will scramble their signal, and then by refusing to look up, thus keeping his face out of range of the observing eye, which we are told later in the film is 155 miles above him. Only specialized knowledge of the techniques of surveillance, something most of us do not have, can protect us from it. The more realistic presentation of the limitations of surveillance in *The End of Violence* is in this way almost refreshingly democratic.[14]

Finally, Ray's character is fleshed out more fully with the minor character of his father, Louis (played by Samuel Fuller). This contrasting character gives Ray a past rather than dropping him out of nothing into a world of high technology. This is important, at least because it makes Ray a character we can empathize and identify with in a way that we most likely will not be able to do with Hackman's portrayal of Harry Caul, though which unfortunately we might be able to do with the techno-geeks in *Enemy*. Though not an "everyman," Ray is still someone we can more imagine as affected by the realizations unfolding before him in a way that we might be affected. We never learn much of anything about Ray's father, though he appears in a number of scenes throughout the film as a kind of naïve confidant to Byrne. It's never clear at all that Fuller understands what is happening to his son, especially later in the film as Byrne is put in danger when he learns of the possible secret uses of the surveillance network. Fuller serves more as a contrast to the high-technology world that Byrne moves in and through. In the scenes where we see him, Fuller is always in the study of the house he apparently shares with his son. Papers and old books are stacked here and there, in a contrast to Byrne's workspace in the observatory, though still similar to it in its chaotic order, and Fuller sits without fail behind an old wooden desk next to a large manual typewriter. As Byrne's chief character contrast, Fuller is portrayed with respect and a kind of awkward dignity as someone unfamiliar with computers, satellite technology, and the like and who has comfortably opted out of the need to understand these new developments.

In a lighter moment, Byrne watches his father tapping out something on his typewriter, one letter at a time, and suggests to him that he instead get a computer. Fuller replies, "No, no! I think the idea of this, is *right*! Not your computer. Oh, no, no, no, no, no, no, no." And then, pausing, he continues, "An old man, is an old man. I have nothing to lose but *that* [pointing to the letters on the typed page], as long as you remain with me." In the character of the father, the life of those outside of this special-ized world of technological knowledge is still represented as a life worth living. Though seemingly occasionally senile, Fuller's character helps to sober us up to the possibilities of resistance to the ubiquity of this tech-nology without lapsing into a form of Luddism.[15]

There is much more to be said here. But other than giving us a more complex character of a surveyor than possibly even found in *The Conversation, The End of Violence* also gives us a more explicit discussion than these other films of the trade-offs that go along with the widespread use of surveillance technology. This argument of the film might be para-phrased as a claim that surveillance itself is a new form of violence be-cause it relies on secrecy in order to be effective. This amounts to a kind of paradox of surveillance: If surveillance is used to create more security, it is always followed by a corresponding lack of security, at least if security is measured in terms of privacy. Or to put it another way, if we really could watch everyone doing everything all the time, and if we had the power to use that knowledge to stop bad acts from occurring, then we might create a perfectly safe world, but at the cost of completely undermining personal autonomy, or, if you will, our own sense of personal integrity, which the preservation of safety is supposed to protect.[16] Unpacking this argument from the film would take a lot more effort, and then evaluating the merits of it would be even more involved, but at the very least the film presents something much richer, and much more enticing in a public medium, than the Hestonite argument that surveillance technology is simply a neutral tool or that the users of this technology are only destined to be unaffected extensions of the tools they employ.

Conclusions

The paradox of surveillance proposed in *The End of Violence* is not just fiction. It is the subject of some of our most important discussions over surveillance today. On June 11, 2001, the U.S. Supreme Court handed down a major decision, *Kyllo v. United States* (No. 99–8508), on the limits of the use of surveillance technology as balanced against guarantees of the maintenance of privacy. The decision was highly unusual for the Court, not least because it cut across the traditional ideological divisions that have been duplicated in the past few years again and again, with Justices Rehnquist, Scalia, and Thomas holding down a conservative and strict constructionist view of the Constitution and Justices Ginsburg, Souter, and Stevens supporting more progressive and liberal interpretations of constitutional protection. In this 5–4 ruling, however, Justices Scalia, Souter, Thomas, Ginsburg, and Breyer joined in the majority while Justices Stevens, Rehnquist, O'Connor, and Kennedy were in the dissent. But even more impressive than the division of the vote was its sweeping nature, aimed not just at limiting a particular surveillance technology but also future technological developments that may erode privacy.

The original issue in *Kyllo* involved a federal investigation of a possible marijuana production facility in a home in Florence, Oregon. On the basis of tips and utility bills, the agents believed that high-intensity lamps were being used to grow the illegal drug. Using an "Agema Thermovision 210," an imager that can sense the intensity of heat sources through walls, the agents detected the presence of several hot spots in the house, and on the basis of the surveillance obtained a warrant to enter and search the home, where they found 100 marijuana plants. No warrant was ever obtained for the initial use of the technology on the house, however. Federal attorneys argued that none was needed because the thermal imaging devices "neither reveal private information nor violate the 'reasonable expectation of privacy' that is the Supreme Court's test under the Fourth Amendment" which provides protection against violation of "the right of the people to be secure in their person, houses, papers, and effects against unreasonable searches and seizures".[17] They cited case law, such as the 1964 decision in *Katz v. United States,* to assert that naked-eye surveillance of a home or other place where privacy can be "justifiably relied" upon is permissible (such as when a passing police officer may see, hear, or smell something that may warrant further investigation), while intrusions into a home "by even a fraction of an inch" are impermissible. Accordingly, the government argued that the investigation in *Kyllo* was not a "through-the-wall" invasion of the sanctity of the home but instead an "off-the-wall" search, where information providing inconsequential details of the heating ratio in a home was obtained and from that a reasonable inference was then derived which led to the arrest.

But in overturning the decision, Scalia and the majority argued that in the home "*all* details are intimate details, because the entire area is held safe from prying government eyes," and so the use of the Thermovision without a warrant was in violation of the Fourth Amendment. Further, this warrant requirement should be applied not simply for a device like this one but any "'more sophisticated system' in use or in development that lets the police gain knowledge that in the past would have been impossible without a physical entry into the home." As Scalia put it: "The question we confront today is what limits there are upon this power of technology to shrink the realm of guaranteed privacy," or, at what point "enhancement of ordinary perception from such a vantage point, if any, is too much." So long as the technology in question is not "in general public use," then its employment by a government to obtain information without a warrant is now illegal.[18]

Reflecting on these issues we might ask the following question: Does a critical reading of the films we have been discussing help us at all in understanding the scope and importance of the June 2001 decisions and future priorities for regulation of surveillance technology? If we were to base our decision solely on *Enemy of the State*, I think our answer would be that the decision might have gone too far—the state has a presumptive interest to police people in the name of creating a guarantee of certain public goods, here, the regulation of drugs, but more broadly, as we have said, maintaining security. So long as technologies, even what the Court referred to as "crude" tools, such as the Thermovision, are in the hands of the right people working in the interest of the public good, our attention should be directed at keeping an eye on the users of that technology, not at banning the use of the technology altogether. But looking at this decision from the perspective offered in *The Conversation* and *The End of Violence*, we may answer with a concern that the decision did not go far enough. Is it really permissible to use such technology even when it becomes publicly accessible, since then its use would not count as an unreasonable infringement of our privacy? Is it permissible for the government or private investigators to use such technology against us even in public settings, such as the Mount Vernon Square scene in *Enemy*, so that its employment would not violate the sanctity of the home? Such conclusions sound naïve: Even if such technologies become publicly available (and it is difficult to imagine how they might not be) then their dissemination only strengthens our panoptic society, where control is maintained, again, by being aware that we are being "watched by unseen eyes."

Additionally, while *Kyllo* did speak to the worries over the tensions between privacy and surveillance at the heart of both of these films, we also could argue by appeal to them that such issues may only be the tip of the iceberg. *Kyllo*, while heartening, raises the fundamental question of whether we want to live in a world dominated by this form of technology with its possible substantive and inherent problems. In light of new imperatives we will face for limiting privacy to counter the security threats made manifest by the events of September 11, addressing such broader aspects of surveillance technology may be even more important now than it ever was before that pivotal date.

3

Wim Wenders's
Everyday Aesthetics

I don't ever want to make another film in which a car or a petrol station or a television set or a phone booth aren't allowed to appear.

—Wim Wenders[1]

Aesthetics, as a philosophical discipline, is aimed at understanding the nature of beauty, much the same way that ethics aims at an understanding of the right and the good. Much work in aesthetics does indeed focus on the products of the traditional disciplines, especially the plastic arts, such as painting and sculpture. But for some time now, philosophers interested in aesthetics have turned to such subjects as nature, in the field now known as "environmental aesthetics," and other phenomena that are not normally thought of as the formal arts.[2] Collectively, many of these new areas of philosophical aesthetics are sometimes referred to as an aesthetics of the "everyday."[3]

An aesthetics of everyday life may be concerned with a broad range of phenomena, from the appreciation of ordinary objects, weather, food, or particular activities like walking to broader arenas such as the aesthetics of built spaces, including parks, skyscrapers, and cities. Further, when we describe someone as "living beautifully"—such as in identifying their inclinations toward small acts of kindness and generosity—we may even be speaking in everyday aesthetic rather than moral terms.

It is not the purpose of this chapter to offer a rigorous defense of an aesthetics of everyday life. Even while many people find such an endeavor intrinsically appealing, others find it difficult to take seriously as a philosophical project. But if there is something to such an idea then what follows should be of interest. The concern is actually not so far off from one we might have about the more formal arts. It has to do with the relationship between the determination that something is beautiful and the question of whether it then follows that we have either a moral obligation to preserve it as such or a social obligation to create practices or institutions dedicated to the preservation or production of such beautiful things.

From the perspective of an everyday aesthetics, I think the same question might be put this way: Does an inquiry into the aesthetics of everyday life tempt a normatively social as well as a more purely aesthetic form of inquiry? For if we can argue that the world around us is beautiful or not, then we beg the question of whether we want to live in a world configured so that it preserves and respects that beauty or else goes on indifferent to it.

In this chapter I explore this intuition with respect to the representation of an aesthetics of the everyday, with strong social (even moral) overtones, in the work of the German filmmaker Wim Wenders. In particular I will look at the narrative structured around the representation of our relationship to built space in his 1974 film *Alice in the Cities (Alice in den Städten)*. My intention here is not so much to examine this film as an aesthetic object itself, but to argue that Wenders's work reflects a broader view of how we should aesthetically understand, and consequently value, certain kinds of spaces encountered in everyday life.

Rather than analyzing this film by itself, I will frame this discussion in the context of a relevant debate currently under way in philosophy of technology, a subfield of philosophy discussed in the last chapter, that ought to be able to say something about the social, and perhaps aesthetic, dimensions of everyday material life, given how imbued that life has become with modern technologies.[4] Here I will look at an unfolding debate between Albert Borgmann and Andrew Feenberg, two philosophers who have written extensively on the possibility of technological reform for the purpose of enriching everyday life. So, in addition to the general issue of what Wenders's *Alice* tells us about the normative dimensions of an everyday aesthetic, it will also be interesting to see if thinking through Wenders's film helps us to better envision the kinds of transformations called for by theorists like Feenberg and Borgmann. Hopefully, situating the film in this philosophical debate will help us to better understand its relevance for assessing an aesthetics of everyday life while also demonstrating again that some films can contribute to ongoing philosophical debates in their own right.

Of course, providing us with novel ways of thinking through the dilemmas of our relationship to built space and technology is not the exclusive focus of Wenders's films. But there is enough there to "startle us," as Stanley Cavell would say, to see the important philosophical content of the films on these questions.[5] What becomes of these images, again following Cavell, is the raw material of film criticism, and in this case, I would say, substantive philosophical inquiry.

Thick and Thin Spaces

As just mentioned, much work in contemporary philosophy of technology is concerned with accounts of how different kinds of technology create different forms of social relations.[6] Certainly, one of the best examples of such a theory can be found in Albert Borgmann's Heideggerian-inspired distinction between devices and things. Borgmann's distinction expresses the intuitive difference between context-filled and contextless artifacts and the different social relationships they can engender. The richer sorts of technologies are called "focal things" (or just "things"). Our active engagement with these things are called "focal practices."

Things, Borgmann has argued, are inseparable from the context in which they are embedded. To stand in some relation to a thing is to engage in the social relations which it helps to make up. The benefits of a thing cannot be reduced to only one identifiable commodity. The social relations created by the wood stove in the frontier North American prairie house is one of Borgmann's paradigmatic examples of the complex effects on human relationships of a focal thing. Each person fulfills a special function in relation to the stove, with some gathering wood, others stoking the stove, and others cooking.[7] The stove is in this sense a medium for family life in at least three ways: It provides temporal regularity for the household, marks the different seasons, and serves as a locus for familial responsibility, and in that respect, part of individual identity.

We can also acquire skill in relation to things, as in the case of the wheelwright or blacksmith. Skill in relation to a thing "molds the person and gives the person character."[8] The skill we get in relation to things helps to shape our identity. Our engagement with the world through focal things potentially enriches our engagement with others as it thickens our own identity.

Conceptually distinct, for Borgmann, is the "device." Here is the foreground of modern mass technologies for which the world of things is the rapidly receding contrasting background: "A device such as a central heating plant procures mere warmth and disburdens us of all other elements. These are taken over by the machinery of the device. The machinery makes no demands on our skill, strength, or attention, and it is less demanding the less it makes its presence felt."[9]

As artifacts that need no particular context, devices do not connect us to particular places, relationships, or forms of agency. We can enjoy devices almost anywhere, anytime, with anyone. Since we do not need to engage with devices in the same way that we do with focal things, they do not require the skills we would have needed to use their counterpart, focal things. As a consequence, however, we lose whatever social identity we might have had through our connection with a similar focal thing. Borgmann's concern was that a life lived with and through devices is diminished, especially as we lose the social relations that we could have had through focal practices. It is because of this focus on the pernicious effects of devices on our social relationships that Borgmann called his theory the "device paradigm."

But how does Borgmann's ontology of technology help us to understand more complex technical systems and relationships? Can the claims of the theory be extended to conglomerations of artifacts—social spaces, both public and private, cities and suburbs?

In principle, we should be able to extend the theory to discussions of everyday spaces. The first reason is that one common method of making an argument for evaluating social spaces is to evaluate their component parts. On this account the overall characteristic of a built space is the result of the material characteristics of its component parts. This is a defensible assumption provided that an important rider is attached: Though such a theory may offer a necessary component of a full description of a space, it probably won't be a sufficient description in most cases. I am not arguing that cities, for example, are solely reducible to their parts. Several writers have pointed out that a full description of a city must include other elements. But an analysis of cities as collections of things and devices is at least an important part of a full account of the character of built space.[10] If a space is dominated by one kind of artifact, and we have a good theory of the normative implications of that artifact type, then a legitimate claim can be made that our understanding of that artifact type offers an important part of the description of the spaces dominated by such artifacts.[11]

Following Borgmann's device paradigm, we can say that there are both *thick* spaces (constituted by focal things) and *thin* spaces (constituted by devices). We might then argue that the world of a homogeneous suburb, dominated at first glance by its devices of convenience, is a thin space, and that a richly textured city, even with all its problems, is a thick space. But such a dichotomy is only the beginning. Although it is certainly true that material spaces can be dominated by one set of artifacts, or one mode of experience, scale adds to the complexity of our understanding of any space. We can expect to find thick and thin (or thing-like and device-like) spaces of many types and many combinations. The challenge from Borgmann's framework is to unearth the terrain of complexity of a space under the weight of the device paradigm, and then to carefully discern the things and devices in each space.

Borgmann's theory is concerned with how technologies affect human identities and human relationships. By extension, whatever can be understood about the dominant artifacts of a space should help us to assess the probable social effects of that space. So by providing a theory for how artifacts socially influence us, Borgmann has already provided us with a way to account for spatially influenced identities and relationships. The preferred normative content of social space, given the device paradigm, should be clear: thick spaces that give us a sense of *place*. This is the second reason the device paradigm ought to be extended to questions of space. Borgmann's theory provides a social account of place and how artifacts shape our sense of place. We are better off, on Borgmann's account, when we attach ourselves to a specific location for specific reasons. One might say that our view of the world is thus enriched by such interaction. Borgmann's is not a theory of how isolated individuals relate to artifacts, but how artifacts shape us in relation to others to form places, or thick spaces.

Let me preempt one possible misreading of this claim. I am not arguing that an extension of Borgmann's account would result in a critique of thin spaces interpreted as meaning sparsely populated. If thick spaces are inhabited by focal things, or at least share the relationships Borgmann wishes us to have with focal things, then thin spaces are those made up by devices, inhabited by devices, or sharing the relationships we associate with devices. A device-generated space need not be sparsely populated. A typical thin space might be an area crowded with the same gas stations, fast-food restaurants, and chain motels that are found all along North American highways. There is little to distinguish these areas as places, and their virtue is that such franchises can be found anywhere and have devoted consumer followings. A thick space, in contrast, could be either a multifaceted, wonderfully crowded urban area or a simple "mom and pop" store in the country marked by its distinct historical and cultural connections to its surroundings.

But as Borgmann's view was not explicitly formulated as an aesthetic of the everyday, we need a further comparison to bolster this account so far. Philosophical reflection on this nexus of artifacts, spaces, and places—on the intuition that an investigation of one of these areas entails, or perhaps requires, an investigation of the others—was central to what Henri Lefebvre was working toward in his *Critique of Everyday Life*.[12] Though too complex to go into here, Lefebvre's target was an "unearthing of the human world that lies buried" beneath the commodified world.[13] Or, following the device paradigm, an investigation of the possibilities of thing-like relationships in thick spaces despite the ubiquity of devices. As Michel Trebitsch has pointed out, Lefebvre's thesis here stands in striking contrast to the approach of other European critics of the first half of the twentieth century who had degraded the everyday. For Georg Lukács, the everyday was *Alltäglichkeit,* or "trivial life," the world of objects that drearily stands in contrast to "authentic life" found in works of art. But following Lefebvre, one can argue that there is an aesthetic to be found in the everyday and that it can be contrasted, not with the arts as institutions, but with a world dominated by Borgmann's devices.[14] Both the fine arts and an aesthetic appreciation of the everyday stand against the homogeneity of thin spaces. One way then of describing a serious reflection on spaces and artifacts, following Lefebvre and perhaps Borgmann, is as an investigation into the aesthetics of everyday life.[15]

But before going further, let us contrast Borgmann's approach to technology, with its implications for an everyday aesthetic, with a different view advocated by Andrew Feenberg. Feenberg's focus was on the potential for modern commercial technologies designed for passive use and consumption to contribute to social injustice. One of his central claims, however, was that public involvement, either in the design process or at the point of consumption, can result in what he called a "subversive rationalization" of those technologies. Successful subversions occur when the social relations embedded in the design process are overcome in an act of "democratic technological change."[16] Feenberg's examples included the subversion of the Minitel videotext system in France from a passive information technology to an interactive network connecting thousands of people for purposes never anticipated by its creators. In this example, the French government sponsored the production and distribution of information retrieval units in private households. For example, train schedules and tickets could be called up and purchased over this primitive electronic mail system. But eventually, users learned to "hack" the Minitel and subverted the social role of the design of the machine for a variety of purposes.[17] The transformed videotext service was used both to clandestinely arrange for sexual liaisons and to organize protests against government policies.

Feenberg's argument assumes a description of technological design that is socially relative. While political intentions can be built into designs, designs also can have unintended political consequences. Artifacts and technical systems need not necessarily exert one form of social control, but because they often do, a critical theory of technology different from Borgmann's is needed to give an account of the peculiarities of various forms of design. We might, however, wonder about the breadth of the processes described by Feenberg's notion of subversive rationalization. Is this process limited only to artifacts, or can it be extended to more complex systems and built spaces as well?

Feenberg's subversion thesis can be thought of as a conscious political strategy: advice to persons living amid technological systems that often appear to shape their lives without consent. His account is supposed to offer hope for resistance to the technologies that often determine how we live, or at least severely limit our options for shaping our social and political relations. But such strategies are surely not the only way to resist the pernicious effects of our technological environment. Following the suggestion of the aesthetic implications at work in Borgmann's device paradigm, we might also consider how artistic representations of technology, space, and everyday life that stand against dominant forms of social organization could also serve the process of subversive rationalization.

But this conclusion leaves us with a bit of a tension. Although Borgmann's device paradigm might in the end be useful for examining the everyday aesthetics of artifacts and spaces, it does not have much room for the transformative potential in some technology that theorists like Feenberg have envisioned. Borgmann has given us a way of describing different kinds of social relations mediated by different kinds of technology, but he has not given us an argument for how we can transform the relations produced by one form of technology to those embodied by another, other than abandoning one set of technologies for an alternative set.[18] How then do we thicken the spaces we actually find ourselves in and improve the social relationships they engender?

Because of problems like this, Feenberg found substantive theories like Borgmann's inherently conservative.[19] Such theories, he argued, tend to embrace a romantic notion of a simpler technological world we have lost, or of the importance of a sense of place that may be out of reach for most of us. Is there instead a way to give particular devices, or systems of devices, thing-like qualities, or at least to expand and open up what we take to be the world of focal things? I think there is. But an account of such transformations ought to do something Feenberg's argument does not always do—it ought to begin with Borgmann's assumptions that there really are different sorts of technology, and hence spaces, which have different social effects. In what remains of this chapter I will argue that Wim Wenders's films provide an example of an everyday aesthetic that encompasses an account of spatial and technological subversion while also clearly marking out different types of artifacts and spaces. They therefore combine the virtues of both Feenberg's and Borgmann's theories and may reconcile and go beyond them in some ways.

In Wenders's work we find an interesting description both of the transformative potential of particular technologies and of new social relations possible within built spaces. Mass commodity devices are subverted in these films to serve the interests of focal practices and thick spaces. New social relations can be created, or at least aesthetically represented, where we do not ordinarily see such potential.

A World on the Road

Many of Wenders's films are driven in part by a desire to reappropriate something that has been corrupted: first, our appreciation of everyday material culture, and second, our sense of place in an environment of increasingly sterile and characterless built spaces.[20] These two tasks are not distinct for Wenders as a filmmaker—he embraces Béla Balázs's idea that film as a medium is supposed to "show things as they are" and, specifically, "*rescue the existence of things.*"[21] Filmmaking itself, for Wenders, can be a heroic act because it halts "the gradual destruction of the world of appearances." He wrote, "The camera is a weapon against the tragedy of things, against their disappearing."[22] This notion explains the quotation opening this chapter. Wenders was expressing the frustration he experienced while making *The Scarlet Letter* (1972). At the production site in Spain, the filmmaker wasn't allowed to show the things and built spaces that would have been anachronistic in the context of the seventeenth-century period depicted in the film. Wenders mentions, for example, a two-story saloon that couldn't be changed to fit the historical requirements of the shots: "We would eat lunch in that saloon, sitting at long tables, but such genuine and arresting images of ourselves in the saloon (which we never shot) weren't allowed to appear in a film from which reality had to be strictly excluded, cut away like a bit of bad apple."[23] Wenders's films then ought to be a good candidate for an analysis of the everyday aesthetics of built space if only because he is so concerned with representing and holding on to the world of focal things.[24] Wenders's films are inextricably linked to some place, not just as a description of the landscape, but as an occasion to call attention to the material components making up the space itself. In a way, Wenders, Lefebvre, and Borgmann have all argued that the positive aesthetic qualities of everyday space should be preserved against erosion by a uniform commodity culture.[25]

Let us examine one of Wenders's films, *Alice in the Cities*, with an eye first toward its commentary on the transformation of built space, and second, briefly, to its appeal to the potential to preserve the focal quality of film itself.[26]

The First Road Trip

Alice is bracketed by two road trips, the first in the United States and the second in Germany. The first trip amounts to an exposition of the banality of the world of devices in American suburban and increasingly urban space. Our protagonist, Philip Winter (played by Rüdiger Vogler), is first seen under an unidentified pier taking pictures with a Polaroid camera, comparing the view with its photographic representation. Slowly, the film provides some sense of location, but only vaguely. A water tower advertising the place as "surf city" puts us on a coast somewhere in the United States. Spanish moss on trees along the highway makes the Southeast a likely candidate for the opening sequences.

Eventually, we learn that Philip is a German journalist on assignment to write an article about America. The specific topic is never mentioned, consistent with the sense that his travels lack focus. Philip is only collecting images by taking pictures, images which, he says, in some of the first lines of the film, "never really show what you've actually seen." But since Philip is never able to accurately express what the images do not reflect, it is unclear if any *thing* is really being seen at all, or any place ever encountered.

The opening sequence captures the banality of American highway culture, an endless stream of monotonous sameness for which there is only one overriding relationship: commodities and consumers. Philip drives through this landscape with increasing frustration. He starts talking to himself in a mixture of English and German, gets frustrated with the babble of commercial radio, and shows signs of coming apart. One outburst goes like this:

> "To shoot pictures." *(In English.)*
> "Mow down anything you can't stand." *(In German.)*
> "Channel 6. WTVR!" *(In English.)*
> (pause)
> "Talking to yourself is more of a listening than talking." *(In German.)*

The theme of searchers getting frustrated out on the road is a common one in Wenders's films. Robert Philip Kolker and Peter Beicken have argued that the common road theme in the films is indicative of Wenders's fascination with searching. But unlike the characters in a film like John Ford's *The Searchers* (1956), a film and a director much admired by Wenders, Wenders's characters are not clearly looking for anything. Kolker and Beicken claimed that Wenders's male characters "rarely gain insight into the traumatizing conditions and the hidden forces that drive them." They search without reason and what they ever find is not altogether clear.[27]

But in this case I think Philip actually has found something. Paradoxically, what he has found is the thin quality of suburban spaces, or perhaps more accurately, the spaces between cities. Later in the film, Philip returns to New York City, from whence, we eventually learn, he had launched his trip. In trying to explain his journey to a German friend, he lets us know what he has found on the road: "Soon as you leave New York everything looks the same. It seems impossible to imagine things being different. I completely lost my bearings. All I could imagine was things going on and on. Sometimes on the road, I was sure I would turn back next morning. But still I went on and on and listened to that sickening radio. And in the evening in the motel, looking just like the previous one, I watched that inhuman television. I almost took leave of my senses." Even if it is true, following Kolker and Beicken, that Philip, as a standard Wenderian searcher, is trapped in a kind of movement without clear reason, one of the apparent consequences of his travels is a discovery of the banality of thin space.

We can ascribe Borgmann's description of the device paradigm to the world on the road created in the opening sequences of this film. But if this were all we could get from this story, it wouldn't be very interesting in the context of the previously mentioned philosophical discussion. There are many texts from which we could draw images that correspond to Borgmann's picture of the world as constituted by devices: Todd Solondz's *Happiness* (1998) and Richard Linklater's *SubUrbia* (1996) come to mind. And hence, there are many places from which we could make the argument that the device paradigm can be used to describe an increasingly uncomfortable quality of urban and suburban space. But the remarkable element of *Alice in the Cities* is that even with the banality of the road, there is something out there that Philip also maintains could have been retrieved as thick space.

New York City

In *Alice* the first indication that Philip might have found something significant on his trip comes out during a conversation with his New York editor once he returns from his seemingly aimless wanderings. In this scene, consistent with Kolker and Beicken's case, Philip seems genuinely confused with what he has come across in his travels. Confronted with the editor, angry that no story has been produced in all this time on the road, Philip shows him his many pictures. These instant images, flawed on Philip's own account, are evidence that he has seen something. Philip maintains that the pictures are crucial to the story he is writing, but he cannot offer any explanation as to their significance. In fact, we never really find out the relationship between the photographs and the article in progress. We can conclude, however, from the opening shots of the film, that their narrative significance rests in their inability to represent whatever it was that Philip thought he saw on the road.

At least Philip's disappointment with the Polaroids is understandable. Instant photographs are a poor excuse for photographs. The images are bad, insofar as they offer a fairly flat reproduction of the world. But if built space really is as thin as Borgmann's device paradigm suggests, ought not such an image suffice? For Philip, it seems that the answer is no. The image is flawed because it does not reproduce the world as he at first perceived it. In the opening sequences, Philip seemed genuinely disappointed with the pictures, not simply because of their poor quality, but because they don't show what he has seen and found worth noting. Interestingly enough, the picture that we first see him complain about is of an old petrol station, which we know Wenders himself would find of interest as one of those things whose existence must be "rescued."

There is other evidence in the film that also suggests that the quality of the images is not the source of Philip's malaise. From at least one other perspective, we have reason to believe that Philip's need for representation is a symptom of a deeper problem. The type of representation really doesn't matter; the problem is Philip. We get this view from Philip's aforementioned New York friend. In answer to Philip's suggestion that he almost "took leave of his senses" on the road, she replies, "But you lost them a long time ago. No need to travel across America for that." Philip's identity, she claims, is empty, perhaps as empty as the open road. So empty, at least, that he needs external confirmation of his experiences to verify them. His need to take pictures on the road is grounded in his peculiar form of solipsism. This she claims is the point of the photographs, that they provide needed proof that Philip really exists: "Your stories and your experiences are handled by you as if you were the only one to experience things. . . . That's why you keep taking those photos," she says, "further proof that it was *really you* who saw something."[28]

Even if this claim is true, the first point raised by the New York friend still needs answering: Why does Philip have to travel across the United States to discover and explore his rootlessness? Why can't he simply wander around New York City taking unsatisfying pictures? In answering this question we should note that the film takes pains to show us particular spaces on Philip's trip, spaces that we may intuitively find as flat and thin as Philip does his Polaroids. While it is certainly true that Philip does not need to travel across America to learn that he has lost his identity, it may very well be the case that we needed to see him do this in order to infer another possible cause of his problems, specifically, a spatial cause. But what does that mean?

Philip's friend clearly sees his solipsism as a sickness, one that is bound up in his stories and photographs. Philip's problem is tied up somehow in the disjunction between what he sees and the produced image, not just in the mere fact that he is taking these pictures. It isn't the case that Philip takes pictures of just anything; rather, he carefully selects the images of spaces and things that he finds meaningful. But the attempt to preserve them as thick spots on a thin field of view falters. Following my twist on Borgmann, the importance of thick space is that it has a grounding effect for our identification with a place. If this is true, then the claim by Philip's friend that he has lost his identity may be spatially diagnosed: Philip has no sense of identity because he has no sense of place. He has no sense of place because there is no space that grounds his identity. At the very least, the searches compound his identity problems when the spaces he passes through suffocate him in their anonymity. Such spaces cannot provide an identity that could pull him out of his solipsism. The New York friend is partly wrong in her diagnosis of Philip's sickness. Philip's need to represent his experience with photographs is not itself the problem. The cause of his malaise may instead be his thin relationship to any kind of spatial representation, which in turn is caused by his susceptibility to the identity problems associated with thin space.

The general worry presented by this film then could be paraphrased as follows: Thin spaces help to produce thin personal identities, which in turn help to dull our attempts to form significant social relationships with those around us. Though Philip may think he sees something on the road, something that perhaps may enrich his identity, the surrounding environment of devices corrupts his access to thicker spatial relationships. If there are thick spaces in the world that can help his identity, he needs some better way of gaining access to them, some more secure way of holding on to their meaning. But more important, the narrative appears to suggest that there is a particular harm that results from the homogeneity of much built space: Thin spaces help to produce a thin self incapable of meaningful human contact.

Working on the assumption that for Philip, and for many of us, built space has implications on the health of our identities, then it is in part through the access to new spaces that we may enrich our identities. On the question of how to gain access to new spaces, the film moves closer to Feenberg than to Borgmann. Philip is not just moved to better surroundings to cure him of his solipsism. He does not realize the spatial cause of his problems and then move to the countryside or a wilderness area to embrace thicker spaces as the solution. Though he does decide to return to Germany after getting back to New York, there is no clear indication that he thinks this change will really improve his state. Instead, following the established connection in the film between spaces and their produced image, Philip will be provided with a new way of seeing the world that will help him to hold on to the thick aspects of the places he encounters. From here on, Philip will see essentially the same world, and the film will use noticeable aural and visual cues to signal the capacity of European spaces to be as thin as North American ones, but it will be seen in a new way. A new lens will emerge that helps Philip to see built space differently, subvert the anonymity of thin space by bringing out the thickness that it masks, and most important, help him to learn to secure the thickness of those spaces to his identity.

Introducing Alice

This new lens is provided by another human—a child, Alice (played by Yella Rottländer), whom Philip meets in New York at an airline ticket agency, where she is trying to get back home to Germany with her mother. Alice becomes the new medium providing Philip with fresh descriptions of the world, even a world on the road. The embodiment of the new lens in another person seems appropriate, as it represents the shift from one of the newest forms of representation, the Polaroid camera, to perhaps the oldest—the descriptions we get of things through the eyes of other people.

Like Lewis Carroll's character, this Alice finds herself in a wonderland, but here, a wonderland of cities. When Philip first sees her, he watches for some time as she plays in a revolving door, perhaps reminding him of how everyday things and spaces can be appreciated in different ways. The city is alive with possibility for Alice, as perhaps it could be for Philip. After meeting, Alice's mother suggests that the three of them spend time together as they all wait for an available flight home. In the interim, Philip becomes reengaged with the city space through Alice. In a wonderful scene, he pretends to blow out the lights of the Empire State Building from Alice's hotel room window, knowing that they will be turned off at midnight. She is thrilled even as she guesses his trick. He later takes her to the top of the building and, surveying the cityscape, has no need to try to capture it in Polaroids.

Still, the picture of this transformation of perspective for Philip is not so simple. It is not the case that Philip is easily drawn into Alice's perspective, or that once her perspective is introduced the film is transformed into a merry, Disney-esque, precocious tyke movie. Philip must be drawn into this new way of seeing, and into this thicker world, slowly and with difficulty. After an initial fascination with Alice, a break comes when Philip returns with her from an excursion in the city to her hotel room. He finds a note from Alice's mother: Something has come up and she had to leave. She asks that Philip take Alice to Europe alone. Alice's mother will follow and meet them later.

The strain of suddenly being left alone with Alice quickly becomes wearing. This new responsibility, though ultimately transformative for Philip, breaks any easy association connecting the way Alice sees things with Philip's ability to recognize thick spaces in the world. In the airport, getting ready to fly home (via Amsterdam because of a ground crew strike in Germany), he finds her absorbed in a coin-operated TV and fascinated by the plastic wrapping on a sandwich. But everything cannot be renewed for him simply by seeing it through her eyes. The film's message about appreciating the everyday cannot simply be reduced to an appeal that we should all see the world through the eyes of children. But even with these awkward moments, there are times in this tense part of the film worth noting. Alice finds a Polaroid image of the sky taken from the plane window lovely because it is blank. But it is not the picture that is lovely, it is the amazing sky, noticed for a moment rather than simply passed through without recognition. Still, Philip resists this kind of appreciation for now. The numbness of pointless travel returns to him with the long flight to Europe. He appears to have nothing waiting for him there, and he is burdened with a child, increasingly restless to be reunited with her mother.

The Second Road Trip

When Philip and Alice arrive in Amsterdam, Alice's mother fails to meet them at the airport as planned. After many tense scenes, the second road trip of the film begins. In desperation to find someone who can take responsibility for the girl, Philip agrees to try to find her grandmother, whom Alice believes is in the German city of Wuppertal.

The trip to Wuppertal begins with a sense of definite direction and purpose. This is not an aimless trip in search of a vague sense of a country, or of an identity, but a search for a particular thing—Grandma's house. All of the predictable metaphors of such a journey at times come into play but usually indirectly. Still, any interesting new way of seeing the world that could be gained along the way is subsumed at first in the more pressing goal of disburdening Philip of responsibility for Alice. After they check into a hotel in Wuppertal, the search begins, first by tram and then by car.

Wenders uses repetitive, rather haunting, guitar music to signal the return of the monotony of the road. This monotony soon appears to affect Alice as it had Philip before. The fascination with the cityscape that Alice had for New York evaporates here.

After driving around the city for two days looking for the house, Alice reveals during a rest break at a hotel cafe that Grandma actually does not live in Wuppertal. This small city, so different from the aimless, nameless suburbia of the first road trip, has now also become subsumed into thin material space. The reason is not for lack of something about the place. It is quite a lovely little city, with narrow streets and old buildings that seem to be ideal as the sort of spaces that Wenders must appreciate. But the significance of any space cannot only reside in its structural qualities but must also rest in part in the role one has in it, which in turn affects how it can be aesthetically appreciated. Like Borgmann's wood stove, the significance of the city is not only in the potential connection we could have with it, but also in the attachment we actually have with it. Like a wood stove in a museum, Wuppertal is interesting but ultimately not actually connected to Alice. After this revelation, we realize that any interesting meaning to this search has been lost, and the closing road trip seems to be as pointless as the one that opened the film. The search for Grandma's house is as elusive now as the earlier search for "America." With the mournful refrain from Canned Heat's "I'm on the road again" playing from the cafe jukebox in the background, and the prospect of another frustrating journey ahead, a now penniless Philip takes Alice to the local police station and leaves her there. Someone else will have to take care of this problem.

A crucial turning point in the film comes next. Philip, after leaving the police station, goes to a Chuck Berry concert. The concert revives Philip. Arguably, the event offers a renewed connection with public spaces for him through participation in a technological practice that makes up that space. This live music, unlike the monotonous radio stations Philip has encountered on the road, can be a focal practice. It is presented as embedded in the context of the site of its performance. The interaction of the audience with the musicians becomes part of the performance. Here, for Philip, a new thing-like aesthetic relationship with the world is stimulated through his participation in the concert space.

The everyday experience of attending the Berry concert is enough to reawaken Philip to the thick world of things, both artifactual and spatial. Lefebvre pointed out in his *Critique* that medieval festivals were both separate from and undeniably a part of everyday life. Similarly, the concert provides an occasion to reflect for a moment not simply upon the relatively straightforward aesthetic experience of listening to music but upon the aesthetics of an everyday space. The camera moves in the scene between Philip and Berry, lingering on both as they are caught in moments of total absorption. By the end of the scene, even though there has been no dialogue, and no overlaid soundtrack or voice-over has indicated a shift in the narrative, we know that a big change has occurred. The everyday aesthetic of the event has subverted the monotony of the experience in Wuppertal, providing a place in which the events of the road trip for Philip, and the film for the viewer, could be reconsidered.

Upon returning to the town, Philip finds Alice again and, rejuvenated, resumes the search. At a rest stop, Alice now remembers that Grandma's house is somewhere in the Ruhr, and she has discovered a picture of it to go on. This simple photograph, on which the continuation of the second road trip is based, is ultimately the key to a reading of the film that completes the narrative's message about space. It also provides an opening for the filmmaker's argument about the technological practice of the medium of film.

Like Philip's pictures on the road in the United States, the picture of the house is an unimpressive image. Yet this picture is imbued with a meaning that Philip's Polaroids never had. Philip, through Alice, has a connection to this photograph because it stands for an end to the search. But now the end seems much more exciting. Although the picture's significance could be reduced to its direct representational value, it is more than that. It is a reminder that searches need not be monotonous or pointless, and that one's identity can be grounded securely in a place. The sense of movement in this part of the trip changes. Though it is a difficult search—there is only a picture to go on and not even a name of a town—it continues for a definite reason. Even the return of the lonely guitar music on the driving sequences here feels different. The act of searching, of traveling through space, has been made more legitimate, and the music is now more soothing than strange.[29]

Now we see, too, that the renewed journey is a road trip in a sense that the earlier part of the search for Grandma's house was not. This is not a seemingly endless drive around a city, but a definite engagement with the open road between places. Philip, through Alice, feels the difference, and the two of them appear to enjoy the trip—comically, they stop at a roadside rest area and perform the recommended calisthenics. Alice's role resumes as the lens through which the world is seen anew. Philip is now able to better appreciate this engaged search, and Alice helps him to retrieve the everyday aesthetic of the artifacts that compose those spaces. The two go to a drugstore automatic photo booth for pictures together, and later in the film even stop for a swim. There is enjoyment and proof of a growing connection between the two searchers.

Philip also knows what the picture of Grandma's house means. There is no confusion as to what role it plays, as there was with his earlier photographs. It is not an image of something he thinks he should appreciate, whose meaning is lost by the time the image emerges. This is an image of something with prefigured meaning, a place that helps form the identity of a person to whom he is now intimately attached.

Finally, with the aid of the picture, the house is found. But just when we think the searching is over, we discover that Alice's grandmother is not there; she has long since moved away and the present occupants do not know where she went. At this point we might expect the film to return to themes of monotony and failed expectations. We might expect this last journey to become as frustrating as the opening journey of the film. But it does not. Even though the ostensible point of the trip, a journey to Grandma's house, has been lost, the larger emphasis on traveling through space for a reason is regained.

The importance of the discovery of the house *without* Grandma in it should not be lost on us. If the point of the film was simply a romantic return to a mythic home (the sort of thing Feenberg worried was the upshot of Borgmann's work), Grandma would have been there ready to welcome Alice. But if the point of the narrative is more complicated and interesting, that somehow our identities can be enriched by the spaces around us, despite the sometimes alienating surroundings in which we find ourselves, then it is enough that Philip and Alice find the house and that the search ultimately enriches them. This is what happens, and to give away a bit of the ending now, the two never make it home in the film. They will continue searching as before, but now with a different sense of the possibilities of appreciating everyday space.

Another point about this scene is crucial: When Philip sees Grandma's house, it is ultimately because the picture was an accurate representation of a thing actually in the world. This is not a picture taken by a solipsist only as an attempt to convince himself of the existence of the outside world. This is a picture of a thing, a place, that is connected to him and to someone whom he now cares about, and so it is important. The house, regardless of its present occupant, is a place embedded with meaning. Here the narrative manages to overcome the limitations of the photographs that had been held up earlier in the film as examples of the flaws of technical reproduction of anonymous spaces. This experience makes it clear to Philip that the outside world really does exist and that its apparent flatness is not caused by the camera. If mechanical reproduction destroys the "aura" of images, as Walter Benjamin claimed, then perhaps Philip has discovered the lesson that artifactual and built space is not susceptible to poor reproduction simply because they were only thin spaces in the first place.[30] The key again, however, is Alice. Without her connection to this place, the anonymity of the spaces Philip found himself moving through would have remained unresolved. Alice is the lens through which the picture and the place can be finally appreciated.

Film as Technology

As we see Philip looking in amazement at the picture and the house in front of him, we can begin to see a new issue raised by the film. This is also a kind of subversion, though now directed at the device-like qualities of image making in general rather than at considerations of space. This issue, though connected to the investigation of the narrative now in progress, is important enough for us to consider on its own before returning to the end of the film. It may be the most direct point raised by the filmmaker here about the relationship between the arts and technology and further make the case for the importance of this film in understanding not only the appreciation of an everyday aesthetics but its representation as well.

Much of the first wave of film theory focused on the technological aspects of film, pointing out how its reproductive capacities both blessed and cursed this art form as compared with other media. More recently, some critical theorists have argued that in Hollywood, for example, the techniques of film have all but destroyed the positive aesthetic qualities of the art.[31] If Hollywood has had a spillover effect on the medium as a whole, as many contemporary theorists worry, then Wenders's work represents a unique challenge to that form of technological dominance.

To understand how this claim works, we will have to rethink the point of *Alice* as how *we* see things, rather than how Philip does. The reproduced images that we are most closely inspecting then are not the Polaroids, or the picture of Grandma's house, but the film itself. Benjamin suggested that "the audience's identification with the actor is really an identification with the camera."[32] In this film, we are first asked to consider the device-like qualities of the Polaroid's images, which in the beginning are the primary form of representation and understanding of the world for Philip. To take Benjamin literally, it is not too much of a stretch to also suggest that we are drawn into a consideration here of the kind of technology film has become as well. If we are critical viewers, then once invited to consider the fate of one form of image reproduction it makes sense to open up the question to others, particularly those with which we are engaged at the moment.

Wenders's images are carefully constructed. It is clear from the beginning that we are watching an artistic text, something other than a standard Hollywood road movie. But the medium of film is unfortunately more associated now with the worst aspects of device culture than with the subtle and rich social commentary typical of art films. Movies often bear no relation to particular places, agents, or communities and often "disburden" us of the complexities of important events in our lives. We go to movies more often to escape everyday life than to be challenged to see it differently. There is also no skill associated with watching mainstream Hollywood cinema; we are instead encouraged not to be critical viewers, but simply to enjoy the images.

Surely there is nothing wrong with easily enjoying a film. But we might worry if the medium of film was only limited to this kind of experience. At least with most of Wenders's films this is not the case. On all of Borgmann's criteria, we relate to these films as a focal practice. First, the texts are rich with meaning, the context is specialized, and when we watch them carefully we are drawn into a relationship with the issues they raise. Second, these films are not escapes from everyday life; they are in and of themselves occasions embodying an everyday aesthetic in which the audience has an identifiable social role. Our identity in the film process is to be an active viewer, and as such our character is in part molded by our willful participation in the film. If Philip discovers the richness of the everyday world with Alice, we also are asked to consider this same discovery with *Alice,* both about the world and about the possibilities of the medium of film. If we are not willing to engage with a film like this in this way, we will most likely find the entire experience boring. Finally, we are asked to acquire a viewing skill rather than only to passively consume the film for its entertainment value. Wenders makes us work through his films; they are not easy to watch. If most audiences do not have an ability to critically view this work, the film's potential is lost, and once we lose our ability to engage with film in general as critical viewers, challenging films will lose one of their most important components—an audience. If there is anything to the intuition that films are made to be seen, that they are produced in order to communicate a message to an audience, the lack of possible receivers for that message is a threat to the institution of filmmaking. But Wenders hopes to reverse this course by making films like *Alice* that sharpen our skills and our identities as viewers.[33]

But if Wenders's work amounts in part to a presentation of films as a focal practice, then it is also a subversion (following Feenberg) of, first, the Hollywood system, and, second, the effects of video and television on the art of filmmaking. As mentioned above, many critical theorists claim that most films serve an ideology of mass cultural consumption. Wenders, and other independent filmmakers, have subverted the current tendencies of the medium by breaking out of the mainstream, producing films that are critical of the commodity culture they often depict, though made with the same technologies. Wenders's films are in part reactions to the artistic restrictions of the Hollywood system. An argument could be made that this system encourages just the sort of indifference to the subtleties of technology and built space that Wenders resists.

Against the effects of commercial television on film, for many an extension of the Hollywood system, Wenders has been very vocal. At the Cannes Film Festival in 1982 he set up a 16mm camera in a hotel room to film the reactions of several independent and commercial film directors on a question concerning just this subject. The filmmakers were asked to enter the room, sit in front of the camera, and answer the following question:

> Increasingly, films are looking as though they had been made for television, as regards their lighting, framing and rhythm. It looks as though a television aesthetic has supplanted film aesthetic. Many new films no longer refer to any reality outside the cinema—only to experiences contained in other films—as though "life" itself no longer furnished material for stories. Fewer films get made. The trend is towards increasingly expensive super-productions at the expense of the "little" film. And a lot of films are immediately available on video cassettes. That market is expanding rapidly. Many people prefer to watch films at home. So my question is: Is cinema becoming a dead language, an art which is already in the process of decline?[34]

This question amply demonstrates Wenders's concern. Notice specifically that part of his worry about the effects of television and large Hollywood productions is conjoined here with a concern that film has become entirely self-referential in content. When Wenders suggested that "life" has dropped out of cinema, it is fair to say that his concern is over the loss of an appreciation of the everyday in film. To make films without passing on such an aesthetic to the viewer would not be very effective if part of the point of film is to create a viewing audience that can appreciate films other than those that predominate on TV and in Hollywood.[35] So, just as Philip sees the picture of Grandma's house as something that has important representational value at last, we are directed to see this film as having subversive potential against what Wenders sees as the destroyers of the film art and hence of an everyday aesthetic.

Conclusions

Now let us return to the narrative and combine these different aspects of *Alice*. Where are we left with Philip and Alice? How is their journey finally resolved? After not finding Grandma at Grandma's house, Philip at first decides to take Alice to his parents who live nearby. Soon, however, he learns that Alice's mother has at last returned to Germany, and the two travelers now continue at their leisure to reunite the girl with her family. The road itself, and the journey, and the aesthetic engagement with the world of thick places, has been retrieved and focused. Philip and Alice continue, more relaxed than they have been for the entire film.

But the film's message, in the end, is not an overly simplified claim that thick places—cities or suburbs—are defined only by our personal connection to them. Something deeper is at work here. Philip has found a different way of understanding the world through a way of retrieving thick places from a thin landscape. Of course, he doesn't learn this lesson in these terms, but as a character he is transformed by an implied form of that understanding. The film ends with a new journey by train, through a landscape in which we can imagine that Philip is finally able to see more *things*. As the train journey begins, we see Philip reading a magazine article about John Ford, possibly pointing out one last time that the film has presented searching as a meaningful movement through space, as still possible. We learn that Philip has decided to go to Munich, and Alice asks him what he will do there. "I'll finish off this story," he replies. His identity as a writer, a chronicler of everyday aesthetics of sorts, has finally been restored.

The final shot shows Alice and Philip opening the window of their train compartment and sticking their heads out for a better look at the landscape rolling by. We, too, are given a better look as the shot slowly pans back to a perspective above the train looking down on the travelers as they move forward. The search music fades back in, and we know that the experience of moving through space for the searchers will continue as before. They are not necessarily going home, or magically resolving their problems. But they are also not suffering as they were before in their misdirected movement from disconnected place to place. In this last shot, the film dramatically brings to life movement forward through a landscape using a completely different perspective from any used in the film before. But not just the physical landscape is recovered; also, the dying terrain (or as Wenders put it in the Cannes question, the "dead language") of film is restored. The last shot shows what a striking role film can play in reviving an everyday aesthetic if it is only employed for that reason.

For Wenders, the journey of the film is his own, matching the subversion of space with a subversion of the film medium. Following Lefebvre, Wenders has unearthed something to be appreciated beneath the world of Borgmann's device paradigm while still acknowledging that there is something to the point that the world of devices is at least initially something to worry about. But like Feenberg, Wenders sees a way out. The film shows how the differences between the two philosophers of technology may be in part resolved. Wenders has demonstrated by example how an everyday aesthetic may be preserved against the thinning out of everyday life.

4

Boyz in the Woods: Los Angeles as Urban Wilderness

One of my most intense memories from when I was in graduate school in Southern California in the mid–1990s was watching the outbreak of what became known as the Rodney King riots. I will never forget the moment I found out about them. It was the evening of April 29, 1992, and I was making extra money by teaching an adult education class at the University of Redlands. The night the riots broke out, I was in the middle of a lecture when a friend of mine who was a student at the university, Julia Pazzi, came to the classroom to get my attention. I quickly excused myself and went to the door. Julia, looking stunned, said simply, "Los Angeles is burning."

It had been a bit over a year since we had all seen the infamous footage of Rodney King, a twenty-five-year-old African American, being beat mercilessly by several members of the Los Angles Police Department. An already racially divided city and region became even more divided as what many had long suspected was common police brutality toward minority residents was finally caught on tape by a plumbing company manager named George Holliday. After a long and caustic trial in Simi Valley, a suburban community north of the city, we had learned that evening that the jury had finally reached a verdict: The four officers accused of using excessive force in the beating of King were acquitted and would be let free. That evening, the riots, or as some would call them, "the uprising," began. Before the night was over, the city would see the worst urban disturbance it had experienced since the 1965 Watts riots. Motorists were taken from their cars and beaten, shops were looted, and an angry crowd gathered in front of the L.A.P.D. headquarters. The chaos would go on for days, the cleanup weeks, and the punditry for months.

After Julia left I turned back to my class and told them what was going on. Some students with family in the city quickly left the room to make phone calls. Those who remained started a disjointed class discussion, but passions were running too high for much by way of a productive conversation. Several of the students were local police officers themselves and admirably tried to offer opinions cautiously critical of both the officers responsible for the beating and the rioters. But since none of us knew any details about the events, we agreed to cancel class and go home. As I drove back to my small place in Riverside (about an hour and a bit east of L.A. without traffic), I listened intently to the radio in my car and then, at home, settled down for a long evening of watching television and calling friends in the city to see if they were okay. There seemed nothing to do but wait this out, like some kind of natural disaster, until it would be possible to help with the cleanup later.

The feelings of intense helplessness I experienced in the weeks that followed have only been duplicated once for me since then, in the aftermath of September 11 in New York City. Though very different, this event stirred two common reactions among my friends: either a feeling of increased fidelity to the city—wanting to do something to help, digging into the community, and reaffirming one's sense of place in that community in a desire to make it better—or, understandably, of wanting to flee. I joined those responding with a sense of fidelity. Journalists, commentators, and other professional media personalities opined that this was the right reaction, and a variety of reasons were given to justify it, ranging from reasoned criticism of the geopolitics that had led to the attack (including outrage at Osama bin Laden et al.) to distinctly less admirable demonization of Muslims writ large and xenophobic jingoism about the power and promise of being American.

The reaction in Los Angeles though at the time of the riots was in many ways more complicated, if even somewhat sinister. Responses among friends included feelings of fidelity or wanting to flee, to be sure, but in L.A. it was more difficult to assess where to lay blame. Fleeing this time risked the appearance of just another wave of "white flight." Meanwhile, the proximate cause of the destruction we watched at home on television was from our own citizenry—it should be remembered, however, that only some 35 percent of those arrested during the riots were black. Unlike New York after September 11, there was a less keen sense of division between enemy and victim, and little by way of a clear idea of why this had happened. Explanations ranged from the extremes of out-

right denial on the Right of the racial elements of the riots, claiming that
what had happened was simply undesirable elements in the community
looking for an excuse to steal things, to an incredulous reaction by some
on the Left proposing that the riots were an urban proletariat revolution—not just a wake-up call for a more egalitarian society, but an actual
attempt to put one in place. The looting on this view was simply a redis-
tribution of wealth.[1] In comparison to both of these accounts, the theory
that the attack on the World Trade Center and the Pentagon was actually
carried out by the CIA, coordinated by a right-wing American cabal,
sounds reasonable.

Trying to figure out a more sober response to the events, the myriad
teach-ins and panels held after the riots provided some clues for a more
helpful explanation of what had created the tinderbox in L.A. that time
around. The text that emerged for me as the most helpful at the time was
historian and geographer Mike Davis's recently published *City of Quartz*.[2]
Although it was not written as a reaction to the riots, it did go further
than almost anything else I had read to explain the racial segregation of
the city and the history of spatial politics that had created a place that was
not so much a single entity (the city of Los Angeles) as it was several
balkanized neighborhoods whose borders were designed so as not to be
easily crossed. Though certainly not providing anything by way of a comprehensive explanation for the riots, Davis did make a good case that the
spatial and racial divisions of L.A. had helped to create a city ripe for
burning (again), so long as the right match came along to ignite it. It
could have been the King incident or it could have been something else.
Los Angeles was a siege city, dividing parts of the population against one
another. When the top blew off, for whatever reason, the community
would consume itself.

Such claims may seem alarmist, and they are certainly incomplete. But
they were attractive enough to me to inspire my own small contribution to
the rest of the literature stimulated by this series of events. In the two
years that followed, I worked on two papers, not so much directly addressed to the riots themselves (though with some reference to them) as to
the background spatial politics that may have helped to create the conditions for them. Of course, we often try to understand such times, especially when we live through them, using the lens of our own interests and
concerns. Perhaps this is a coping mechanism. As I had been working in
environmental ethics, the philosophical subfield devoted to the question
of whether we have moral obligations to protect and restore nature, partic-

ular things jumped out at me. Reading the transcripts of the King trial, and listening to the post-riot commentary, especially when the city was still smoldering, I noticed first a word and then a set of related terms being used over and over again: "wilderness," "wild," "savage," "jungle." King was a wild animal, referred to both as a gorilla and a bear at different times in the ordeal; the cops chasing him were working in a wilderness, or jungle, where danger lurked around every corner.

I had, of course, heard such language before, but coupled with my reading of the Davis book, it seemed worth investigating the issue a bit further. What did it mean when a city was described as a wilderness? Was the use of such language only metaphorical, or was it natural to use the term to refer to something other than the dark green places on a National Park Service map? Or was this another means for continuing the spatial separation of the city? I was beginning to be troubled anyway about the term "wilderness," joining a growing chorus of other voices at the time, led by the historian William Cronon, who had argued that "wilderness" was not only empty of an actual referent, in part because of growing evidence that Native Americans had long transformed the North American landscape in substantial and dramatic ways prior to white contact, but also harmful as a management strategy.[3] And I was also just beginning to think that it was odd that environmental philosophers rarely if ever wrote anything about cities, which, after all, were environments as well, and we ought to be able to say something about their preservation or restoration, too.

I called my topic an investigation of "Urban Wilderness."[4] In the two papers I attempted to describe in philosophical terms how some contemporary discussions concerning the American city had become bound up with what geographers call a "classical" designation of wilderness. This claim was predicated in turn on a comparison with another historical understanding of wild nature, namely, the "romantic" idea of wilderness, such as that held by figures like Henry David Thoreau and John Muir. The romantic view was arguably much more influential on my colleagues in environmental ethics who were determined to come up with a theory of natural value that would justify an ethic of wilderness preservation. This view sees wilderness as an untouched space whose purity human contact corrupts and degrades. But the earlier classical view instead identified wilderness not as something to be admired, respected, and preserved, but as something to be feared—an area of waste and desolation inhabited by wild animals, savages, and perhaps even supernatural evil.

Certainly, these two ideas of wilderness are not exhaustive of descriptions of wild nature, nor are they easily distinguished by history. Classical and romantic views of wilderness emerge in many different places at many different times, sometimes in combination. My focus in these papers, however, was to more clearly distinguish classical wilderness from other descriptions of wilderness and then follow the referential history of a classical understanding of wilderness from a focus on nature to a focus on cities.

We can see the classical use of the term "wilderness" in turn-of-the-century urban social-reform literature, such as Upton Sinclair's *The Jungle*. But there, the city is called a classical wilderness for benevolent reasons: The language is supposed to motivate our moral outrage against the abuse of the urban poor by greedy capitalists (more on this point below). But today we find the language of the urban wilderness used more often than not for very different reasons. As in the case of the more regressive discussions of the L.A. riots, it is used to stigmatize inner-city residents. If the city is a wilderness, then those of us outside the inner city are justified in separating ourselves from it and from the people who inhabit it. The language used to justify the beating of Rodney King was consistent with this usage of "wilderness" and related terms.[5] My view was that tracking the different uses of this term might help to unpack the language I had noticed in the events around the L.A. riots, which, in turn, might make a contribution, from a field that wasn't saying much about these events, to understanding them better.

The purpose of this chapter then is to further my earlier argument by looking at examples of the language of urban (classical) wilderness in film. My motivation is similar to the one that inspired my analysis of films about surveillance technology in chapter 2: Movies have an astounding amount of power to shape popular discussion and popular opinion on important moral and social issues of the day. If a popular film passes off a harmful or naïve understanding of an important subject as a view that we should accept, then it may serve more harm than its entertainment value justifies. In this case, I think that some films about Los Angeles help to support the harmful racial and spatial politics just mentioned. Although surely they don't do anything as powerful as actually cause events like the King riots, they do inform our understanding of them and help to shape our interpretation of these events and eventually our response to them.

So, while the purpose of this chapter is not to make a direct contribution to the literature on the King riots, those events are related to the issues dealt with in most of the films that I will discuss, and hopefully the films in turn can help us to understand what some of the responses to the riots have been and to think about other, more nuanced responses. But beyond King and Los Angeles, this chapter should also be understood as an attempt to take on a broader issue, namely, the demonization of inner-city inhabitants and cities themselves beyond just this one example. The language of urban wilderness is found in many places. Although it may mostly be innocuous in terms of its effects, it still presents a distorted picture of cities and encourages harmful, prejudicial responses to their inhabitants. As in the case of surveillance technology, there are films that do a better job of representing the difficult moral and social questions at the heart of this phenomenon.

So, first, I will revisit and summarize my original arguments about classical wilderness. Then, I will look at the film *Falling Down,* which portrays the wild city from the perspective of whites seemingly trapped in an urban environment. In this film, our acceptance of the breakdown of an antihero is parasitic on a depiction of Los Angeles as a classical urban wilderness. From there, I will look at another, more hopeful set of films that use implicit appeals to an urban wilderness in portrayals of cities, again with a focus on L.A., from an African-American perspective: the work of John Singleton and Albert and Allen Hughes. Their depictions of urban life usually mirror the early social-reform use of the language of urban wilderness when they appeal to its imagery, though with a more direct acknowledgment of the racial and racist overtones of the description. Finally, I will briefly suggest some films about city life that avoid entanglement with the language of urban wilderness altogether.

Classical Wilderness Defined

As just mentioned, at least two conceptions of wilderness are identifiable in the literature in geography: the "classical" and the "romantic" views.[6] Again, the classical view sees wilderness as something to be feared, an area of waste and desolation inhabited by wild animals, savages, and perhaps even supernatural evil. Here, human society is the standard by which the world is measured, and hence conquest over the nonhuman areas, the wild areas, signals a form of human achievement, or, as John Rennie Short has put it, "a victory over the dark forces and a measure of social progress."[7] By contrast, on the romantic view wilderness is that form of nature that has remained close to its "pristine" state, and so it has not been "corrupted" by human intervention. Accordingly, many have tried to form an ecological ethic around the romantic idea of wilderness, claiming that experience with the wild results in an improved understanding of the relationship between humans and nature.[8] Despite the fact that today, at least in places like the United States, Canada, and Australia, we are largely neutral between these two views in the language we use to describe wilderness, and possibly at the extremes are pseudo-romantics, the idea of an unknown evil at the edge of civilization still haunts us. The only question remaining is where that evil now resides. To understand this point, though, we need to know more about the referent of classical wilderness.

The classical view, and perhaps all versions of wilderness, to a large degree revolves around what I want to call a "cognitive" understanding of wilderness.[9] By this I mean that "wilderness" does not just designate a particular place, or a kind of place, but instead a set of categories describing how that kind of place shapes our self-understanding, and in turn how we should understand others who come into contact with that kind of place. Further, designations of "wilderness" suggest a socially normative account of how we should act in relation to such places and their inhabitants. On the classical understanding of wilderness, it is a place that is marked as the realm of the savage, who, in addition to other things, is thought to be distinct from the civilized human in terms of his rational faculties. The savage is that which civilized people are not. Part of what makes civilized people not savage on this view is our possession of reason or control over our passions. The savage, on the classical view, has no control over his "wild" passions and so can never really escape the wilderness. If the savage leaves the physical space of the wilderness, he is still wild because of the wilderness within. The cognitive dimension of classical wilderness refers then to the idea that those who are part of the wild are never fully rational. On this view, the physical surroundings somehow environmentally determine the mental states (or limitations) of their inhabitants.[10]

Many historians and geographers have argued that the classical view, with this version of a kind of cognitive environmental determinism, was the prevailing view of wilderness that traveled from the Old World to the New and helped to shape early Euro-American perceptions of Native Americans. For example, John Smith described New England in the seventeenth century as "a hideous and desolate wilderness, full of wild beasts and wild men."[11] So uncontested was the assumption of a strong cognitive dimension to the gap between the civilized and uncivilized in early

American history, with a few notable exceptions, that different thinkers developed radically different views of the potential for civilizing various kinds of savages given a range of conditions, but including their different environments, without ever questioning the grounds for their debate. While some believed that the African "savage" could be made to be civilized with appropriate guidance and training outside of their "wild jungles," they held for various reasons that others—most importantly Native Americans—were beyond hope. Some, such as Thomas Jefferson, reversed this conception.[12]

The language of classical wilderness was also a way of designating a state of spiritual impoverishment for the new peoples encountered by Europeans. Wilderness was thought of as a kind of hell. One cannot help but think that the classical wilderness was, for at least the early Puritans, a projection of their deepest fears of what they would become in the New World if they were not careful. As Short put it, "The [classical] Wilderness becomes an environmental metaphor for the dark side of the human psyche."[13] If one entered the wild without succeeding in destroying it, one risked succumbing to one's own wild, evil side.

It is important, however, to be more precise about this characterization of the classical view. My more unique claim in this literature is that classical wilderness can be summarized as encompassing three related and often overlapping theses:

(T1) Separation. Since the wilderness is bad, evil, cruel, etc., it must be separated from humans—it must be marked off as distinct and kept separate from civilized spaces.

(T2) Savagery. The inhabitants of the wilderness are nonhuman, more akin to beasts, and are to be treated as such.

(T3) Superiority. In contrast, civilization and its inhabitants may be celebrated for their superiority over wilderness and its inhabitants.

I will continue to refer to these theses throughout this chapter in order to demonstrate the representation of classical wilderness in several films about Los Angeles.

As we might expect, the idea of classical wilderness is constantly changing, and so these theses, as applied to specific places or texts, represent an idea in transition. For example, one could speculate that as Euro-Americans began a concentrated effort to eliminate Native Americans in the nineteenth century, the relevance of T2 diminished for a time while the savage was driven out of many places. Nonetheless, the wilderness still existed as a place inferior to white civilization (T3). It could also be argued that the process of westward expansion encouraged a gradual move from T1 to T3, that is to say, a shift from fear of the wilderness to triumph over it. Still, the stimulation for conquering wilderness, as a process demanded by our superiority, was our fear of it (T1 and T2).

With this description of classical wilderness in hand, we may again inquire as to the nature of the term. Certainly, the classical account of wilderness is a cultural construction with an identifiable history.[14] My claim, however, is not that everything is a cultural construction (as some social constructivists might argue), or even that all referring expressions to parts or processes of nature are cultural constructions. To pick just one example, on my view the actual process of photosynthesis is not a cultural construction. But the things or places picked out in the world by "wilderness" are different in kind than the process of photosynthesis. Although wilderness certainly does contain things that are scary and harsh, the experience of which helped to form the classical ideal, it can also be other things. It can be a source of special transcendence, for example, as some romantic poets have claimed (though I do not think there is a necessary causal connection here). Surely, though, the reality of the wild must lie somewhere in between these poles of terror and bliss: Wild nature is both dangerous and a source of positive values, but not exclusively either all the time or for every person.

Whatever the case, for good or for bad, "wilderness" is a culturally constructed term whose referent is dependent on the social context in which it is used. Given my argument that classical wilderness entails a particular cognitive frame, rather than only a description of types of spaces, the word does not refer so much to a thing in the world as such as it marks a set of comparisons between an idea of civilization and its inhabitants and a contrast to it. While I think such a claim is true, I will not attempt a more rigorous defense of it here.[15] Assuming, though, that a successful argument for this understanding of classical wilderness, and perhaps all notions of wilderness, could be mounted, then the next question is, Why is such a claim important?

Wilderness is about any place that we fear, natural or not. It's more telling use is more metaphorical. Nothing strongly grounds this term to a description of particular places, or even kinds of places. It can easily be used to describe any place that we might find alienating, threatening, evil, and powerful enough to have a corrupting influence on its inhabitants, according to a folk account of environmental determinism. So we ought not be surprised to see the language of classical wilderness used to describe things that we would not consider to be wild nature. The full metaphorical force of "wilderness" will be evident when it is cut free from its apparent moorings in descriptions of wild nature, since it never accurately picked out a kind of natural space from the beginning.

Something like this claim helps us to make sense of the evolution of the terminology of classical wilderness from its common references in the early American colonial period to its use today. As Euro-Americans came to think that wild nature was no longer a threat, the romantic view was able to gain more acceptance. But the classical view persisted in some rather unusual domains. I maintain, and I am not alone in this contention, that the metaphorical legacy of classical wilderness is now found in the use of "wilderness" (along with a set of related terms) to describe urban areas and events, such as the King riots. Along with this legacy has come the cognitive dimension of wilderness as applied to cities. What is "out there," still for us to fear, is an "urban wilderness," a savage inner city.[16]

We should be wary of drawing any clean historical lines concerning the designation of an urban wilderness. Still, as suggested above with reference to Upton Sinclair's *The Jungle,* one can track the use of urban wilderness in America first as a term used by turn-of-the-century social reformers to raise issues concerning the deplorable living conditions of recent immigrants in the inner city.[17] To motivate the public's moral outrage over these conditions, a new face was put on the old evil: Savage Indians were replaced by savage capitalists (a reserved application of T2); threatening, dark landscapes were no longer in the realm of the supernatural but the result of the naturalization of an exploitative labor relationship in an industrialized factory environment. But in using the language of urban wilderness, the social reformers continued the classical understanding of wilderness as uncivilized space even while they changed the usual referent "wilderness." Sinclair, for example, wanted the people of his time to be repulsed at the conditions of those working in the Chicago stockyards and butcher houses and living in "packingtowns." He wanted them to see these places as unfit for full members of the human community. Sinclair used such language in hopes of motivating us to attack the poverty and savagery of the urban wilderness out of a sense of revulsion.

The problem, though, as mentioned above, is that we have come back, at least in the United States, to a description of urban areas as a classical wilderness using a more straightforward application of the three theses that I suggested earlier. Instead of subverting separation (T1) to motivate support for benevolent reforms, we now employ T1–T3 to vilify urban inhabitants and urban spaces in the same way that aboriginals and natural spaces were vilified in the past. We can see this problem in several contemporary American films.

Los Angeles as Urban Wilderness

Given the way it is spoken about and represented in a variety of media, Los Angeles is one of the premiere urban wilderness areas in the United States today. We may even think of L.A. as something of a wilderness preserve because it maintains as clearly as possible a separation between white suburbanites and inner-city racial minorities in concrete jungles. Many films have played on a sense of L.A. as a dangerous place full of corrupted inhabitants, but one of the most fascinating uses of themes of urban wilderness is the 1993 release *Falling Down,* directed by Joel Schumacher and written by Ebbe Roe Smith.

In this "tale of urban reality," as it was marketed, we follow the last day in the life of an out-of-work L.A. area white-collar defense worker, played by Michael Douglas. The character goes through a series of crises as he moves through the landscape of a predominantly Hispanic area of Los Angeles, in the process transforming from an easily angered, but as yet nonviolent, average Joe to a gun-toting killer of the scum of the city. During the course of the film, which is divided neatly into ten episodes, Douglas takes on the persona of a warped Odysseus trying vainly to find his way home from an urban war. But acting as a strong arm of middle-class sensibility necessitates going through the urban wilderness, and there he becomes tainted by it, consistent with some of the Puritans' worries about the corrupting effects of the wild in their version of T1. As the film progresses, Douglas's character loses his everyday attire, changes into a black military outfit, and becomes a twisted image of the new white hope of the inner city. The three theses of urban wilderness are prevalent throughout this journey.

Separation (T1)

If *Falling Down* is about anything it's about the separation of parts of Los Angeles from itself. L.A. is, as Mike Davis argued, a city transformed by a process of "Ulsterization," deeply divided along seemingly intransigent lines.[18] The opening sequences of *Falling Down* clearly rely on the acceptance of this separation. The first scene shows Michael Douglas's character sitting in his car on a hot day in a traffic jam somewhere on a highway in East L.A. Pressure builds in the scene as he stares at a child seemingly out of a Third World relief poster who stares back at him from another car. The heat of the day is pervasive; his air conditioning doesn't work, his window won't roll down. With an extremely short military-style haircut and a cheap white shirt and tie, he looks like an annoyed missionary in sub-Saharan Africa. We have no idea who this man is, but he's definitely in a spot none of us would like to find ourselves in. Finally he breaks. Douglas abandons his car and walks into a shrubbed embankment into the city. Our only clue to his identity is a personalized license plate reading "D-FENS," and though we later learn that his name is Bill Foster, even the credits list him by the name on the license plate.

D-fens turns out to be an engineer who made a career in Southern California's once booming aerospace defense industry. A victim of the end of the Cold War, he was fired over a month ago and is now unemployed. Somewhere along the way he lost his wife and child in a divorce, and since then he has been living with his mother. Today is his daughter's birthday, and he is determined to make his way across town to Venice Beach to give her a present, clearly over his ex-wife's objections and against a no-trespassing court order (the ex is played by Barbara Hershey). A product of the military-industrial complex, he was a strong believer in his profession and his country. As his mother explains later to the police, under the misperception that her son is still going to work every day, "He's building important things to protect us from the Communists."

It is telling that our antihero is a defense worker. Now that America's greatest enemy has been defeated he is no longer needed. While our global political landscape has greatly changed today, when this film came out the attention of Americans was turned more inward. This was before the Oklahoma bombing, and white racist militias seemed to be on the rise. In this climate, D-fens views the inner city as a new enemy territory, and his journey through it gives him a purpose for perhaps the first time since losing his job to protect us from the Communists. At the end of this day, D-fens, who has presumably lived his whole life in the area, expresses surprise at what he has found in his journey through the city as if he had never been there before. In response to his wife's plea that he is sick and needs help, after he finally catches up with her in Venice Beach and holds her hostage at gunpoint, D-fens retorts, "Sick? You wanna see sick. You ever walk around this town? *That's* sick." His bizarre adventures have woken him up to hate the city he once took for granted. He has fully experienced his environment at last, but it is an experience tainted by the lens of classical wilderness.

The thesis of separation comes out sharply in two persistent themes of the film: (1) the inner city is just as dangerous, violent, and chaotic as the most uninformed outsider's perception of it would have us believe, and (2) the separation of one part of the city from another is justified and rational. The first theme is pervasive, especially early in the film, soon after D-fens leaves his car on the highway. In his first stop, at a dingy Korean-owned convenience store in a Hispanic neighborhood, we see D-fens surrounded by the decaying, graffiti-covered barrio. The overwhelming yellow and brown tones of the cinematography (shot by Andrzej Barkowiak) evokes a sense of an overwhelmingly ugly, smelly, and generally vile place. Though surely such areas are impoverished, the mise-en-scene suggests that they are uniformly unappealing. There is no room for any urban aesthetic here until D-fens finds his way through the barrio to a rich neighborhood, and later in the colors of his showdown with the police on the Venice pier.

But not only is the place itself uniformly disgusting, the inhabitants are also depicted as one-dimensionally violent, irrational, and unforgiving. In the Korean convenience store, D-fens immediately has to deal with a rude foreigner who doesn't appreciate what, he claims, "America has done for Korea." More rude service people are encountered later at a fast-food restaurant. But unfriendly service is only the tip of the iceberg. All of the Hispanics encountered in the city seem to be gang members intent on robbing or killing D-fens. Even though a vague attempt is made to balance this portrayal with the inclusion of a Latina police officer in a parallel story line (involving the cop who finally tracks down D-fens—a detective named Pendergrast, played by Robert Duvall), it is important that every brown-skinned urban resident D-fens encounters is some kind of unreasonable savage. This wouldn't be the first time, of course, that a big-budget Hollywood film has profited from prejudiced and overly simplified characterization. What is important here, though, is how these characterizations reinforce descriptions of the urban wilderness as unequivocally cruel and dangerous.

But many spaces can be given an undesirable description. The wilderness metaphor comes across more distinctly in the second theme mentioned above, that because the inner city is dangerous, white L.A. residents must separate themselves from it. There are at least two ways in which the force of the propriety of separation is portrayed in the film: D-fens's own expressions of the territorial nature of his adventure, and external observations made by the police asking why this man is in the inner city at all.

After leaving the Korean store (an episode I will return to shortly), D-fens walks to a vacant lot in the Hispanic neighborhood. He has taken a baseball bat from the Korean store owner, which he used to smash things in the store during a rant about how the owner was overcharging his customers. He sits on the concrete remains of a staircase to a house no longer there. Then he is approached by two young Hispanic men visibly marked as gang members. The two men immediately tell D-fens that he has to leave the lot. He's sitting on private property, they claim, identifiable by a crude gang symbol painted on the concrete block.

The camera perspective here is telling. As the young men threaten D-fens, they begin to circle him. In an earlier establishment shot we saw that the abandoned lot is open and affords a broad view above the smoggy L.A. cityscape. But as the young men circle D-fens, the camera moves to a continuing tracking shot circling outside of the men who are circling D-fens. From this perspective, the open lot becomes a cramped space and the young men and D-fens appear trapped within a closing circle rather than on a vista overlooking the city. The suggestion is clear: As in a "nature" film, D-fens is the prey trapped by circling predators.

Finally, fed up with this threat, D-fens condescendingly assesses the situation: "This is a gangland thing. I've walked into your territorial dispute. I've wandered into your pissing ground or whatever it is." He knows he has crossed a line, that he is now in forbidden territory, but D-fens has decided that here he will begin to take a stand. Like Medieval monks who burned European forests to exorcise them of the devil, D-fens decides to begin cleaning house in the hood. Shouting about how he doesn't care about this "piece of shit hill," D-fens begins beating the men with his baseball bat. Clearly evoking his desire now to cross back into his home territory and leave the wilderness, D-fens shouts at one of his victims, "I'm going home, clear a path you motherfucker, I'm going home!" Later, these same characters try to kill D-fens in a drive-by shooting. They completely miss him, kill several bystanders in the process, and then immediately wreck their car against a telephone pole. Chastened, D-fens saunters over to the wreckage and takes a duffel bag full of guns from their car. He shoots one of his assailants in the leg for good measure. D-fens carries this bag of guns through the rest of the film, using them to terrorize a wide variety of urban inhabitants.

The theme of D-fens's status as a territorial outsider is repeated explicitly at least twice in the film. Once, in a public park, he is approached by a panhandler who lamely tries to con him out of money. As the more rational character, D-fens easily sees through the pitch and rebuffs the man. As D-fens walks away from the scene, the panhandler shouts that D-fens has no right to be in *his* park. D-fens laughs and continues on his journey. Later, after leaving the barrio, D-fens must cross through a rich neighborhood in West L.A. to finish his journey to Venice Beach. He takes a shortcut through a private golf course and interrupts two old men who are trying to finish their game. When one of them begins yelling at him to get off the course (again, a mark of territory), D-fens becomes the conscience of the working class, arguing that this space should be open for kids and families and not reserved for old men with money. D-fens shoots the golfers' motorized cart and it rolls into a lake. One angry golfer begins to have a heart attack and pleads for someone to get his heart medicine out of the now submerged cart. While this last portrayal of territoriality is in a more affluent area, the sense of savagery is no less acute. One could argue that just as Upton Sinclair recognized the wild overtones of a kind of Social Darwinism at work in the attitudes of the owning classes in *The Jungle,* here the urban wilderness encountered by D-fens contains similar hazards. Below, however, I will suggest a more plausible reading of this part of D-fens's journey that makes this scene more consistent with my reading of the earlier parts of the film.

The police observations further demonstrating this separation theme emerge as they pursue D-fens. As Detective Pendergrast puts together different reports of violent episodes across the city, he slowly develops an intuition that it is the same man who is causing trouble. The theme of separation comes out after he realizes that it is a white man who is shooting up East L.A. As Pendergrast explains his theory to other police officers, he is rebuffed. Why would a white man even be in these neighborhoods? The film parades a series of ethnic detectives in front of Pendergrast—Hispanic, African American, and Asian—all of them dismissive that the assailant on the Korean grocer, the object of a drive-by shooting, and the man who was walking around the barrio with an automatic machine gun shooting up phone booths and fast-food restaurants could be the same white person. Pendergrast voices this dismay himself, finally shouting, "Yeah, what would a white guy be doing in *gangland*?" The separation of the city, so common and accepted even by the police, prevents them from believing that a middle-class white person could possibly be in the area.

What is going on in the separation of L.A. into territorial spaces determined by racial and ethnic factors in real life is an even deeper problem. What this film does with the theme is to simply repeat the assumption that there is nothing wrong with keeping parts of the city separate from one another. It is almost as if the urban wilderness, like the natural areas covered by the U.S. Wilderness Act, has become an object of preservation. But the film's representation of L.A. reverses the romantic view that the wilderness should be set aside because its good qualities deserve protection. It is as if once we have conquered the "green" classical wilderness, we should preserve the urban variety as a quaint reminder of the cognitive environment to which we have not succumbed. Or, more consciously, we must encircle the inner city because it is beyond salvation. There is no Sinclairian reform instinct here: "We" would not even think of allowing "them" into our areas, so we ought to just control this wild place and keep it separate as best we can and as long as possible. Davis, and some others, have argued that this process of separation, along with its effects on the inhabitants of the maligned areas of the city, helped to fuel the violence of the King riots. If true, this film only perpetuates the sense that such separation was justifiable. I will return to this point later.

Savagery (T2)

Why must this separation be maintained? Because the savagery of the inner city corrupts those who find their way in. This is the message of *Falling Down*. The title alone evokes a descent into chaos, along with a descent into violence, which D-fens finds himself committing in ever escalating circumstances. I have already mentioned the uniform depiction of inner-city inhabitants, particularly nonwhites, as violent, irrational savages; the suggestion of corruption from exposure to this environment is the most evocative of the effects of wilderness on the civilized in the film.

D-fens announces early on that he is on a journey home. He knows he has crossed a border and thinks that he will have to defend himself to make it from East L.A. to Venice Beach. Still, he may not yet realize how violent he will have to become in order to make it back to civilization. It is clear by the end that he has not made any conscious decision to become a gun-wielding fanatic; nevertheless, this is what he evolves into through his journey. When a break comes in the violence, and he is able to reflect on how he has changed, he realizes that he is no longer a member of civilized, rational, polite society.

Though the film was criticized on its initial release as a crude vigilante film thinly disguised as social satire, it is more complex than it was given credit for in its use of the metaphors of urban savagery and the corrupting effects of the city on the civilized. D-fens does not just descend into a personal madness and then start shooting up Hispanic neighborhoods. There is a clear connection implied by the film between the landscape he moves through and the person he becomes. While D-fens starts the film carrying a briefcase and wearing a shirt and tie, by the end he is wearing combat fatigues and carrying a duffel bag full of guns. He does not just collect these artifacts; he becomes proficient in their use as a part of his savage environment. With all of this violence, however, we can only be sure that D-fens is the direct cause of one death. Perhaps to try to counter the worst possible interpretation of the film, as a justification for vigilante racism, the filmmakers put D-fens in a situation where he must kill a neo-Nazi. This scene, however, more than any other, shows how our central character has been transformed in his journey through the wild.

At the beginning of the film we see D-fens looking at a hole in one of his shoes. Several times we see him struggling through this discomfort and so it seems plausible for him to later wander into an army surplus store to buy a pair of walking boots. While it is important for my reading here that D-fens buys outdoor boots rather than another pair of street shoes, it is more interesting to note the character with whom he interacts in this episode (which, as it turns out, is in the middle of the ten episodes on his journey).

The owner of the shop, named Nick (played by Frederick Forrest), is a white supremacist who immediately takes an interest in D-fens when he enters the store. Nick has been following reports describing a white man involved in several shootings in the inner city over a police scanner and pegs D-fens as the suspect given his clothing and demeanor. Seeing D-fens as a kindred spirit, Nick tries to impress him by loudly insulting two other customers marked as young gay men. D-fens does not show any visible signs of endorsing or condemning these insults, only seeming to ignore the store owner. But when one of the detectives on his trail enters the store, D-fens hides in a changing room and Nick covers for him, telling the detective that he hasn't seen anyone fitting D-fens's description.

After the police officer leaves, Nick openly embraces D-fens as a comrade in arms. From the account he learned on the scanner, Nick has decided that D-fens has been "kicking ass" in the city and so must sympathize with his neo-Nazi affiliations. In a bizarre parody of show and tell, Nick takes D-fens into a back room to show him his private collection of Nazi paraphernalia. There, Nick pulls out a stash of war surplus equipment, culminating in a can of Zyklon-B, the chemical used in the gassing of Jews in concentration camps during the Holocaust.

Clearly amused with himself, Nick the Nazi remarks, "I wonder how many kikes this little can took out?" Nick gives D-fens a heat-seeking shoulder missile that is used later in the film. When D-fens asks why he is getting this treatment, Nick explains, "I know you. We're the same, you and me. We're the same." Certainly, from what we have seen so far in the film, and what little we know about D-fens, such a claim is not implausible. Especially given D-fens's nationalistic comments in the Korean grocery store at the beginning of the film, it could easily be assumed that he holds extreme racist views and that they just haven't been divulged by the film as of yet. Wouldn't this help to explain why he unhesitatingly takes up automatic weapons and uses them to plow his way through East L.A.? But D-fens denies the comparison: "I am not a vigilante, I'm just trying to get home for my little girl's birthday." And then, "I'm an American, and you're a sick asshole!" Duly insulted, Nick tries to handcuff D-fens and take him to the police. D-fens responds by first stabbing Nick and then shooting him several times.

What can we make of this scene? Clearly, we are not being encouraged here to equate D-fens with Nick, nor to explain D-fens's actions so far by appeal to extreme racist views. D-fens is just an average person with average conservative politics, and here he is given a chance to clarify himself; he isn't a sophisticated racist like Nick. But we still need some explanation for why he has suddenly become so violent. The obvious choice presented by the film is that D-fens is suffering from stress and some sort of mental breakdown. But such an answer only begs the question of why D-fens must go on this particular journey to have this breakdown. We would be remiss to discount the effects of the environment through which he is traveling and the supposed effects of this landscape on his change in perspective over the course of the film. Moving through this particular landscape, as opposed to some other, somehow makes it permissible for this loyal American to break even the most mundane conventions of the society at large. His journey must help explain D-fens's savage turn. Certainly D-fens had to be on the edge to begin with, but no more so than many people today. In fact, this is a large part of D-fens's appeal: He is the quintessential 1990s down-on-his-luck average guy.

It seems then no accident of the plot that D-fens is wandering through the inner city and that the city releases his passions. Consistent with the early Puritan view that all people have an evil side to them, the urban wilderness has brought out the worst in D-fens, just as it has corrupted its everyday residents. One could have made a similar film where a character like D-fens had a similar breakdown in a suburban New Jersey bedroom community and then started shooting his middle-class neighbors. But *Falling Down* is not just a film about the internal collapse of one man; this is a film where the journey through the urban environment is itself a trigger for D-fens's savage turn. Even if one wants to question this interpretation by appeal to the fact that D-fens eventually makes his way into an affluent area and continues his rampage—in the scene at the golf course mentioned above—it is important that he begins in East L.A. It is the urban wild that corrupts him and it is this corruption that he carries back into the civilized sections of the city. It is in Hispanic L.A. where he gets the guns to shoot the golf cart. As in the colonial view of Native Americans, a savage is still a savage after leaving the wild. I have little doubt that this presentation of a kind of environmental determinism was not intended by the filmmakers. It does, however, shine through as a vestige of the idea of urban wilderness in American society that we can plausibly speculate influenced the direction of the film.

This account is supported by the transitional moment of the scene with Nick. When D-fens leaves the Nazi's store, he feels that he has crossed another kind of line, that he has been completely transformed into a product of the inner city where guns can be used to settle any dispute. D-fens has made his first kill and is now part of the inner-city tribe. As mentioned above, D-fens leaves the store dressed all in black, a dark warrior in the wild terrain. If there is any doubt that he has made a significant change, D-fens calls his wife from Nick's store before leaving and in the process tells the audience that he has recognized his own corruption. He remarks to her that he is "past the point of no return" now, which he explains as "the point in a journey where it is longer to go back to the beginning than it is to continue to the end."

Though this last observation by D-fens may seem to romanticize his situation by making his adventure into some kind of journey of positive discovery, we are afforded an opportunity to observe him taking one step back from his transformation to look in horror at what he has become. Running from the scene at the golf course, D-fens comes over a security wall into the back yard of a Westwood mansion. There he encounters a

family having a barbecue and swimming in a pool. We learn quickly that
these are not the owners of the house but the caretaker and his family.
Hearing police sirens, D-fens grabs the caretaker's young daughter and
runs for the house, waving his gun at the family to come along. Hiding in
an alcove of the house, the family waits nervously for this strange man to
make the next move. Convinced that D-fens will kill his daughter, the
caretaker offers himself as a hostage and begs that his family be let go.

At this moment, D-fens breaks down for the first time in the film.
Realizing that the caretaker thinks he will harm the girl, D-fens explains
that he is supposed to be with his own daughter on her birthday now,
"having a barbecue, like you guys." D-fens is confronted here not by East
L.A. gangsters, neo-Nazis, or indifferent capitalists, but people more like
himself. D-fens acknowledges that he has become something other than
what he should be, that the city has remade him. He realizes that the
caretaker and his family must see him as a savage, an outsider. Though he
does not fully understand his transformation—at the end of the film he
remarks to Pendergrast, "I'm the bad guy? How did that happen?"—in
this particular scene he appears to be granted a moment of clarity to ab-
sorb and be horrified at what has happened to him.

One could claim that at these points the film is encouraging us to also
be appalled at what D-fens has become. No matter what cinematic guilty
pleasures we have derived from watching this adventure (and some of the
scenes are truly funny), at the end of the day we need to confess, along
with D-fens, that what he has done is wrong. But even if that is true, as I
have been arguing, the film still portrays the environment D-fens has
traveled through as both unambiguously bad and as the thing that has
transformed him. D-fens has become a savage through his experience;
he's no longer just a frustrated and angry human being who has lost his
job and family. Even if we empathize with him at the end and feel sorry
for him, we must also realize that we could be transformed by the wilderness, too. I find the message clear: Stay away from the inner city, and support attempts to cut it, along with its inhabitants, off from the rest of us.

Superiority (T3)

Even in his descent into savagery, D-fens tries to maintain his superiority—the superiority of middle America—as he makes his way through the
environment. At several moments in the narrative, D-fens opines how
he thinks the world should be. For example, in a signature scene from

the film used in many previews, D-fens shoots up a fast-food restaurant because they will not serve him breakfast three minutes after the transition to the lunch menu. Though certainly humorous, such scenes belie the film's support of D-fens's complaint that such establishments should be more flexible in their service and so need to be set straight. Even the press materials that accompanied the film were filled with reminders that D-fens stands as a representative of a correct middle-American perspective on the world. Michael Douglas remarked that the film represented a "loss of our middle class." Joel Schumacher suggested that the film is about how society "seems to give people today a general sense of having been cheated or shortchanged." But again, the force behind such themes in the film is provided by the inner-city environment in which D-fens is placed. This is not a film about the general loss of the middle class and middle-class sensibility in the suburbs: This film contrasts such a sensibility with an inner-city hazard.

At the beginning of the film, in the scene where D-fens smashes up the Korean grocery store, his actions are supposed to be instigated by his outrage at the prices being charged by this foreigner. It all starts when the owner, Mr. Lee (played by Michael Paul Chan), refuses to give D-fens change for a pay phone unless he buys something. D-fens brings a can of Coke to the cash register and is told that the price is eighty-five cents. This begins an argument and a sustained outburst by D-fens about how grateful the Korean should be for everything that America has done for the latter's country. D-fens mocks the man for his accent and inability to speak English, and after terrorizing him and destroying much of the store's merchandise with Mr. Lee's baseball bat (grabbed from the hands of the owner), D-fens formally says "Pleasure frequenting your establishment" and exits the scene. The contrast here is noteworthy. D-fens holds the upper hand as the nostalgic representative of a time when the simple amenities of life were reasonably priced. The problem appears to be that foreigners have come in and somehow caused inflation. D-fens not only knows how this man should be running his business, but more important, better grasps the language of exchange.

The presumed superiority of D-fens's position is again evinced at the scene in the fast-food restaurant. There D-fens is put into a position where he is asked to accept rude treatment, presumably common in our anonymous consumer culture. Standing up for what is right—namely, that he should be able to get breakfast at 11:33 when the restaurant stops serving it at 11:30—D-fens blows his top. But when D-fens pulls out an automatic pistol to emphasize his complaint to the store's manager, he is quickly transformed to the stance of a crazed assailant. His position is superior, as it is most reasonable, with regard to how to run a fast-food restaurant, though he has already become too corrupted by the urban wilderness to maintain his cool. Still, the film takes the point of view that D-fens has a justifiable position.

All three theses of the classical wilderness I picked out at the start are at work in *Falling Down*. The social implications of this view are consequently distressing. Films like *Falling Down* encourage a dismissive attitude toward the real problems of urban life instead of seriously considering them and in failing to address these issues exacerbate the conditions that helped to cause the King riots, reinforcing our continuing failure to reconcile those problems in post-riot L.A.

As briefly mentioned above, before the riots, Mike Davis chronicled the growing balkanization of Los Angeles in *City of Quartz*. Throughout the book, he used the imagery of the three theses of urban wilderness:

> The carefully manicured lawns of L.A.'s Westside sprout forests of ominous little signs warning: "Armed Response." . . . Downtown, a publicly-subsidized "urban renaissance" has raised the nation's largest corporate citadel, segregated from the poor neighborhoods around it by monumental architectural glaciers. . . . In the Westlake and San Fernando areas the L.A. police department barricades streets and seals off poor neighborhoods as part of their "war on drugs." In Watts . . . a panopticon shopping mall [is] surrounded by staked metal fences and a substation of the L.A.P.D. in a central surveillance tower.[19]

Even though works like Davis's help to reinvigorate critical discussions of the legacy of the disastrous post–Watts riots' urban policies, we should not find it surprising that the overwhelming response to the King riots was in part to continue to view the inner city in the context of T1–T3, rather than to begin to publicly address the sources and reinforcements of the demonization of the inner city. Police abuses (including several questionable shootings by the L.A.P.D.) continued against inner-city residents. The perspective that youth gangs are the savage enemy within the city, consistent with a justification for separation, was reinforced. Separation efforts were redoubled in an attempt to protect threatened white suburbs at the insistence of the post–King riot Warren Commission (impaneled to investigate the causes and effects of the events). Successful arguments were made in the California State Legislature to justify increased criminal penalties in order to further the state's control over urbanites, and aid to rebuild the city remained at a standstill for some time. Davis argued later that a consensus was forming in the business community that the region as a whole had slipped backward into a "neo-Disney, plastic Stone Age."[20]

But even if it is true that the city is the new inheritor of the reference for classical wilderness, worries about the effects of this shift on the inhabitants can be easily ignored. A simple "law-and-order" stance is all that is needed to argue that, just as the idea of the classical wilderness was in part motivated by the real dangers of wild nature, fear of the urban wilderness is justified by the actual dangers of life in American inner cities. Still, there is good reason to believe that such savage baiting causes harm beyond whatever cautionary benefits it might bring. Acknowledging a danger is one thing; unnecessarily dehumanizing the source of a real or only perceived threat is quite another. Without the designation of the inner city as an alien, savage place, is it not plausible that a more reasoned discussion of its problems could be accomplished across the board, and given my interest here, also on film? If a film like *Falling Down* actually is a "tale of urban reality," it more accurately reflects the prejudices of suburban and rural populations, raised on the myth of urban wilderness, against the cities. Its damage may be realized too late.[21]

Boyz in the Woods

What are the alternatives to the imagery of urban wilderness in depictions of the city? One answer can be found in the African-American urban cinema of auteur filmmakers such as Spike Lee, John Singleton, and Allen and Albert Hughes. Each of these filmmakers responds to overly simplified portrayals of urban life without romanticizing the problems of the inner city. They recognize that the city is a dangerous place, though certainly most dangerous for its own residents rather than for white outsiders. And just as any depiction of wilderness must acknowledge the actual danger that inspired the classical view, a sober portrayal of the inner city must realistically describe its dangers. But they reject the simplistic imagery of inner cities as an urban wilderness filled with savages, bringing out more complex causes for the dangers they acknowledge.

Lee's films are perhaps the most mainstream, and he has dealt with the widest array of topics. Here, however, I want to briefly discuss the first films of both John Singleton and the Hughes brothers, which unlike Lee's

New York–based films, are set, like *Falling Down,* in Los Angeles. (I will, however, return to Lee in chapter 6.) Although they may not be directly aimed at responding to portrayals of the inner city as a savage space, both *Menace II Society* (Hughes Brothers, 1993) and *Boyz N the Hood* (Singleton, 1991) contain implicit and explicit commentary on these themes.

Menace II Society begins with actual footage of the 1965 Watts riots, placing the film into a more precise historical and social context than is found in *Falling Down,* where violence appears to be simply a natural part of the urban landscape. A voice-over from the film's protagonist, Caine Lawson (played by Tyria Turner) explains, "When the riots stopped, the drugs started." The film follows Caine, a minor drug dealer, in his attempt to extricate himself from these surroundings. Unlike the main character of *Boyz,* the college-bound Tre (Cuba Gooding, Jr.), Caine begins the film fairly satisfied with his surroundings. But after he sees his cousin killed in a carjacking, Caine begins to doubt the sustainability of his environment as well as to rethink his expressed nonchalance about the possibility of his own death. He begins to contemplate a move out of the city, eventually committing to move to Atlanta with an imprisoned friend's wife and child. Rarely does the explicit imagery of the three theses of urban wilderness come up, even though the film depicts Caine's surroundings as extremely violent. Here, however, it is violence that has at least been historically oriented and so partly explained.

Two scenes are especially interesting. In one, the father of one of Caine's friends (played by Charles Dutton) urges him to leave the city. His point is not that L.A. is dangerous in and of itself, however, but that the state of race relations in the United States has helped to create these violent conditions and directs this violence at black citizens: "Being a black man in America isn't easy. The hunt is on and *you're the prey.*" Because this scene is immediately followed by one of extreme police brutality, the comment does not seem to be an expression of T2 (that the inhabitants of the wilderness are nonhuman, more akin to beasts, and are to be treated as such); rather, it suggests that it is the police, the strong arm of a majority government, not the inner-city residents, who are the savages. Similarly, one of the most threatening characters in *Boyz* is a black police officer who has become an irrational and indiscriminate hater of inner-city youth evidently because of his position over them. Still, to even suggest that Caine and his friends are prey is to use a characterization of inner-city inhabitants as nonhuman animals. Such language relies in part on the imagery of an urban wilderness in order to turn the tables on it and represent the police as a threat, thus, à la Sinclair's *Jungle,* motivating a concern for the young black inhabitants of the city.

There is a danger, however, in this social-reform use of urban wilderness. The Dutton character's comment easily resonates with other, less charitable, animalistic representations of African-American men. For example, in Robert Gooding-Williams's account of the rhetorical strategies of the defense attorneys in the first Rodney King trial, the language of classical wilderness is thick:

> After inviting jurors to see events from the point of view of the police officers, the defense attorneys elicited testimony from King's assailants that depicted King as a *bear,* and as emitting *bearlike groans.* In the eyes of the police and then again in the eyes of the jurors, King's black body became that of a *wild "hulk-like" and "wounded" animal, whose every gesture threatened the existence of civilized society.* Not surprisingly, the defense attorneys portrayed the white bodies which assailed King *as guardians against the wild, and as embodying a "thin blue line" that separates civil society from the dangerous chaos of the essence of the wild.* . . . *This animal,* claimed one of the jurors, echoing the words of defense attorney Michael Stone, was in complete control and directed all the action. Still, somehow, the *forces of civilization* prevailed, preserving intact human society as we know it.[22]

One question then becomes whether the majority audience for such a film as *Menace* (a white audience) can distinguish the positive and negative uses of such language of savagery. To their credit, the Hughes brothers inserted a scene that more straightforwardly rejects the imagery of T2. When visiting an old street mentor in jail toward the end of the film, Caine says that he didn't visit before because he didn't want to see him in a "cage." His friend quickly retorts, "You think I'm some kind of animal?" and Caine says no. Such a quick reply, however, may not be enough to demonstrate the film's rejection of the less responsible imagery of urban wilderness in other films. Skirting such problems is something that I will return to below. Suffice to say for now that this film, like others made by the Hughes brothers, stands as a strong response to the one-dimensional portrayal of inner-city life found in films like *Falling Down.*

Boyz starts with a historicizing moment too, but one more personal than the opening of *Menace.* We begin with a view of our protagonist, Tre Styles, as a small child stumbling onto the scene of a shooting on the way to school one morning. It is the first shooting he has ever witnessed. Tre appears to be a very bright but somewhat argumentative child. After he gets in a fight at school, his mother decides to send him to live with his father, Furious (played by Laurence Fishburne). After a few scenes involving Tre as a child, the film jumps seven years to Tre as an adult. In large part, the film focuses on Tre and his interaction with two neighbors, the brothers Dough Boy (played by rapper Ice Cube) and Ricky (Morris Chestnut). Ricky is a rising football star on his way to a college career at USC; Dough Boy has been in and out of prisons and seems, like Caine from *Menace,* both thoughtful and violent. Tre, however, is the most reflective of the three, and though ambivalent at the moment, we learn by the end of the film that he will eventually attend Morehouse College in Atlanta.[23]

Themes similar to those found in *Menace* play through this film, in particular the violence directly toward inner-city neighborhoods. One unique scene occurs toward the end of the film when Furious takes Tre and Ricky to Compton (one of the most notoriously violent black neighborhoods in L.A.) to give them a lesson on gentrification. Even though we have seen these characters in extremely hostile environments, both Tre and Ricky are afraid to be in Compton. As though he is responding to the uniformly negative imagery of films like *Falling Down,* Furious tells the boys, "It's the '90s, we can't afford to be afraid of our own people anymore."

Furious goes on to give a sophisticated critique of the claim that south-central L.A. has become run down at the hands of its own black residents and them alone. As he goes on, and a small audience gathers, he asks us to consider how it is that crack has made its way into the inner city and why gun and liquor stores are on every street corner. "Because they want us to kill ourselves!" explains Furious. Even if we disagree with the conspiracy theory at the heart of Furious's argument, this scene successfully asks us to reconsider the stereotypes that cause us to fear the city and its inhabitants and to examine the ways in which we simplify issues of violence in our urban centers. In a similar scene at the very end of the film, after Ricky has been killed in a drive-by shooting, Dough Boy tells Tre that he has just seen a television show about how we "live in a violent world." Expressing dismay about the show's focus on foreign places, Dough Boy suggests, "They don't know, don't show, or don't care what's going on in the hood." But "they" do show what goes on in the hood—only from afar and through a lens that demonizes the inner city and those who reside there rather than contributing to a solution to the problem of urban violence.

Both of these films focus on the African-American experience of the inner city from an African-American perspective. They are representations of the inner city's perception of itself and its own problems. *Falling Down*, by contrast, is very much a voyeuristic film, dropping an agitated white man into East L.A. to see what happens, and supplying a white perception of the city. Although both *Menace* and *Boyz* contain characters who seem to be able to rise above their situation as well as characters mired in failure, neither film resorts to an external critique from the perspective of a white audience or an appeal to old prejudices as the basis for their depiction of violence in the city. The focus of both films is black-on-black crime. (To drive this message home, public service spots at the beginning of the videotape editions of both films feature commentary about internal violence in the black community.) But in depicting both the historical context and the present motivations for some of that violence, neither film degenerates into the environmental determinism of the classical view of wilderness that we saw in *Falling Down*. What allows a character to resist or fall prey to the real dangers of inner-city life are as complex and various—social forces, economic conditions, political problems, personal fortunes, and moral luck—as would be true anywhere.

One final remark. As I suggested earlier, one can compare the portrayal of urban wilderness in these films to that used in turn-of-the-century social-reform literature. Both employ the language of wilderness to serve a call for urban improvement and social justice. Significantly, the imagery of urban wilderness that is most closely rejected in both films is T2, savagery. The films strive to show that inner-city residents cannot be easily dismissed as savages. The violent images and themes of drive-by shootings and gang activity go hand in hand with scenes of police brutality and harassment. The feel of the two films may be consistent with the highly tense atmosphere of *Falling Down*, at least in focusing on the violent aspects of city life. However, *Menace* and *Boyz* are both about the very real problems of violence in the city. The violence in these films is not gratuitous but serves a larger purpose of social critique. *Falling Down*, in contrast, gives us violence as a source of guilty pleasure, à la *Rambo*.

Nonetheless, a problem these portrayals share with a film like *Falling Down* is their implicit appeal to the terms of classical wilderness in their rejection of T2. Even though they present a more subtle understanding of the city, by using the terms of classical wilderness they may perpetuate a false view of the supposed physical referent of such a term. As an accurate description of the external world, the classical view fails when it is revealed to be a cognitive projection more than a physical description. If the portrayal of the inner city as a classical wilderness is to be rejected, it may not be wise to try to retrieve the imagery of the old social-reform strategies. After all, it was the availability of this idea, as brought forward and applied to cities by authors like Sinclair, that in part gave power to the pernicious imagery of urban wilderness found in films such as *Falling Down*.

What makes the portrayal of the city as a wild, savage place plausible to us is at least found in part in our "cultural memory" that the city can legitimately be described as a jungle. My feeling is that it would be better to entirely reject the metaphors of urban wilderness and focus our understanding of cities through themes that reflect the more complicated diversity of urban life. This is not to say that *Menace* and *Boyz* should be rejected as social commentary. It is only to say that in our search for a full answer to the imagery of urban wilderness, we may need to look to those films that do not employ it at all.

Conclusions

Fortunately, there are plenty of filmic representations of cities that do provide a more comprehensive view of urban life. For example, Darnell Martin's *I Like It Like That* (1994), a film set in a Hispanic area of the Bronx, rejects overly simplified portrayals of the city by placing an almost traditional comic-drama in an inner-city setting. Unlike the representation of the Bronx in the earlier, more well-known *Fort Apache: The Bronx* (1981), in *I Like It* the Bronx is a place, like any other place, where people live, love, and die. But the setting is undeniably the Bronx, and it is significant for the character development in the film that it is set in this particular place. It is not a nameless place that could be anywhere in the United States. The main character of the film, Lisette (Lauren Velez), a young mother who must find a job for the first time in her life after her husband, Chino, is arrested, wears a Bronx baseball jersey in much of the film. The focus is not the city in the abstract, but the lives of people in the city who are clearly part of their landscape. This portrayal, which also includes obligatory references to the violent drug trade that was more a part of New York City at the time, nonetheless works against the T2 stereotype of portraying inner-city residents as savages.

Other place-specific films, such as *Smoke* (1995, directed by Wayne Wang and set in Brooklyn) and *To Sleep with Anger* (1990, directed by

Charles Burnett and set in Los Angeles) could also be mentioned. But perhaps in a different category are those films which not only normalize portrayals of the city as a background landscape but take on the complicated postindustrial legacy of urban America as the center of the plot. In that respect, John Sayles's *City of Hope* (1991) is one of the most important films yet made in America to address the multiracial and multicultural problems of city life in a context outside of the legacy of urban wilderness.

In the first few minutes of this film we see a full array of inner-city residents: bigots, liberals, crooks, nationalists, bums, and just ordinary people. All races also seem to be represented. But there are no stereotypes here, no easy depictions of media-hot problems. There are just signs of city life, city politics, and city issues. This mid-sized city, which is never identified directly, though several cues would place it in New Jersey, is not a stand-in for anything other than the urban home of different people with different forms of interaction. Although there is designated central character, Nick Rinaldi, the son of an Italian-American developer, his story alone does not move the plot of the film. The film is about the problems of any city with an identifiable history and the movement of different groups within it as they strive for political recognition and economic well-being.

On Sayles's view cities are spaces where different communities must try to work through the problems of occupying the same place. This is not a romantic picture of different communities easily coming together, but a portrayal of the hopeful potential of city life as a site where different groups of people can acquire the power to forge a home for themselves and solve their problems. The central problem in the film is the challenge to the Italian-American power structure of the city by black and Hispanic residents. An African-American city council member, Wynn (played by Joe Morton), is the elected leader of the community trying to convince those in the city's power structure to recognize their problems, focusing on affordable housing and jobs. But many of the city leaders are corrupt and unwilling to hear these voices of dissent.

Still, no community here is portrayed as homogeneous. Wynn, for example, must constantly spar with black nationalists who control the local community center and urge a much more confrontational strategy than he is willing to take. Members of the city elite constantly argue over the right course of action, remembering that they only recently came to replace the Irish Americans who once ran the government. Even members of the police force argue amongst themselves, in a much more realistic portrayal of police brutality than is found in *Boyz* or *Menace*. The overall effect is to portray the city as a complex place. It may be unique in some respects and not in others, but it is a place that deserves attention untainted by easy characterizations and stereotypes.

A closer reading than I will provide here would be needed to better tease out the virtues of this film. In the next chapter, however, I will provide a close analysis of another Sayles film that also does a superior job of representing the tensions of race and class in a particular location, with attention to the history of those tensions, but without resorting to dogmas such as forms of environmental determinism. As I will point out, Sayles is one of the most politically astute filmmakers in America today, and he is also one of the few who is highly sensitive to the importance of place in his films. In interviews surrounding the release of his brilliant film about personal risk in relationships, *Limbo* (1999), set in Alaska, Sayles made much of the point that he finds it disturbing that most films can be set anywhere: Their locations are insignificant to the stories told in the film. Those films lose the important relationship that emerges between people and the specific places they inhabit. This is not to say that the argument in *Limbo* about the risks of relationships is limited only to Alaska, but that the setting of the film in Alaska is not incidental to the plot and important for bringing the broader message of the film home to us. How films depict a place, as uniformly bad or good, or whether they are indifferent to the specificity of their location, is something that we should pay attention to.

The continued rehearsal of suspect fears of the inner city is an important obstacle to a meaningful discussion of the very real problems of urban life, inclusive of problems that exacerbated the King riots, and then going beyond them to discover solutions and to lay the foundation for a more positive future. Given the enormous power of film to shape our perceptions of ourselves and our communities, blame must be incurred by those who would continue the representation of any space as a classical wilderness. Praise should in turn be given to those who would resist this legacy and move us forward to a more responsible portrayal of urban life.

PART TWO

Film, Group Interests, and Political Identity

5

John Sayles on Class Interest

"You know there ain't but two sides in this world—them
that work and them that don't. You work, they don't."
— Joe Kenehan in John Sayles's *Matewan*

John Sayles is arguably one of the premier independent filmmakers in the United States, and certainly one of the most politically important. He has never hesitated to dive directly into difficult topics, including controversies over race, gender, and class conflict, as well as the problems of how communities come to constitute themselves through argument, disagreement, and negotiation, with a full recognition of the weight of their historical past. Sayles is the closest thing we have in America to European directors such as Margarethe von Trotta (e.g., *Rosa Luxemburg,* 1996) or Ken Loach (e.g., *Land and Freedom,* 1995).

This chapter focuses on Sayles's independent film *Matewan* (1987) and its representation of working-class interests. Those unfamiliar with this film may know Sayles's other works (which, by and large, he has written, directed, and edited), including *Return of the Secaucus Seven* (1980), *The Brother from Another Planet* (1984), *Eight Men Out* (1988), *City of Hope* (1991, briefly mentioned at the end of the last chapter), *Passion Fish* (1992), *Lone Star* (1996), *Men with Guns* (1997), *Limbo* (1999), and *Sunshine State* (2002).

Sayles is particularly important for me for a number of personal reasons. I'll say more about this later, but one reason is that it was one of his films, *The Brother from Another Planet,* that first helped me to understand the potential of independent cinema to make substantial contributions to contemporary social issues. The reason was that it was also one of the first independent films I ever saw. Visiting my closest cousin Paul in Atlanta when I was a teenager, we somehow stumbled into *Brother*, knowing nothing about the film or the filmmaker beyond the movie's cool title. The experience was a revelation to me. This film was grittier and less polished than any I had seen before, yet it was so much more powerful, taking on the legacy of race relations and slavery in the United States using a very smart, low-tech, science-fiction story that was both funny and poignant.

Coming from a small town outside of Atlanta at the time, a place where VCRs and cable had not yet taken much hold, didn't afford me much of an opportunity to see anything other than the standard Hollywood fare. Although I had seen some independent and cult films (mostly the work of Woody Allen and *The Rocky Horror Picture Show*), I was not at all prepared for *Brother*. Coming out of that theater, I knew that I had been exposed to a whole new world of film: Evidently, when unfettered by the restrictions of the big studios, they could both be entertaining and make powerful contributions to critical moral, political, and social debates. The fact that *Brother* is about race relations, and that I had grown up in the South and was now watching this film there, only brought this point home stronger.

Among Sayles's films, *Matewan* is surely one of the most explicitly political; some would even say it openly embraces a form of socialism. The plot is set in the coal-field wars in southern West Virginia in the 1920s, focusing on the story of an attempt by a union organizer to try to unify white, black, and recently immigrated Italian miners against a coal company intent on using racial prejudice to break a wildcat strike.[1] After the local white miners begin to organize and walk off the job, the coal company brings in skilled black and unskilled Italian miners as scab labor.

The quotation that forms the epigraph to this chapter is indicative of the strong, no-nonsense, jargon-free approach of the film to class politics. This is not a script by a frustrated academic, loaded with opaque references to high Marxist or postmodern theory. This is a film written and directed by someone with a feel for class politics from the inside. Before turning to fiction, then later screenwriting and filmmaking, Sayles worked in factories and hospitals in the rust belt. He was not a film school graduate, and he was steeped neither in the techniques of the trade nor in the theoretical commentary on it. Sayles was instead someone with keen progressive political instincts, and, as he put it, a native talent for "thinking in pictures."

For Sayles, even when he was writing fiction, ideas for stories came first as images, sequences of movement, and ideas for characters and a sense of how they might interact, and then only later developed as written text.[2]

Sayles tells the story of the development of *Matewan* as beginning with a hitchhiking trip through West Virginia and eastern Kentucky in the late 1960s. There he came across the story of the 1920 "Matewan massacre," involving a bloody shoot-out between striking miners in Mingo County, West Virginia, led in part by an honest chief of police named Sid Hatfield and gun thugs from the private Baldwin-Felts security agency, which had been hired by the local mining companies. The conflict left eleven people dead and, as David Alan Corbin put it, transformed the Mingo County strike into the "Mingo County war."[3] Although accounts of the incident, according to Sayles, were few, largely biased to one side, and lacking in eyewitness testimony, several characters emerged for him from the stories who would later make it into the film. Sayles saw the action in pictures that could convey the rage, despair, and sliver of hope of a time in a more engaging way than had been achieved in its representation in history or fiction. Sayles hoped that the film would convey to the viewer the visceral experience of the conditions of the miners, their arguments over strategy and tactics, and the conflict over race that came into play. It could make the understanding of the political and social issues less abstract. As Sayles put it: "Politics are always at the mercy of human nature and custom, and the coal wars of the twenties were so personal that they make ideology accessible in a story, make it immediate and emotional. It was this emotional immediacy that made me think of making a movie about the events of Matewan."[4]

But at first glance, one might find the plot of the film, which ends up reconciling the different racial groups in a unified strike against the coal company prior to the shoot-out that ends the film, almost fanciful: Was such solidarity across racial lines really possible, and even if it happened in this case, wasn't it the exception rather than the rule, which partly explains much of the failure of unions over the past century? Surely a politically savvy, progressive director shouldn't have picked such a story to try to say something substantive about the history, and possibly the current state, of class politics in America, given that this tale comes across as more an aberration than an opportunity to struggle with the actual dilemmas of race and class. The "emotional immediacy" that Sayles was trying to capture may, in the end, degenerate into a bad form of romanticism for a lost time that does not speak to our current troubles.

Kenehan's quotation above is a good case in point. On first reading, while attractive, it sounds like an overly simplified slogan about complex social questions. We know there are more than two sides to this world, and there are certainly other divisions besides class division that are relevant to understanding where one sits on the political spectrum. If progressives of all persuasions have recognized anything, it is the historical, theoretical, and strategic mistake of reducing all political differences to exclusive issues of class. Isn't Sayles then substituting the representation of a romantic impulse for political substance in the creation of an explicitly working-class film image? And isn't this surprising coming from a filmmaker who has taken up the peculiar ways in which problems of race complicate questions of class politics, in such films as *The Brother from Another Planet*, and more recently, *Lone Star*?

My purpose here is to defend Sayles against such a charge of romanticism and political naïveté and to dispel the notion that *Matewan* argues that class solidarity can in and of itself resolve problems of racial and gender differences. I will do this mainly by giving a close reading of one scene in the film that I find most evocative of its overall political position and most telling of the problems we might have with that position. I will use two foils to motivate the virtues of the film. The first is the theoretical debate on the Left about how to reconcile class politics with the politics of race, gender, and other identities. I will give a brief argument in the next part of the chapter that, while skeptical of some of the more fashionable philosophical positions on the politics of identity, suggests that no pragmatic progressive project can avoid the challenge of taking up these relationships if it hopes to rebuild some form of unified Left. Because I treat the issue of a politics of identity in depth in the next chapter, I will only briefly discuss it here. I hope to portray Sayles as offering a practical approach to reconciling the problems of class with other forms of identity through a focus on motivating a common class interest over the demands of particular political identities.

Matewan offers this vision of common class interest, and overcomes worries about being overly romantic, by presenting a series of literal (not theoretical) interruptions and reconciliations in the film. In these scenes, a representative of racial interests, in the form of the leader of the black miners, interrupts an Old Left dialogue that appears to be focused on class divisions between workers and capitalists to the exclusion of any other concern. This is where my other foil comes in. To prepare us for the analysis of these interruptions in *Matewan*, I will briefly look at Richard

Linklater's cult generation-X film *Slacker* (1991), which includes a contrasting depiction of a representative of class interests as an interruption on a postmodern cultural landscape.

The power of Sayles's films as depictions of working-class history and struggle emerge not only from their emotive moments, but also because they are directed forward at the current viewer, encouraging a more sober conception of class identity that is relevant to social and political problems today. Sayles is no formal dialectician: Like the Old Left's "Wobblies," members of the Industrial Workers of the World (IWW), an anarcho-syndicalist union that did not discriminate against any worker seeking to join a movement for labor solidarity, he is more a folk theorist of sorts, more concerned with using media to forge practical links between workers than in demonstrating the existence of class consciousness as a law-like force in history. We should not be surprised, then, that the union organizer, Joe Kenehan, the main character of the film, is introduced as a former Wobbly. Through Kenehan we can understand Sayles as arguing that a common class interest practically is the same thing as class consciousness. Sayles's motivation is pragmatic, answering the question of how to identify a union, and a class, given the contingencies of the labor relations of the moment. In *Matewan* we do not just get a representation of the emotional elements of a class-based ideology, as the film also depicts a sound understanding of politics, and it is not ignorant of the complexities of racial, gender, and other community divisions, either.

Class Interest and Practical Philosophy

Is there a way in which class interest or affinity can have a place in contemporary concerns with other forms of political identity? In the next chapter I will distinguish between the formal literature on identity politics and a more general politics of identity, which is simply the attempt to understand how different individuals and communities see their political interests as connected to their personal identities, not just aspects of identity such as race, but also specific concerns with particular social issues. So, another way of putting the question just asked is whether class politics can be reformed to speak more informatively to questions of racial, ethnic, gender, or other forms of political identity or affinity.

Several schools of analysis oriented toward thinking through the relationship between class identity and other forms of political identity have arisen over the years. I will briefly mention only one, without going into too much detail: the group of theorists loosely referred to as "post-Marxists," a name derived from their attempt to fuse postmodernism with Marxism. Its leading theorists were such figures as Ernesto Laclau and Chantal Mouffe, authors of *Hegemony and Socialist Strategy*.[5] These thinkers, plus others from various disciplines, have argued for a reconstruction of Marxist philosophy to respond to other forms of identity politics. But to say that these theorists were interested in reforming Marxism to deal with contemporary problems of political identity may not be quite accurate. Though I will not purse the argument here, some have claimed that what they have provided instead is a rationale for leftists to abandon the traditional ends of class politics in favor of what they call "radical democracy," leaving behind economic class as a foundational category of social and political philosophy.

Whatever they were up to, the language of the post-Marxists was often criticized as alienating, and the philosophical moves as too abstract to be of much direct use in overcoming the more practical hurdles that arose for the project of reconciling class interests with other forms of political identity. If this criticism is true, they certainly would not be the first theorists in the Marxist tradition to use overly complicated philosophical moves and arguably abstruse dialectics in their work. But such worries about this particular branch of Marxist theory, combined with claims that the pursuit of a radical democracy amounted to, in Ellen Meiksins Wood's words, a "retreat from class," caused many on the more traditional Left to be highly critical of it.[6] They felt in part that this kind of approach abandoned Marx's own proclamation in his eleventh "theses on Feuerbach" that we should seek to change the world rather than only interpret it.

But it is not my intention here to fully assess the post-Marxist literature or the criticisms of it. I only use this example to highlight the point that even if one were enamored of the literature of identity politics, one would obviously need at some point to admit that at least some of it, especially of the postmodern and poststructural varieties, has severe limitations for practical political and social questions. This is certainly not a profound point, and it could be levied against many other schools of thought in this literature as well. Even so, if we were inclined to reject the post-Marxist answer to the question of how to reconcile class politics with other interests, how should one respond to a progressive political sphere often dominated by the language of concerns that are not oriented around class politics? How can those interested in class politics add to the discussion of a politics of identity writ large in a constructive manner? Perhaps the answer is to reject the rejection of economic class as a fundamental category of social analysis and again pursue the project of reducing other political interests to class interests, or to argue that other political interests must always take a backseat to questions of class conflict. We could then spend our time continuing to fight out these debates in academic books and journals: Many social and political theorists do just that, taking variants of these positions. But would even a sophisticated denial of the importance or relevance of other political identities really get us anywhere if our concern was to make a contribution to actual political conflicts and social questions?

I do not think so. The reason is that I think that important issues of political identity warrant consideration in and of themselves if we are interested in actually resolving, rather than just discussing, political and social questions, especially at the progressive end of the spectrum, simply because political groups oriented around different identities still are so predominant. Such a project requires a more practical political or social philosophy. By this I mean a political philosophy derived from actual problems at hand rather than in the application of theoretical answers to political or social problems. Or, in other words, perhaps we could do our philosophy from the "ground up," as it were, rather than from the "top down."

I draw this idea from Bryan Norton's distinction between applied and practical philosophy in environmental ethics. Briefly, environmental ethics is a relatively new subfield of philosophy (around in philosophy departments since the early 1970s) concerned primarily with making arguments demonstrating the value of nature independent of the value that humans attribute to it because of the resources it supplies for our use in meeting human needs. Pragmatists in this field, such as Norton and I, have argued, however, that pursuit of this philosophical account of natural value in and of itself actually may impede environmental ethicists from making a relevant contribution to the formation of a better moral basis for environmental policies.[7] I don't need to go into the details of our reasons for taking this position now; those readers who are interested can investigate the papers I suggest in the notes cited in this chapter, but suffice to say that, for Norton, a more pragmatic philosophical approach to this set of issues entails a distinction between doing environmental ethics as a form of "practical philosophy" and seeing it as a form of "applied philosophy."[8]

On Norton's account, to merely apply philosophy is to impose a philosophical scheme on a problem in the world from the top; practical philosophy, in contrast, "is problem-oriented; it treats theories as tools of the understanding, tools that are developed in the process of addressing specific policy controversies." Practical philosophers therefore do not assume that "theoretical issues can be resolved in isolation to real problems."[9] Where Norton and I disagree is on the warrant for such an approach. Whereas he appears to find such a form of philosophical practice generally defensible, I have argued that either a clear goal or another set of conditions involving the area of our philosophical inquiry must justify the move to a practical philosophy.[10] For many if not most philosophical questions, a more abstract approach using the traditional tools and reservations of philosophical analysis is best. The reason we might want to change our approach in environmental ethics is that we can mount a specific case that improving our treatment of the environment is based on a strong practical warrant, namely, that environmental problems are critical right now and must be more immediately solved to relieve much present and possible human and nonhuman suffering. So, in addition to figuring out the moral value of nature, environmental ethics ought to also offer philosophical tools that can more readily be used, without debating them for another generation first, to help in resolving these very pressing problems now. To generalize Norton's intuitions to other forms of practical philosophy requires having a clear goal or set of conditions pertaining to a problem to direct this shift in our philosophical methodology.[11]

It is likely the case that this practical and pragmatic approach could be justified for many areas of social and political philosophy. In the case of how a political or social philosophy should engage with the pressures of consideration of a politics of identity, a warrant for a practical approach would be that a substantial amount of political activity in fact is generated out of political positions that are grounded in identity. This is particularly true on the Left, and so philosophers interested in making a contribution to progressive politics could not simply ignore other aspects of identity for practical reasons, in the sense of the term as used by Norton, even if they took the position that economic class and the interests that follow from them really were the best category of analysis for social and political problems. Feminism, race-based politics, and the politics of sexual orientation (and as I will argue in the next chapter, environmental politics and other so-called "special-interest" concerns as well) do not have to be based in a politics of identity but often are. For good or for bad, even if one finds the politics of identity fragmentary, either for the Left in particular or for the larger political sphere in general, at least in the industrialized north, the politics of such identity positions has garnered a great deal of attention on the progressive agenda and will continue to do so even as more formal versions of an identity politics itself are rejected.

I, for one, have been more often than not frustrated by the excessive focus on a politics of identity of late (in the next chapter I will explain how my own views in social and political philosophy have gravitated toward more traditional notions of "citizenship" rather than identity), but I still think that as a practically oriented philosopher I must look to the terrain of group identities as presenting a series of questions that need to be answered in a way that respects the legitimacy of those positions. This is not to say that I necessarily agree with the grounds of the positions themselves, or with their implications, but that even if I reject either those grounds or their implications I cannot afford to simply reject these identities as such, since many people would describe their political commitments in these terms. Criticism of existing movements and political strategies is part of a practical philosopher's task, but if that same philosopher is interested in building a coalition to actually take on real political problems, this criticism must be oriented toward the goal of unity and convergence of interests toward more progressive political formations. Solidarity across diverse interests and beliefs is never guaranteed, even with such a methodology, but its aspiration requires empathy with our fellow's political priorities, where possible, as they are important to them. This is not a hard and fast rule but a recommendation for doing philosophy in a particular way. Other principles can certainly supersede it, so I'm not in any way suggesting that a practically oriented philosopher, or anyone else for that matter, has to empathize with Stalinists or others who deny minimum levels of dignity and respect for others.

As implied above in the worries suggested about post-Marxists, another part of making philosophy more practical in certain contexts is to expand its message so that it speaks more easily to as broad an audience as possible, not just other philosophers and academics. Such a task involves more than simply clarifying our arguments; it also involves making them through mediums of communication that have a broader appeal. Film, as I have said many times in these chapters, is an excellent medium for achieving this goal because films often offer important insights on social issues that are philosophically interesting. It certainly helps my suggestion here that there is a long tradition of utilizing film to express substantive progressive positions; moreover, it provides a forum to debate the Left's portrayal of itself.

Some of Sayles's films are good examples of a kind of practical philosophy on screen, not just because they will be seen by a broader audience than any philosopher or political theorist is likely to reach, but because, in the case of the issue being discussed here, they appear to endorse the practical answer to the challenge of a politics of identity. Sayles does not simply reject a politics of identity, nor does he capitulate to it, but especially in *Matewan* he recognizes such group identities and then tries to reconcile them with a common portrayal of class interest. Before turning directly to Sayles's treatment of these issues in *Matewan*, I will briefly examine a contrasting cinematic moment that may express a more dismissive view of the role of class interest on the contemporary political landscape.

Class as Interruption: *Slacker*

Except for in the work of filmmakers like Sayles, Loach, Mike Leigh, and a few others, working-class politics is not found very often in the artifacts of today's popular culture. Even in hip independent cinema, depictions of class issues are few and far between, and when they are found, the language of class politics often comes off as outdated and unimportant. Richard Linklater's film *Slacker*, which I otherwise greatly admire, is a case in point.

Slacker is a series of loosely connected vignettes all set on the streets of Austin, Texas, and largely involving twenty-somethings doing exactly the sort of pointless things that we have come to expect twenty-somethings to do in films of this genre: discussing 1970s television shows, hanging out in coffee shops, and mostly talking about rather than having sex. But this low-budget independent film is much more sophisticated than its Hollywood equivalents. As Douglas Taylor suggests taking a cue from the structure of Luis Buñuel's *La Voie Lactée* (1969), *Slacker* follows characters from one scene to another, quickly losing people along the way. No one character makes it through more than a couple of scenes. This is both an extremely enjoyable piece of film art as well as a paradigmatic postmodern text, with no clear narrative or theme, offering instead a pastiche of images sampling different moments from daily life.[12] But we are often called by the film to try to recognize cultural cues representing different segments of the population. A fairly close reading of the film can yield some interesting conclusions for questions of the representation of a politics of identity. One thing to get out of it is a glimpse into how the identity of youth culture is building to a kind of political critique. Kellner commented that:

The slackers . . . appropriate media culture for their own ends, turning articles from conservative media sources into material for radical social and political critique, while using media technology for their own purposes (as does
obviously director Linklater and his team). The slackers are not passive
products or media effects, but active participants in a media culture who use
media to produce meaning, pleasure, and identity in their lives. The ubiquitous T-shirts often have logos or images derived from media culture, and TV
and music are constant backgrounds for the cinematic events of the film.[13]

Occasionally, there are glimpses of more traditional political commentary in the film as well, with shades of the Old Left sneaking in. For example, in a scene where University of Texas philosopher Louis Mackey
plays an aging anarchist who catches a college student breaking into his
house, the interchange between the two is given perhaps the longest continuous segment in the film. Mackey goes on for some time about anarchist politics and history, moving effortlessly between tales of the Spanish
Civil War to the 1966 shootings from the University of Texas clock tower
by Charles Whitman that left fourteen dead and thirty-one wounded.
But one scene, where a vagrant (played by Charles Gunning, one of the
few professional actors in the film) makes a comment about what he takes
to be the real relationship between commodity production and the identity of workers, is a unique moment in the film.

A man walks by a hip Austin coffeehouse, looking very disheveled. We
do not know anything about him except that he had bummed a ride into
town from an auto junkyard and reported during the drive that he had recently been to his stepfather's funeral. He walks up to one of the outdoor
tables at the coffeehouse and asks to bum a cigarette, clearly annoying
some students reading what appear to be sophisticated theoretical texts.[14]
A student film crew approaches and requests to interview the man. He is
asked if he has a job, and when the students find out that he does not, they
inquire as to his prospects. The man responds flippantly that he's not worried because he's "makin' it" and is only waiting to receive "the true calling"
for something. When asked if he has anything else to add, the man says he
does, responding with an outburst, "To all you workers out there: Every
single commodity you produce is a piece of your own death!" After an
awkward pause, the camera operator asks the man about his relationship to
his father, and he walks off abruptly, saying, "End of interview." One final
shot shows us the students' puzzled, if not bemused, expressions.

In the context of the scene, and the larger film, this outburst about
working-class interest seems entirely alien to the conversations of the

nearby slackers. The awkward reception of the man's outburst by the students (who could stand in for the crew shooting the film as well) comes across as a dismissal by youth culture of any kind of working-class perspective. The vagrant's outburst is a literal interruption, interjecting a strong claim about the social position of the proletariat under capitalism, against an otherwise sterile depiction of the development of cultural identity among the slackers. But as an interruption, the outburst is a failure: The film proceeds as before without any questioning of the role of class conflict in this postmodern landscape. The class perspective is not presented on the same level as other forms of media politics in the film; it is instead seen as an archaic, even obnoxious interjection of a presumed dead language on a political terrain that has moved onto more sophisticated cultural territory.[15]

Although it would be unfair to try to describe this scene as a depiction of the post-Marxist approach to class issues against other claims concerning political identity, there is a resemblance to the criticisms of that approach, fair or not, that is illuminating. For if it is actually true that some post-Marxists reject more articulate claims along the lines of the vagrant's outburst, then class interests are pushed out of the public sphere on that account. The dismissal in this scene of class interests through this caricature could be seen as a popular version of that approach. The vagrant's claim is reductive, applying to all workers, regardless of their race, gender, sexual orientation, point in production, or other aspect of identity. Working-class interests are out of place in this film as a relic of a previous period of history that we should move beyond.

Race as Interruption: *Matewan*

From its beginning we can expect that the focus of *Matewan* will be on the class issues only alluded to in *Slacker*. The plot is steeped in labor history. The central character of the film, Joe Kenehan (played by Chris Cooper), is an itinerant union organizer hired by a national union to aid in a wildcat strike by coal miners in the small Appalachian town of Matewan. As I said before, early in the film we discover that Kenehan is a former Wobbly, that he was imprisoned for draft resistance in World War I, and that he is now barely hiding his former anarcho-syndicalist affiliations to work for the new coal miner's trade union which would one day become the contemporary United Mine Workers, or UMW. Like many radicals who survived the first purge of American socialists and anarchists

at the turn of the century, Kenehan has gone into mainstream union organizing. He finds his activities no less dangerous than his old days in the
IWW.[16]

The scene where Kenehan makes the claim about the two types of people in this world, cited at the beginning of this chapter, comes early in the
film. Having just arrived in Matewan, Kenehan is attending his first secret
meeting of the loosely organized white miners who have just recently
walked off the job. Kenehan listens quietly as plans for industrial sabotage
and armed resistance are debated. Given his past, which is cleverly established by the film in an impromptu history test given to Kenehan before
he can enter the meeting, the viewer familiar with labor history can wonder whether Kenehan will endorse such plans, particularly given the early
advocacy by some Wobblies of industrial sabotage. Or will Kenehan object to such tactics out of an understanding of how futile violent resistance
had been up to that point in the American labor movement?

Before we can learn Kenehan's position on this crucial question, the moment is, again, literally interrupted. The cause is the entrance into the meeting of a black worker from Alabama who, along with other African
Americans and some newly immigrated Italian workers, has been brought
up by the mining company to break the strike. The worker (played by James
Earl Jones) introduces himself as "Few Clothes" Johnson, an acknowledged
leader of the black miners (based, according to Sayles, on a historical figure). Few Clothes has experience with unions and wants to assess for himself the grievances of the striking miners before crossing an increasingly
militant picket line. His entrance has the effect of breaking a scene evocative of the traditional debates inside the industrial Left, and his presence
collapses any simple dichotomy we might see between the white workers
struggling against the oppression of their "wage slavery" and the black itin-
erants standing in as representatives of the "reserve army of the unemployed," ready to do the capitalists' bidding. Like the vagrant in *Slacker,* Few
Clothes interrupts the discussion of class politics and strategy, but here with
the problem of racial differences as a hurdle for class solidarity.

The strategy of hiring scabs based on their racial or ethnic difference
was a typical union-busting move in the late nineteenth and early twentieth centuries in the industrialized world, particularly in North America.[17]
Racial intolerance is used to serve the interests of capitalists as a tool for
dividing workers. The ire of workers is turned toward those they are predisposed to be prejudiced against, rather than toward those who are creating unfair labor conditions. Exploiting racial difference also helped to

prevent the creation of a unified movement among the working class, since, more often than not, whites refused to allow blacks or immigrant workers into their unions.[18] Based on this history, the reaction by the miners in this scene to Few Clothes's interruption is predictable and historically accurate: Race baiting begins, accusations and insults are thrown, and violence against the black worker is imminent.

But Kenehan now steps in and provides a new interruption to what appears to be an inevitable breakdown between the workers: "Union men, my ass!" he charges. "You want to be treated like men? You want to be treated *fair*? Well you ain't *men* to that coal company, you're *equipment*, like a shovel or a gondola car or a hunk of wood brace. They'll use you till you wear out or you break down or you're buried under a slate fall and then they'll get a new one, and they don't care what color it is or where it comes from."[19]

Continuing, Kenehan argues persuasively, for now, that the racial divisions between the workers are not the real issue here; the "enemy" is not "this man," he claims, pointing to Few Clothes, but those who are behind the encouragement of racial conflict in order to impede labor solidarity. For an effective worker struggle, as the Wobblies were renowned for arguing against the early skilled-only unions, they should be focusing not on black versus white, native versus foreigner, or community versus community, but "them that work and them that don't," that is, owners of the means of production versus those who are forced to sell their labor in an unfair labor market. In full, Kenehan's outburst reads: "You think this man is your enemy? Huh? This is a *worker*! Any union keeps this man out ain't a union it's a goddam *club*! They got you fightin' white against colored, native against foreign, hollow against hollow, when you *know* there ain't but two sides in this world—them that *work* and them that *don't*. You work, *they* don't. That's all you got to know about the enemy."[20]

Watching this stirring scene, for a moment we may be convinced. The only thing that really is important for workers in such a situation is to remember that their class enemy is identified by their own role in production, rather than by any other aspect of political or personal identity. In the struggle, that is all that is important. Few Clothes even appears to agree with such a position. After he is accused of being a scab by one of the white miners, he reacts by asserting his right to be recognized, too, based on his role in production: "I been called nigger and I can't help that, the way white folkes is, but I ain't never been called no *scab* and I ain't startin' up now! I go ton for ton loadin' coal with any man here an when I do I spect the same dollar for the same work!"[21]

We also might be persuaded by Kenehan's rationale: At the point of industrial production aren't workers treated just like a piece of machinery, regardless of other aspects of their identity? Aren't they simply the parts of mechanical processes that have reproductive organs (which marks their peculiarly inefficient method for continuing their role in the production process)? Perhaps Kenehan is right that the owner doesn't care what color the cog in the wheel is, only that it works, and the owner knows that problems arise if that cog doesn't fulfill its role.

As the grandson of two West Virginia coal miners, another reason why this film is particularly important to me, I found that this scene had a particular appeal. My grandfathers, Jack Light and Carmine Pellegrino, both came from completely different backgrounds. Jack was a native-born American from a working-class family that had labored for generations on the land in a variety of agricultural and extractive enterprises. He grew up as part of that class in a region of the United States that never treated its workers very well. He had little choice in what he was to do with his life; he went into the mines at an early age and stayed with it in some capacity until he died, though he did rise eventually through the ranks to become a state mine foreman examiner. Carmine was a member of the Italian proletariat. Like many of his countrymen, he immigrated after World War I in an attempt to find both work and a better life. After first going to Brazil to work on plantations, he made his way to West Virginia and went into the mines. There, working for years, he was paid by the ton of coal he could move in a day until he had made enough money to bring his wife and children to America. He, too, worked the mines until he retired.

Each of these men faced a peculiar set of social problems brought about by their different backgrounds. Jack lived and died in his native country, always at home among his people; he was never made to feel like an outsider within his own class. Carmine came to this country a stranger, living mostly inside his own immigrant community, and no doubt was sometimes discriminated against by locals throughout his working life. Italian immigrants like Carmine, in *Matewan,* are brought in with the black workers as scab labor and uniformly despised by the whites in the early part of the film as those "dagoes" they would never get near. But by the end of the film there is hope, and the whites, blacks, and Italians begin to not only work together but accept each other's cultures. As I watched the film it was easy to imagine my grandfathers engaged in similar situations and similar discussions. And as the film progressed I saw the gulfs that must have existed between them evaporate: Kenehan is right, they both are workers, and from the perspective of the labor struggle their differences really aren't that important.

But, of course, though appealing, this is all too simple.

As the tensions between race and class do not come into conflict again in the film as severely as in the scene described above, one could take this scene to be a romantic look at one of the mistakes that almost every contemporary progressive social or political theorist now acknowledges: Proclamations of class interest often reduce the problems of race to problems of class, or more generally, reduce any identity to a class framework. The unique problems and forms of injustice that racism or sexism brings to class conflict should not be overlooked and ignored.

Isn't Sayles then deliberately ignoring the historical failures of class politics in order to create a filmic fantasy of class consciousness that subsumes other forms of personal identity like race, gender, and nationality? It would seem that the interjection of Few Clothes—into this scene in particular, and in the film's general portrayal later of the cooperation of three distinct groups of workers in the struggle against the bosses (white, African-American, and recent Italian immigrants)—is only window dressing for a fairly traditional, even naive, portrayal of the plight of workers. As such, the interjection of race, though perhaps more interestingly realized in the film, has no more influence on the political message of the narrative than the outburst of the vagrant in *Slacker*. The vagrant interrupted the pastiche of postmodernism with a claim about the interests of workers but soon fades into the background of the play of other images. Class is made irrelevant by the frame of the story. Perhaps with Sayles, the problems of race and class are simply reduced here to the priority of portraying a fantasy of class politics. The most charitable reading of *Matewan* then would be that it only portrays a historical view of labor relations, now as arcane and politically impotent as the vagrant's outburst in *Slacker*.

But this conclusion risks missing the depth and complexity of Sayles's narrative. Given Sayles's other body of work, we would do well to further push our reading of this film and its political argument. For in a strong sense, this film does constitute a textual argument (or set of arguments) for some proposition concerning the history and future of race and class relations. But what is that proposition?

Class as Reconciliation

We should note first that the very inclusion of race in *Matewan* is not necessary to the unfolding of a traditional narrative of class struggle. If this film was supposed to be a romantic reconstruction of labor history, then Sayles could have made it a lot less complicated by not introducing the problem of the dialectic between race and class. But in the present film, race relations form at least the most important subplot. More important, we can give a reading to the film that calls into question its seeming flirtation with a caricature of vulgar Marxism. [22]

Kenehan's argument about how the sides to the labor struggle are to be identified serves the greater goal of an argument for solidarity among the workers and for encouraging empathy with each other's plight. The white workers have a particular history of oppression that includes the loss of their traditional lands to the mining company; the black workers have a particular history that includes the legacy of slavery and displacement, which led to the search for work in the north; and the Italian workers have a particular history involving their displacement by industrialization (they are presented in the film as former skilled shoemakers), which has forced them to come to a foreign country and become unskilled labor in a new trade. It is crucial for Kenehan to get across to the workers that, whatever their history, they are in their particular predicaments because they are now put in jeopardy by a common oppressor. But this argument is not made in order to ignore the aspects of their identities outside the labor process, but rather to point out that their different forms of oppression have a common origin, or at least that their different legacies of oppression are now being exacerbated to maintain the power of the owners. Therefore, they have a common class interest despite whatever other differences they may have. Those differences should not always be subsumed to class interest, but they can be pragmatically reconciled in many instances. But to make this point Kenehan must argue from the bottom up, from this particular situation, in order to make his pitch to the workers more effectively. Like the practical philosopher, he must appeal to the interests of the different workers and reconcile them, not ignore their various interests and push a principle from the top.

Kenehan is careful not to lose the opportunity to show how racial differences have become a necessary part of the owners' strategy of union bashing. Using other native-born whites as scabs would not have the desired result of drawing fire away from the company. Therefore, the blacks and Italians in the film are uniquely being made to serve the owners' interests in a way other whites could not. Making these other groups the object of this form of site-specific discrimination is thus a unique form of oppression that they must endure in the production process. The film then takes the position that oppression differs within the same class depending on other parts of a worker's identity, a point that would not serve a simple reduction of race to class. Critically, if the white workers can be made to realize this point, then they will see that their class interests extend to respecting the identities of the black and Italian workers in order to more effectively resist the threat to themselves by the bosses.

Realizing the situation he is up against, Kenehan argues that the point of a union is not just organization by a class for the self-interest of its individual members, but instead to help form a community of interest across these differences. In this sense, class interest helps to reconcile competing individual interests and the interests of different identity groups. It offers a set of concerns with other parts of society where various people can realize their common interests, not for all time, and not in just any situation, but in this particular kind of struggle. But this is not just a struggle against a common foe in one or a series of discrete incidents, but a continual struggle to create a community across the divisions among workers that are exploited by others. Such a community in struggle does not dissolve the particular forms of oppression that each person may face—the black workers, after all, must still fight racism as it is exploited against their interests; it only clears a common ground upon which all of those struggles can take place. And hopefully, the recognition that parts of these various struggles can be shared will help create alliances across those different interests. The film offers not a retreat from class in the face of the needs of other identity groups but instead a practical redescription of it. The labor struggle, especially in, first, a strike, and then, "war," as Corbin described the events in Mingo County, is the common end that warrants the pragmatic reconciliation of competing interests, even though they are also a motivation for a common struggle.

In explaining his strategy against the option for violence, Kenehan alludes to such a position, claiming that the process of building a union around a shared, but not necessarily identical, struggle creates more than acts of isolated violence can ever hope to achieve:

And you say you've got guns. Well I know you're all brave men and I know you could shoot it out with the company if you had to. But the coal company don't want this union, the state government don't want it, the federal government don't want it and they're all of 'em just waitin' for an excuse to come down and crush us to nothing! . . . So we got to pick away at it, we got to plan it and prop it and keep an ear out for how it's working and we got to work together—*together*—till they can't get their coal out of the ground without us cause we're a *union*, cause we're the *workers* dammit and we take care of each other![23]

Even though this monologue may appear to privilege the role of class interests above other identity interests, the other aspects of the scene as it is filmed suggest otherwise.

As I said above, when Few Clothes enters the room with the other workers, he becomes the "voice" of race interrupting a portrayal of class struggle. We see Few Clothes as a powerful man, and the focus of the scene pivots on him. Several other point-of-view shots establish Few Clothes as the center of the film and the center of much hostility. But gradually, as the scene progresses, Few Clothes becomes a part of the group of miners as they all listen intently to Kenehan; he no longer seems like a foreign element. So, while it is clear that the film celebrates the history and politics of the working class, it does not do so in a manner indifferent to other social concerns. In another scene, shortly after this one, once all of the workers, white, black, and Italian, have joined together in a strike camp (as they have been kicked out of the company-owned houses), the separate cultures and identities of the different groups of workers is maintained. In the evenings, each group still plays its traditional music for entertainment, as they did separately in prior scenes, but now at times they come together to play as a group, combining guitar, blues harp, and mandolin. But this process occurs only gradually, and not with a preference for the white workers' style of music.

Even with such scenes, the film does not ignore the continuing prejudices that inevitably persist among the workers even when they have united in their struggle. For instance, it returns again and again to a spot in the camp where an Italian and white family have pitched tents next to each other. But the focus in each case is on the mothers in each family. Throughout the film, the two women are reserved, even hostile toward each other at times, and we are afforded a view of the deep cultural differences between them. It is only at the end of the film, through the recognition of the common sufferings that each endures for similar reasons (the focus is on their mutual interest in the welfare of each other's children), that the two finally come together. Significant for my reading of the film, they unite based on their common identities as women and mothers, and not necessarily as members of the same class. Class struggle is simply the medium of their interaction; we can imagine other mediums that might also bring them together as women. If this film offers a romantic look at older forms of political struggle, there is just as much evidence that the object of this romance is multiculturalism, or perhaps even identity politics itself, rather than class politics.

But slipping now from an analysis of the film, which I think contains something like a political proposition about class interest, to the question of the motivations of the filmmaker, we can ask why Sayles chose to complicate what could have been a celebration of working-class politics and history in the way he did. *Matewan* is in a sense a cultural artifact, not only of labor history and working-class culture, but also of the problems of a politics of identity as outlined above.

Sayles, as both a filmmaker and a novelist, has been involved in leftist politics since the 1960s, and in his work there has been an arguable recurrence of themes involving the problems of differing group interests.[24] *Matewan*, though a period piece, was not made without an appreciation of that history, and Sayles, as a politically savvy filmmaker, directed it as much toward an understanding of the past as toward a reading of present social concerns.[25] The political propositions of *Matewan* concern how cooperation between different groups is possible, given a certain amount of empathy, understanding, and recognition of the similar material conditions binding the groups together. The film is unique, however, in that it reintroduces questions of class into the discussion of political identity by reading questions of gender, race, and ethnicity *backward* from the present into a narrative ostensibly about class struggle. The spirit of Sayles's project is therefore practical: The Left needs a representation of its history that would serve a reconciliation of class concerns with a recognition of the importance of the politics of identity. *Matewan* could be seen then as providing the cultural artifacts of such a reconciliation, something that political progressives could use in actual struggles to appreciate each other's concerns in a practical and pragmatic way.

Sayles provided an apt metaphor for the overall thrust of this work in a description of how he managed to finish a particularly tough shot in the making of *Matewan*. The scene involved a crucial moment in the film when the white, black, and Italian miners all face each other at a midnight standoff. The company owners had forced the blacks and Italians into a late-night shift while the whites were asleep, but the white miners realized what was going on and charged up to the mine, ready for violence against those whom they still see as scab labor. Sayles needed a master shot to establish the scene. He considered a high crane shot looking down on the approaching miners, from all the different groups, ultimately merging them into one cohesive mass. This would set the stage for the dramatic moment in the scene when all three parties decide to work together, strike, and turn against the coal company. But he chose not to use this shot. He reflected on his decision: "This master shot would cover all the pertinent action but distance us from the individuals. In a Socialist-realist drama about the glory of the masses this might be appropriate, but at this moment in *Matewan* we have a bunch of individuals all straining to go in opposite directions, and we have to find a way to give a flow to the scene as a whole while touching base with each of them."[26]

I understand Sayles's goal in this scene as similar to the one I would associate with the practical philosophical approach on the themes of this film: to provide a way of understanding the knot of issues at the heart of the connection between class interest and the politics of identity that shows how they can better fit together in a pragmatic context, while at the same time recognizing the tendency of both groups and individuals to pull in opposite directions. Certainly, portrayals like Sayles's here will not insure that various groups that may have a common interest won't pull away from each other, but in offering us a vision of how they can, this film encourages us to rethink our past to inform our present in a form that we can come back to again and again for inspiration.

6

Spike Lee, Chico Mendes, and the Representation of Political Identity

As mentioned briefly in the last chapter, the 1980s and 1990s saw a flurry of interest in "identity politics," a conceptual framework dealing with the role that aspects of personal identity (especially, but not limited to, race, gender, and sexual orientation) play in formulating particular political, social, or even moral outlooks, and their legitimacy as serving a claim to justice. Many important political and social theorists have often argued that such identity positions do in fact afford special claims to political recognition and possibly even rights. Figures such as Judith Butler, Iris Marion Young, Wendy Brown, Patricia Williams, and a host of others advocated the merits of this position.[1] At times, these claims overlapped with other areas in moral and political philosophy, such as traditional work in feminism and race-based politics (e.g., Cornel West), work on the ethics of care (e.g., Joan Tronto), and debates among liberals and communitarians over claims to "group rights" (e.g., Will Kymlicka).[2]

As a student at the time I was drawn into this literature, and I taught a good deal of it as a teaching assistant in a department of ethnic studies which didn't have its own graduate program, so employed TAs from other departments. My original intention for my dissertation was to write on this topic. I was especially inspired in this regard by work that I had been doing with Carole Pateman, the eminent feminist political theorist at UCLA, whose own work was actively engaged with many of the concerns brought up in this literature. But I eventually decided not to pursue this thesis topic for a variety of reasons, perhaps the most important of which was that I was fortunate enough to find both intellectual and institutional support for my primary interest in environmental philosophy. But my curiosity had certainly still been sparked, and although I was shifting the focus of my dissertation I held onto the ideas I had developed in that work and eventually published a few papers in this area.[3]

Still, I have since grown more skeptical of the literature on identity politics and have lost faith that working through it will in the end be the best contribution that philosophers can make to debates over questions of rights and justice in the areas to which it is purportedly directed. My own views have gravitated back toward more traditional conceptual frameworks in political philosophy, such as civic republicanism, which puts an emphasis on more robust notions of citizenship over the arguable fragmentation represented by an emphasis on identity, and in a manner that I hope is more useful for actual debates over group interest and competing notions of justice. In recent essays on environmental politics, I have explicitly rejected an identity politics framework for understanding the relationship between humans and the environment and outlined a specific critique of the limitations of that approach for making a productive contribution to the resolution of actual environmental issues.[4] I hope it unnecessary to say that this does not mean that I have abandoned the goals of making a philosophical contribution to achieving a more just and equitable economic and political order. I only think there are more straightforward paths to such ends.

My turn away from identity politics is not unique. Various other worries have surfaced about this approach by important philosophers and political and social theorists, and it is now most likely on the wane in the academy. As we will see in an example to be offered later in this chapter, critics of identity politics raised the concern that political movements oriented around identity, in their most extreme forms, might claim that special rights should be accorded to some groups based on particular forms of discrimination and oppression that they have suffered, but that a unified political sphere could never grant full recognition to such groups. Worries were raised over arguments that those not in a particular identity subject position could not in principle understand the needs and concerns of those in that position, and possibly could not even share in their struggles for recognition. Critics argued that the only thing identity politics offered was a politics of fragmentation, celebration of difference for difference's sake, and a turn away from the goal of equal rights, recognition, and, most important, responsibilities for everyone in a community.[5] The result might be a kind of balkanization of politics.

But giving up on *identity politics,* as something like an argument that one's identity position entails a particular claim to justice that others outside that position must respect without being able to be in that position, does not entail that we should give up on trying to understand the *politics of identity* in a more reserved sense: that is, simply trying to understand how people can see their political interests and motivations as extending from some aspect of their identities, not just race and gender, but other aspects as well, such as their affinity with particular issues of the day. Why hold onto this sense of the politics of identity? Because, in a more restricted sense than some of the proponents of identity politics would put it, any political or social theory today must engage with issues of race, gender, and other forms of identity or else be woefully incomplete. As I suggested in chapter 5, to make this claim is not a wholesale capitulation to identity politics; it is only to recognize that many people will form interests (especially historically based interests) and will be motivated to act out of some aspect of their personal identities. Although I have no doubt that some work in identity politics entails this more limited thesis, I think that some critics of identity politics have confused the two, assuming that any appeal to political identity entails an appeal to a form of politics that necessarily fragments the public sphere around questions of identity.

The purpose of this chapter is certainly not to try to settle these issues. Those who have stayed in these debates are in a better position to continue them than I am. What I am interested in is how some films present political identity and how these presentations inform these ongoing debates. I will proceed first by reviewing my preferred framework for understanding what a claim to a politics of identity means. In the process, I will offer a distinction between two kinds of political identity, neither of which warrant the fear of a necessary fragmentation of political life, though which still might be rejected as a framework for understanding a particular sphere of politics for other reasons. I will use this distinction to try to sharpen Douglas Kellner's reading of the films of Spike Lee (especially *Do the Right Thing,* 1989), and also to mitigate his worries about Lee's representation of the politics of identity. Finally, I will look at an important film about the life of Chico Mendes, the murdered, some would say martyred, leader of the rubber tappers union in Brazil, which famously has fought to help preserve the Amazon rainforest. This film arguably portrays the relationship between political identity and moral motivation in the arena of environmental protection and labor rights. In contrast to other films representing environmentalists, the film about Mendes does not take political identity for granted but shows how it can evolve to potentially heroic heights.

What Is a Politics of Identity?

Very generally, one can describe a politics of identity as a politics where subjects ground their self-conception as political agents in some aspect of their identities. Often this identity is defined negatively: One is socially marked as possessing an identity trait and then subject to different forms of oppression as a result of that trait. A political identity may be based in specific historical claims about the nature of that oppression and then assert the subjectivity of the marked trait as a justification for a unique set of political positions. For example, where a legacy of oppression based on race exists, an identity politics of race can be formed in opposition to that specific form of oppression and perhaps serve as a foundation for racial pride, partly in resistance to that oppression. This does not mean, however, that a concern for and a commitment to racial justice (either from a member of an oppressed racial group or from someone outside that group) must be expressed as a politics of identity. It is simply one option for expressing that position. But for those embracing a politics of identity in this sense, different descriptions can be given of the meaning of one's identity and the political implications of that identity. There is no necessary content to any particular political identity, and the attribution of the meaning or content of a political identity is usually thought to involve the community of those who embrace that identity. Collectively, the groups that have defined their views around an embrace of a politics of identity are often referred to as the "new social movements."

The way that I see such political frameworks is not limited only to the kinds of policies and issues they embrace but extends to the way this kind of political framework is structured. This kind of political identity, even if not of the robust form of identity politics distinguished above, has what I will call a "constitutive profile." This profile helps us understand which character trait justifies an embrace of a given political identity and explains how the content of that identity emanates from this particular trait. The constitutive profile of many forms of identity politics is relatively straightforward (setting aside for the moment the issue of mixed identities, which, admittedly, is a huge issue to set aside). For example, race-based political identities stem from one's identification with a range of interpretations of the distinct political issues associated with one's race in relation to the larger racial politics of one's society.

Constitutive profiles of a political identity, have a "subject," namely, the person embracing the identity, and an "object," or the realm of politics that the subject finds important because of his or her subject position. In the constitutive profile of a racial identity the subject and object are the same; there is no gap between the subject's identity and the object of his or her politics, as this political identity is about the position in which one finds oneself in a society because of that identity. The identity trait that a subject sees as a politically significant category—for example, being black in America—marks the object of one's political concern, as well, here, the political issues endemic to the African-American community. Part of a subject's political and moral motivation are also explained in this frame-work: If part of one's personal identity helps to define both one's subjec-tivity and the object of one's political concerns, then it makes sense that what helps to explain the motivation behind personal ethical choices and the ends of political deliberation is this political identity. We can attribute the reasons for the decisions made by a person embracing a politics of per-sonal identity to the fact that they have embraced that identity. If we could not, then the embrace of the identity would have no role at all in our description of them as a political or moral agent.[6]

But not all forms of what we might think of as a motivating political identity fit so neatly into this description of the relationship between po-litical subject and object. Let us take as our central example of this prob-lem the question of whether environmentalism can be counted as a politi-cal identity in this sense (the importance of this example will become clearer later in the chapter). What sort of identity is constituted by envi-ronmentalism (or, as I will also call it, an "ecological identity")? What character trait justifies an embrace of that identity, and how does its polit-ical content stem from this trait in those who embrace it? At first glance, environmentalism does not seem to have a clear constitutive profile be-cause it appears to be at best a kind of empathy (or perhaps care) for na-ture as some sort of subject of mistreatment, and not necessarily a politics of the self. Still, despite such conceptual difficulties, Stanley Aronowitz, among others who write on this topic, has included the ecology move-ment in discussions of the politics of identity and the new social move-ments for some time.[7] More ambitiously, other authors, such as Catriona Sandilands, have explicitly argued for an environmental identity politics, in a full-blown sense, in order to join environmentalism to the broader call for "radical democracy" as the basis for a unified identity politics.[8]

But simply listing environmentalism alongside these other movements of political identity is insufficient as a reason to think that it is the same kind of thing. An ecological identity more representative of the broader environmental movement describes a general connection between an embrace of one's personal identity as an environmentalist and some nonhuman thing or things in nature (or nature in general) as an object of political concern without necessarily finding this identity in a trait akin to race or gender. That is to say, calling oneself an "environmentalist" may only amount to a claim about one's empathetic stance toward nature rather than a claim about one's own given identity as somehow intimately connected with the oppression of nature. So, unless one holds a radical view of human ontology as indistinguishable from nature (that we are simply a part of nature like any other part of it), there is a gap built into the idea of an ecological identity not found in some other forms of identity politics: the gap between the subjectivity of the identity trait of the individual and the object of the politics of that identity.[9]

In contrast, if an ecological identity is a politics of empathy or care for nature, then the object of concern, here "nature," is distinct from the political subject, or at the very least, much more different than the subject-object constitutive profile of the more traditional political identities. But this intuitive difference between an ecological identity and other forms of political identity only further raises the question of whether many other forms of political identity succeed in closing this subject-object gap. For example, male feminism, as, generally, a politics engaged in by men involving empathy with the oppression of women, or care about the male domination of women, would also suffer from this same problem. The object of the identity politics of male feminism—women's political issues, such as their equal treatment—is not the same as the trait that gets them this position—their own empathy with the oppression of women. Should we then say that such men are not feminists? For similar reasons, would we discount the possibility of an ecological identity?

As just suggested, one way of interpreting an ecological identity to avoid this subject-object gap would be to argue that the only environmentalism that counts as a political identity in the sense we have been discussing is one that holds a conception of human personal identity as completely coextensive with nature. Indeed, there are some environmentalists who ground their politics in an argument about their own identities as indistinguishable from nature. Specifically, some in the environmentalist camps known as "deep ecology" and "ecofeminism" (though far fewer of the latter) claim that they are intimately connected to nature in this way. For deep ecologists, this account is grounded in a recognition and defense of a "transpersonal self," through which we can come to see that human ontology is part of a larger ontology of nature. Recognition of this transpersonal identity usually involves some transcendental experience in nature.[10] For some "essentialist" ecofeminists, an ecological identity is grounded in their account of a necessary connection between women and nature as objects of the exact same kind of (or the same) oppression by men and a male-dominated (androcentric) society.[11] For both schools of thought, the subject-object gap of an environmental identity is overcome by an account of how the subjectivity of the individual is indistinguishable from her object of environmental concern. Like the constitutional profile of a race-based identity, the subjective aspect of an ecological identity is the trait of being a part of nature on some explanation, and the object of the concern of that trait is nature as well.

But setting aside the plausibility of these views, which I have disputed elsewhere, we must admit that if only those holding a radical view of human ontology can be counted as having an ecological identity, then the content of environmentalism as a form of political identity is very narrow.[12] Such an ecological identity would be so narrow that it could not be what Aronowitz and others have in mind when they include environmentalism in the rubric of political identities making up the new social movements. Even the combination of these two restricted views of environmentalism (transpersonal deep ecology and essentialist ecofeminism) would not make for much of a movement, nor would it exhaust the moral motivations of the vast array of environmentalists engaged in political activity. So, again, the problem remains: If the primary form of ecological identity embraced by most environmentalists is one involving a kind of empathy with nature (or another, less occult, form of identification), rather than a coextensive identification with it, how can environmentalism count as a kind of politics of identity like feminism?

To answer this question, I would argue that a politics of identity, though perhaps not a formal identity politics as such, seems to be crudely divided between those forms which are *attached* and those which are *detached*. Attached political identities are those involving a claim to a thick connection between a subject's chosen identity trait (or traits) and the object of the politics of that identity: for example, feminism as a politics of women; race-based politics as a politics of people from a specific racial group; gay male politics as the politics of homosexual men. This does not mean that the content of the attached identity position is determined, or even that it must be the same for all subjects embracing that position. Rather, attached identities can be distinguished only for the strong connection they evince between their subject and object, as explained above.

As it turns out, many attached identities are also those which we might think of as not necessarily chosen, such as race or gender, taking into account claims that these categories are socially constructed. But even though this observation helps us to understand this distinction, it is not its basis. I will not defend the argument here that all forms of political identity are embraced, though I think it is intuitively true.One is clearly not a feminist merely by virtue of being a woman. An important part of the ontology of attached identities is that they involve a choice by someone to transform a personal trait into a political position whose object is the politics of that trait.[13]

"Detached" identities, in contrast, are not necessarily conjoined to some material or personal aspect of political identity; nor are the subjective traits they emphasize the object of their politics. For the sake of argument, assuming that men can be feminists, they engage in a form of feminism best understood as an ontologically detached form of identity. Men are not materially connected to feminism in the same way that women are, and the object of their politics is not primarily concerned with issues involving the treatment and welfare of other male feminists. Without getting into the theoretical debates concerning the legitimacy of male feminism, at minimum there is some argumentative security in the intuition that a step is needed in identifying as a male feminist that is qualitatively different from a woman's embrace of feminism. The simplest characterization of this difference is that male feminism embraces the identity trait of empathy with women's political issues, and not empathy with other men who empathize with women. Empathy is only the means to the actual political object of male feminism, such as resistance to continued forms of sexist power relations. Even though the activities of some male feminists may be more inward looking (for example, engaging in self-criticism for taking advantage of the culture of misogyny), the motivation for and ends of such actions are grounded in concern over women's issues. Again, this is not to say that male feminism is weaker or shallower because it is ontologically detached in this sense, but only that it is structurally different.

The attached-detached distinction itself does not necessarily imply any normative difference between these two broad types of political identities (a point I will return to below when I look at the representation of political identity in film). Despite the somewhat unfortunate language of this distinction, to me attached identities are not socially or politically better than detached ones, they are simply ontologically attached to the object of their concern. But if this attached-detached distinction is accepted, then we no longer have the problem mentioned above of including the different kinds of, so to speak, direct and indirect forms of political identity under one category.

In the example I have focused on of a detached political identity, determining the constitutive profile of an ecological identity does not mean that all environmentalists can now be described as holding an ecological identity in this sense. Environmentalists do not have to articulate their politics as one primarily involving identity.[14] My point is only that a detached identity is the kind of political identity open to most environmentalists who choose to embrace a politics of identity for their environmentalism for whatever reason.[15]

Media Politics and Attached Identities: Douglas Kellner vs. Spike Lee

The attached-detached distinction should be helpful for understanding the representation of political identity in film and for engaging with those critics of film who have looked at its role in promoting the politics of identity. As in the previous chapters, this philosophical discussion will sharpen our critique of films, helping us to distinguish between films that are better or worse with respect to their treatment of this social phenomena, and at the same time demonstrate that some films can help us to deepen our understanding of philosophical arguments.

Of the philosophers who have looked at questions of the representation of identity in film, few are as prolific and influential as Douglas Kellner. His book *Media Culture* focuses explicitly on the role of traditional and new media technology in shaping cultural and personal identity, especially as a possible locus of identity politics.[16] Following the damning critics of identity politics, Kellner argued that one of the most pernicious influences of media culture on politics is in its effects on the politics of identity. Kellner saw culturally based forms of identity politics, both in *Media Culture* and in other work, such as in his coauthored books with Steven Best, as potentially a politics of fragmentation.[17]

The argument in *Media Culture* is that film and other mass media can exacerbate the fragmentary effects of identity politics, specifically by encouraging the formation of political identities of style rather than of substance. According to Kellner: "The mere valorization of 'difference' as a mark of opposition can simply help market new styles and artifacts if the difference in question and its effects are not adequately appraised. It can also promote a form of identity politics in which each group affirms its own specificity and limits politics to the group's own interests thus overlooking common forces of oppression. Such difference or identity politics aids 'divide and conquer' strategies which ultimately serve the interests of the powers that be."[18]

But his worry is even more specific than a concern with vague "powers that be." The filmic representation of an identity politics, rather than only its theoretical discussion, can serve very specific capital interests. In earlier chapters I emphasized the power of film to shape public discussion over important social issues simply because of its reach, especially in its Hollywood varieties, to huge numbers of people in a form that is easily digestible and enjoyable to watch. Kellner has expressed a similar worry, though in this case it is about how popular films may encourage us to directly link who we think we are in a political sense with particular images and products: "Producing meanings can create pleasures that integrate individuals into consumer practices which above all profit media industries. This possibility forces those who valorize resistance to emphasize *what sort of resistance,* what effects and what differences does the resistance make."[19]

The thrust of Kellner's argument is that the most fragmentary versions of identity politics are encouraged, and sometimes even produced, by media culture, and in that sense those identities serve what he has taken to be the pernicious interests of global capital. If media can produce a sense among a group of people that they share a political identity, it will be easier to attach to that identity a range of commodity choices: clothes that they should wear, places where they should go, music that they should listen to.[20] So, feminists, black nationalists, and gay advocates are encouraged through the media to dress a certain way, listen to a certain kind of music, and thus be able to identify each other as belonging to the same political identity. For Kellner, these commodity choices serve the interests of capitalists rather than advancing any significant political project that might resist the dominant culture. Since it is the Left that is by and large dominated by these identity positions, identity politics ironically becomes more a tool to further capital interests than an alternative political vision for a culture dominated by commodity production.

There are two issues that I want to raise about Kellner's discussion of identity politics and its representation in the media. First, I want to take on the broad target at which Kellner's critique is aimed: the politics of identity. Though he may protest otherwise, Kellner has sometimes run together in his analysis the mere representation of a politics of identity, in the more modest sense in which I have been discussing it, with a full-blown identity politics that risks the fragmentation of the public sphere.[21] As such, I think that in *Media Culture,* some of his criticisms of representations of identity are on the mark and others are not. It is one thing to critique the promotion of a commodity version of identity politics in a television show like *Miami Vice* (one of Kellner's examples), and another to critique the films of Spike Lee. For in Lee's work, I think, we have a representation of political identities rather than identity politics as such; if this is so, then the elements of Lee's films that may appear objectionable under Kellner's analysis may in fact be epiphenomenal elements to what is otherwise a serious and important discussion of how far a politics of identity, especially for African Americans, should go.

The second issue I want to take up goes back to the distinction between attached and detached identities raised in the last section, and in particular, to the claim that the attached-detached distinction was ontological and not normative. Attached identities aren't any better or stronger than detached identities. But even if this is true, one might wonder whether the *representation* of those identities entails any different normative concerns that might be worse for attached identities. Though not the particular worry I will raise about this issue, what if one thought that manipulating the identity of African Americans was somehow worse than manipulating the identity of male feminists, or environmentalists, because it is somehow more of an affront to portray a black man to sell a product than to portray an environmentalist to sell the same product? If that were true, then the kind of criticism Kellner leveled against manipulation of the media identity politics may be much more pressing in the case of attached identities because a successful manipulation of an attached identity would of necessity play off of the attachment itself. I will take these issues in order in looking at Kellner's discussion of Spike Lee.

According to Kellner, Lee's films are focused primarily on the identity politics of African Americans, though certainly other forms of identity are represented in these films as well. Kellner's critique of Lee is that Lee's notion of identity politics is often reducible to a politics of fashion with little substance. This diagnosis fits perfectly with Kellner's overall thesis on the media production of some political identities: "The central problem with Lee's politics is that he ultimately comes down on the side of a culturalist identity politics, which subordinates politics in general to the creation of personal identity."[22] This shortcoming, according to Kellner, marks a clear social and political indictment of Lee's project: "Lee tends to reduce politics to cultural identity and slogans. *School Daze* ends with the message 'Wake Up!' proclaimed by the black activist hero of the movie and *Do the Right Thing* begins and ends with the DJ Mister Señor Love Daddy proclaiming this. Fine, wake up. But to what, and what does one do when one is awake? Such concrete politics seem beyond the purview of Lee's vision and suggest the limitations of his politics."[23]

For Kellner, simply asserting one's cultural identity is not in itself a substantive political position. It gets worse. Kellner also argued that in *Do the Right Thing,* Lee's "primary focus on black identity" operates in a binary opposition between "us" and "them" that may oversimplify political issues: "None of the various characters were involved in any political organization, movement, or struggle, and . . . the boycott of Sal's Pizzeria is a pathetic caricature of the real struggles by people of color for rights and survival."[24]

Here is where I begin to depart from Kellner's reading of these films, given the first issue I mentioned above over distinguishing an identity politics from a politics of identity. Recall for a moment the plot of *Do the Right Thing.* Taking place primarily over a single scorching day in the Bedford-Stuyvesant neighborhood of Brooklyn, known locally as simply "Bed-Stuy," the film depicts the racial tensions that have historically emerged in the neighborhood, which eventually explode later that evening. Episodic in its structure, there is no single overarching story, though there are several subplots culminating in a final climax. The action of the film centers around Sal's Pizzeria, a small business in the neighborhood owned by an Italian-American patrician, Sal (played by Danny Aiello) and operated with his two sons, Pino (John Turturro) and Vito (Richard Edson). Spike Lee plays Mookie, a delivery boy for Sal.

Sal's Pizzeria is an establishment in the neighborhood with a history. Sal is proud of the place and his role in the community. But with the change in demographics that has occurred in Bed-Stuy over the years, the neighborhood is now overwhelmingly African American and Hispanic. Sal and his sons stick out now as apparent outsiders. Sal maintains the pizza place as a stronghold of sorts for a lost community in the neighborhood. He does this primarily through his "Wall of Fame" featuring photos of famous Italian-American movie stars and other personalities. His sons, however, are unhappy coming into the neighborhood to work every day. They see it as increasingly hostile to them, but it is unclear whether this hostility is real or simply a projection on their part.

As the film unfolds we meet several other characters in the neighborhood, all with some kind of relationship to Mookie. There is Radio Raheem (Bill Nunn), a strong, silent type who walks around the neighborhood all day playing Public Enemy on a huge boom box; Buggin' Out (Giancarlo Esposito), a self-styled cultural and political radical who demands that Sal put pictures of African Americans on the Wall of Fame, an issue that partly instigates the riot that closes the film and causes the looting and burning of Sal's store; Smiley (Roger Guenveur Smith), a mentally impaired adult who wanders in and out of scenes selling copies of one of the rare photographs of Martin Luther King, Jr., and Malcolm X together; Mookie's sister, Jade (Joie Lee, also his sister in real life), who is supporting him; Tina (Rosie Perez), with whom Mookie has fathered a child, although he does not live with her and they are rarely seen together; two village elders (Ruby Dee and Ossie Davis) who serve as a connection with the past; and a Greek chorus, of sorts (Paul Benjamin, Frankie Faison, and Robin Harris), who offer a running commentary on the events of the film and the larger social and political changes that have affected the neighborhood with special focus on a Korean-owned convenience store across from the pizzeria. There are many others as well, all of whom represent particular interests in the society depicted by the film, including Samuel L. Jackson, who provides narration of some of the action of the film as the D.J. Señor Love Daddy, mentioned above in the quotation by Kellner.

Lee clearly represents some characters in this film as standing in for a politics of cultural and political fragmentation, most particularly Buggin' Out. But this character is balanced in the film by Jade, who actively tries to discourage the position taken by Buggin' Out with respect to Sal's Wall of Fame. All of the characters in the film undeniably are shaped by the neighborhood they inhabit, but this may only suggest a more modest politics of identity with the concerns of the black community, as most of the characters do not share Buggin' Out's position. Lee's film practically hits us over the head with disagreements over the limits of a politics of identity, by actually putting it literally in the script in the interaction between Jade and Buggin' Out.

But although the film is clear in this representation, it is more obscure with other issues in the film. Kellner questioned the "wake up" call, which is common in Lee's films, and which appears vacuous given that there is no particular thing that the characters should wake up to. But I think this is an unfair characterization, at least of this particular film. *Do the Right Thing* is bracketed by two important sets of images that may be seen as suggesting that while the black community must wake up and take its future into its own hands, there are no easy answers to the questions that must be addressed. This is not a cop-out by Lee, but instead, I think, a sober and realistic assessment of the gravity of the problems at hand for this community.

The first of these images is the sequence that appears during the opening credits. We hear the signature song of the film, Public Enemy's "Fight the Power," playing in the background and see a studio street scene lit in bizarre and unreal colors. In the center of the images is Rosie Perez wearing boxing gloves and gym clothes and rapidly hitting the air. As the credits continue, we see her from many angles; some shots are close-ups of her face, but in all instances she is strenuously fighting. The question is, What is she fighting? The first shot of the film after this sequence is of Mookie abruptly opening his eyes in bed as Señor Love Daddy screams "Wake Up!" on the radio.

The ending sequence of the film is similarly arresting, though very different. Just before the credits begin to appear, we are offered two long quotations on the screen, one from Martin Luther King, Jr., advocating nonviolence and the other from Malcolm X suggesting that violence in the name of self-defense is actually "intelligence."

The ending sequence directly suggests the absence of easy answers to what it means to be black in America: The black community has several choices about how to respond to the threats it faces, and there are important and divergent traditions from which it can draw. Neither of these quotations is supposed to answer the question of whether it was right or wrong to burn down Sal's Pizzeria. Instead, appropriately, the contrast between the two opposing views calls the action into question as possibly one or the other, but not unambiguously either.

The opening sequence is harder to interpret, though ever since I first saw the film I have guessed that Mookie is having a dream about Perez's character Tina. We learn later that she is an intimate part of his life, and so an obvious candidate for a dream. And in dreams, of course, people often do strange things for no particular reason. The odd lighting of the opening sequence adds credibility to this interpretation, as does the first shot of the film after the opening credits, which shows Mookie having just been asleep. But, again, what is Tina fighting? Racism? The powers that be? Or Mookie himself? I wouldn't want to suggest that the film invites us into a psychoanalytic interpretation of Mookie's dream, but rather that the representation of struggle in the opening sequence, the last time Mookie will sleep before the events of the day depicted in the film, is indicative of the film's position that the black community needs to wake up to the struggle and conflict that it is in. This struggle involves hard choices rather than assuming that one should embrace simple answers, be it a politics of fragmentation based on identity, nonviolence, or anything else. The theme of waking up is not an indication of the limitations of Lee's politics, as Kellner would have it, but rather a hint that Lee is considering the limitations of an overly simplified politics.

But what about Kellner's more specific worry about the commodification of Lee's images? Lee's films are certainly full of references to the consumer culture that has been directed at African Americans by the media. Kellner has pointed out that many of the characters in this film are wearing Nike shoes and are engaged in substantive conversations about these goods as fetishized commodity objects.[25] Read against the background of Lee's appearance in Nike commercials, Kellner's worries may be legitimate. Another precursor to the racial violence that closes the film is an altercation between Buggin' Out and a white character who accidentally blemishes Buggin' Out's new pair of Nike Air Jordan basketball shoes with a bicycle tire. Kellner also noticed a pattern to the T-shirts worn by the characters in the film: Radio Raheem wears one that says "Bed-Stuy or Die," proudly proclaiming his black identity and community solidarity, Mookie wears a Brooklyn Dodgers T-shirt emblazoned with Jackie Robinson's number, situating himself as a character bridging the white and black worlds, which is partly his role in much of the film, and the aforementioned white character, living in a predominantly African-American neighborhood, wears a Larry Bird Boston Celtics T-shirt, which establishes him as the last "Great White Hope" of urban integration.[26]

From this evidence, Kellner concluded that the identity politics of the film amount to a kind of sloganeering cultural identity and little more. It is not clear in the film what follows from accepting an African-American identity politics, or any other for that matter, other than wearing certain kinds of clothes.

No one could dispute Kellner's identification of these commodity references in *Do the Right Thing*. But before trying to answer this charge, I want to return to the second issue I raised above, whether the misrepresentation or even manipulation of a political identity is worse in the case of attached identities than it is in the case of detached ones. If it is, then the problem Kellner has brought up may be even worse than he has suggested, since the commodity images would not only belie a consumerism in Lee's films (which one could, after all, dismiss by arguing that there is nothing inherently wrong with consumerism in the first place) but perhaps also a weightier manipulation of an identity group.

Why would a manipulation of an identity group be worse in the case of an attached identity than in the case of a detached identity? Not, I think, for the reason I alluded to earlier—that there may just be something inherently worse about misrepresenting a subject or group with an attached identity. Instead, I think the reason might be that manipulation of a political identity, through its representation for a prurient end, like simply selling more T-shirts, is a kind of infringement on the autonomy of the members of that identity group who are constantly in the midst of asking themselves the hard questions about what to care about as a community and how to respond to the threats to their community. Why? Because one does not engage in a politics of identity in a vacuum.

As mentioned in the first section of this chapter, identity positions have constitutive profiles that are determined not simply by a single agent deciding what will be important to them but in conversation with a larger group facing the same questions, questions the group has faced throughout its history. A self-described feminist is practically always in conversation, at least in some limited fashion, with other self-described feminists who are trying to figure out what is important to them as feminists. Feminists must do this as a community in part because they are all trying to define what it means to hold this political identity, as opposed to some other one, and their individual definitions of the meaning of their identity are constantly challenged by others holding that identity. They may agree to disagree on some issues, but even in disagreement they must always go through a process of discussion and debate, either personally or through organizations, periodicals, or other forms of communication. In addition, they are all in conversation with the past, not just metaphorically, but in two other senses as well. First, because what past feminists have decided on, and disagreed about, concerning the meaning of feminism is something they must take into account in current deliberations over the same set of issues, and second, because, as suggested earlier in this chapter, it is past oppression and discrimination which partly defines the constitutive profile of political identity in the first place.

With this point in mind we could conclude the following: To manipulate a politics of identity in the way that Kellner has suggested (perhaps for personal gain by Lee) takes advantage of this process of political self-formation.[27] Specifically, it takes advantage of a conversation that members of that group must have in order to be constitutive of a discernible political identity at all, rather than one that they can simply opt out of. If detached identities do not require the same kind of ongoing process, let us say for now because of their subject-object gap (I will return to this issue below), then manipulation of attached identities is somehow worse in taking advantage of a situation in which its members find themselves. *Do the Right Thing*, on Kellner's reading of it, takes advantage of a kind of captive audience who will be attracted to the film not necessarily because of its commodity references but because it masks itself as a contribution to that process of self-formation. Others will be attracted to the film as well, but the film partly offers itself to members of a particular identity group asking itself these questions. If there is anything plausible about this worry, then it may strengthen Kellner's critique of Lee by adding additional force to it.

But one problem is that the attached-detached distinction also points to how we must be more charitable in our assessment of the attempts of attached identity groups to form their own politics of identity than Kellner's view may allow for. Therefore, the potential addition that the distinction makes to Kellner's critique also helps us to mitigate that same critique. This will take a bit of explaining.

For reasons offered above, I find Lee's films, in particular *Do the Right Thing*, to be very reasonable discussions of political identity. At a time when conservatives in the United States were content to reduce all racial tensions to mere problems of crime, drug abuse, and general hooliganism (remember that this film came out during the height of the Reagan-Bush years), Lee's film portrayed the politics of an inner-city riot as something that had origins in real racial tensions, themselves originating in something more substantial than mere thuggery.[28] As a film offered for mass consumption, it did not pull punches or overly simplify the problems of political identity. In a Hollywood distribution system dominated by films portraying one-dimensional and overly simplistic politics of race relations (such as those discussed in chapter 4), Lee's films argued for a more complex national discussion of these issues. So, the beginning of an answer to Kellner would be that because the existence of the history of these tensions is, as I argued above, part of the constitutive profile of a politics of identity, Lee's film can also be read as an important step in the assertion of a basis for an African-American politics of identity that calls members of that community to actively debate its priorities, principles, and future.[29]

But there is another related point that may go further in softening Kellner's worry about consumer and commodity images in Lee's films. One difference between attached and detached identities is the degree of their permeability. Consider the following example: I can embrace an identity of "environmentalist," as can my friend Bill Lawson (who in fact does, and also happens to be both a philosopher and African American). But while Bill could embrace his black heritage as a focus for a politics of identity, I could not. Certainly, there are parts of my identity that I could form a politics around that Bill could not, but the point remains that the attached identity open for Bill is not one open for me, whereas my strongest detached identity is open to him, and everyone else for that matter. Although it is no doubt true that "race" as a category is socially constructed and nothing like a natural category of division of persons, a point that others have explicated further, it is still a historically meaningful category of analysis around which a politics can be formed given the way that it has been used and responded to by others in the past.[30]

The relative impermeability of attached identities warrants a certain amount of deference to these groups when it comes to questions of how they choose to go about understanding the basis of their own identity. Though I am not arguing that those outside of an attached identity cannot critique the politics of it, I do think we ought to embrace certain limitations to that criticism. Using the case just offered, I might put the point this way: Although I might disagree with some product of the deliberations of the African-American community about what it means to be black in America, or with particular policy choices that they might make out of that identity, so long as their process of figuring out these issues did not infringe on or cause harm to others, then I should defer to the terms of that process as it takes place in their community simply because I am not a part of that community.[31] This is not to say that I can't understand the terms of their debate, as an extreme identity politics view may hold. I can certainly show interest in their process, but I think it better for me not to criticize that process since the identity formation is in principle closed to me. Again, this is not to suggest that racial justice is a concern only open through a politics of identity. My assumption in this example is that my interaction is with those members of the African-American community who see their politics as constituted through an attached identity.

Lee's choice as a director to include Nike shoes and the like may be seen as either reasonable in this light or at least as something that those of us outside of the political community ought not to get too exercised about so long as there are arguable readings of his films to show us that there is something else going on with them. Even further, I would argue that *Do the Right Thing*, as a successful film, constitutes what Andrew Feenberg called a "subversive rationalization" of the Hollywood system (as discussed in chapter 3). If one can make an argument that Hollywood is predisposed to producing films with a certain kind of portrayal of race relations, and it is the case that this portrayal serves certain political interests—no doubt all uncontroversial theses for Kellner—then Lee's films are courageous political acts. They are subversions of the design of the Hollywood system in their successful portrayal of a complex account of racial tension. If mass distribution of Lee's films through corporate chain theaters encourages or even requires him to spice up his message with references to popular culture in order to make these films more attractive to distributors, I can see little room for critique of those minor parts of his narrative, especially given the comparatively small audiences for more authentic portrayals of racial problems that ignore the baggage of media culture. And this does not imply that smaller independent films playing only in "art houses" should not be made on topics like these. They should, and as one could predict from the films discussed in previous chapters, I love many of these films. But if a film can be made more popular by appeal to mass culture, this is not an intrinsic limitation of the film.

Finally, what harm is really being done here? It's not as if the primary vehicle for mass marketing of Nike shoes to the African-American community, or any other community for that matter, is a Spike Lee film, nor is it likely that if Lee did not use such images in his films we wouldn't buy those products. It might even be the case that all political expression in a media-dominated world gets filtered through different forms of commodity culture at some point. To critique expressions of political identity as merely a politics of fashion is therefore to offer a nonunique critique. And as for the T-shirts used to identify different characters, it seems even less worrisome to me that Lee would simply have wanted to give us an easy way of identifying different positions in what is ultimately a large ensemble cast portraying a complicated morality tale.

If Lee's portrayal of identity politics is saturated with the visual cues of a commodified society, this is ultimately an accurate portrayal of political expression more generally in our culture. It might even be the case that he is doing this for ironic reasons—should Buggin' Out really get in a fight with the Larry Bird character over a scuffed shoe? We know in fact that people do get into serious fights about such things, but the film gives us some distance to laugh about the importance we may place on such items. At bottom, at least with attached forms of identity, some of us should give a wider berth to the forms of representation that these kinds of identities embrace, as long as other aspects of the films involved encourage a more careful consideration of those identities. These are, after all, expressions of political groups coming to self-awareness against the backdrop of a media culture that more often represents a more uniform American social sphere and typically eschews the portrayal of the complexities of different political identities.

Representing Detached Identities: Chico Mendes and *The Burning Season*

In discussing Kellner's critique of Lee, I suggested that if detached identities do not require the same kind of ongoing process of negotiation of what it means to hold them that attached identities arguably do, then manipulation of an attached identity is worse than a similar representation of a detached identity. But I think that this is actually not true, or if it is, it is not for the reasons that I offered above. A manipulative or overly simplified representation of a detached identity is just as bad as its counterpart representation of an attached identity on the grounds I have provided. The reason is simple: Members of detached identity groups go through the same process of both communal and historical discussion, debate, and disagreement over what it means to hold that identity that less permeable, attached identities go through. Although the permeability of the identity may make this process harder to carry out (it is extremely difficult, for example, to pin down exactly who can count as an "environmentalist," and in the end there may not be any very helpful answers to that question), the process itself is no different. This is not to say that I think that manipulation of an attached identity for selfish, harmful, or otherwise objectionable reasons is not wrong; it is wrong, because it interrupts that process of identity formation. But I would maintain that the same is true of detached identities.

Using the example of the representation of environmentalists, to be consistent with the example used in formulating the attached-detached distinction, I will first quickly critique a film that badly portrays an environmentalist because it gives short shrift to the complexities of that identity, and then close with an example of a film that, better than many others, respects those complexities and the process of constantly making and remaking the implications of a political identity. Those who find my criticism of film thrillers as foils for deeper philosophical issues in earlier chapters (such as *Enemy of the State* in chapter 2, and *Falling Down* in chapter 4) unfair will no doubt chafe at the object of my critical comments here. They are directed at Steven Seagal's action movie *Fire Down Below* (1997, directed by Félix Enríquez Alcalá and written by Jeb Stuart). Despite those possible objections, and I can almost see the (hoped-for) reader rolling her eyes right now, I will compare this film with *The Burning Season* (1994, directed by John Frankenheimer), which portrays the true story of the life and martyrdom of Chico Mendes.

There is not much good that can be said about *Fire Down Below*, other than that one may derive a perverse delight from watching someone purported to be part of the U.S. Environmental Protection Agency using sophisticated martial arts techniques to cause great pain to despoilers of the environment. Especially at a time when George W. Bush has gutted the EPA, it is amusing to imagine that there could be rogue agents in the field working behind the scenes to bring down evil heads of extractive industries using obscure legal techniques and swift body blows.

The plot is very simple: Jack Taggart (Seagal) is an EPA agent with an attitude. As the film opens, his boss is directing him to go down to a small town in rural Kentucky. There, another agent has been killed investigating a possible case of illegal cyanide dumping. Once he arrives, Seagal goes undercover, in a manner of speaking, taking on the mantle of a volunteer Appalachian rural assistance worker. Seagal goes from house to house offering to fix people's porches for free, hoping in time to gain their trust since he is warned that the locals "don't like to talk." His ultimate goals are to find out whether the illegal dumping is indeed taking place and to figure out who has killed the other federal agent. In the meantime, the illegal dumpers, led by the son of Orin Hanner, Sr. (Kris Kristofferson), a coal-mining company president who also claims to politically own the state of Kentucky, continue with their business. They are protected in this work by a private army of hillbilly thugs, a cooperative sheriff, and the silence of the public.

Perhaps because he wears what appear to be a series of $5,000 designer leather jackets all about town, even when he is mending broken porch steps, or because he is asking too many questions, Seagal eventually draws suspicion. After the hired thugs make several attempts to intimidate him, though, watching as carefully as I could, I never saw anyone lay a finger on Seagal, then our EPA agent drops the ruse and begins to make an overt appeal to the community to turn against the evil mining company and stop the illegal dumping for the health of their children and their land. There are several dramatic showdowns and the obligatory love interest to seduce (Marg Helgenberger), but eventually Kristofferson is taken into court. For reasons that are never clear, he gets off on a technicality and is only fined $50,000, a pittance since he claims to be making $13 million off the illegal dumping scheme. Seagal finds a loophole, and with the help of the FBI, serves Kristofferson with an arrest warrant and the promise of jail time along with a threat of buggery by an inmate acquaintance. The angry and indignant Kristofferson pulls a gun on Seagal and is, predictably, killed by the EPA agent.

In the context of the foregoing discussion, one thing that is objectionable about the depiction of EPA agent Jack Taggart is that we have no idea what motivates his actions and what role his evident environmentalism plays in that motivation. His environmentalism is not one grounded in a community; he is instead a lone wolf. This film is simply *Matewan* meets *Die Hard* (a film which, incidentally, was also written by Jeb Stuart), with no historical context at all. The problem is not the lack of historical context in the portrayal of the townsfolk that Seagal is interacting with, but in the portrayal of Seagal himself. The film offers no clues, not even small ones, about why he takes the interest in his work that he does. In this vein, the opening sequence of the film is particularly odd. We see shots of Seagal flying to the small town on a turbo-prop plane cut with flashbacks, evidently from his memory, of previous work with local agents trying to ferret out the mystery of the illegal dumping. But none of these flashbacks are ever unpacked so as to explain any of this. There is so little offered in the film for what motivates Seagal that one wonders in watching the opening whether the flashbacks are taken from some prior film that *Fire Down Below* is a sequel to, and which provides some explanation for the character's motivation.[32]

One explanation is that this film is not really about an environmentalist; the plot is just an empty vehicle for action, and anyone wanting to be entertained by that action should just not be troubled by such issues. In this way it would be similar to *Enemy of the State,* discussed in chapter 2. But the film had to be about something, and it focuses on an environmentalist instead of something else. What, after all, makes this character so passionate about the environment, as opposed to some other area where he could use his talents against other evildoers employing similar armies of gun thugs, like stopping terrorism, fighting the drug trade (which Seagal does in *Marked for Death*), rescuing American POWs who remain in Vietnam, or the usual fare of such films?

Perhaps the film is trying to spread this genre out into new territory beyond that covered by the thin plot vehicles of other action films. But then, still, why the environment? Why not human rights? Why not abortion rights? Imagine Steven Seagal entering a town rife with beefy anti-abortion protesters, where he now must kick ass in the name of a woman's right to choose. Why not? Perhaps because such issues are more controversial than illegal dumping by an evil mining company. But it actually doesn't matter, because even with whatever merits we may find in the portrayal of Seagal as an environmental hero, his identity as an environmentalist is just a fact that we must accept without any question. Is it permissible for an environmentalist to use any force of arms in the service of enforcing environmental laws? Presumably, yes, for this film, but there is no development of the historical arguments about environmental protection (versus, in this case, rural development) that could help us understand why this character acts the way he does. If the answer to my concern about this film is that it just isn't an important issue, then I have a good reason to protest that the identity and work of environmentalists, especially in poor, rural areas like this one, is important enough not to be used as mere window dressing to allow Seagal to beat up some people for our entertainment.

But another answer could be that we are simply lacking pertinent information. Perhaps there is actually no good reason to criticize the film's portrayal of an ecological identity oriented toward a set of political positions. Imagine that the scenes establishing Seagal as an environmental do-gooder are on the cutting-room floor and just never made it into the film. In the full script, say, we would get a better sense of what motivates Taggart. But it wasn't an affinity with nature, or an empathy with it, or even a direct, attached, deep ecological consciousness or anything like that which produced this character. What motivated him instead, perhaps, was an extension of a liberal rights scheme about our obligations to future generations to protect the environment so as not to harm their health, or more immediately the health of our children (this is, as suggested above, the appeal Seagal makes most directly in the film, and we get a shot early on of him examining a young kid with a strange red rash on his arm). In this same lost footage, perhaps we learn that the reason Seagal chose this extension of liberal rights rather than another issue was some accident of his background—he was a love child raised by a Navy SEAL father who taught him how to beat up people a thousand different ways and an oceanographer mother who was a devotee of Rachel Carson.

But I think that a claim that no part of Seagal's identity may play a role in why he is doing what he is doing in this film again raises the issue of a distinction between a robust notion of identity politics and a prosaic sense of a politics of identity (either attached or detached). Any kind of politics that involves an attached or detached identity in some minimal sense is motivated by a personal commitment that is, at least partly, connected to the self-conception of agents as persons with a particular set of interests operating in a political sphere. So, if we want to know why Jack Taggart is an environmental advocate, it would not make sense to ignore the question of whether there is not some part of his identity (either conscious or unconscious) that makes him the environmental hero that he is. This doesn't mean that if we could understand that component of his motivation it would necessarily mean that Taggart couldn't reject a robust identity politics in favor of a more traditional liberal conception of environmentalism. It would only mean that we understood his environmental concerns as a moral commitment directed at a particular sphere of the world.

So, one of the things that is so deeply unsatisfying about this film is that Taggart's motivation appears haphazard. The message is that anyone could or should have this commitment to the environment, just as anyone could or should have a commitment to any issue of social justice. It's just a matter of how you decide to spend your day, or in this case, your Aikido prowess. Because Taggart's identity is left so empty, we can conclude that there really is nothing distinctive about the identity, or minimally, about the motivations of environmentalists. But such a conclusion is of course absurd. And perhaps more important, it is an affront to real environmental heroes who have put their lives at risk, and sometimes lost them in the process, in defense of their beliefs.

An excellent portrayal of such a story is the HBO production *The Burning Season,* which gives us one of the richest and most challenging portrayals of an environmentalist on film. It tells the true story of Chico Mendes, for some time the leader of the Rural Workers Union in Brazil, the union that organized peasant rubber tappers in their struggle to prevent the clearance and burning of the Brazilian rainforest to make room for cattle ranchers, who in turn found a market for their products in the bellies of American fast-food customers. While the film is arguably flawed in many ways, and certainly does not supplant two important documentaries on the life and legacy of Mendes—*Chico Mendes: Voice of the Amazon* (1989, directed by Miranda Smith) and *Amazon Journal* (1995, directed by Geoffrey O'Connor)—it does an extremely good job of portraying an environmental cause as grounded in the particular struggles of a community rather than emerging out of nothing. It certainly is not fair to directly compare *The Burning Season* with *Fire Down Below,* but the flaws of the latter film should help us to see more clearly some of the virtues of the former.

In my discussion of *Do the Right Thing* I argued that the film's portrayal of the conflicts over the content of an African-American political identity and the consequences of that identity was one of its chief virtues. For in representing that conflict, both directly and indirectly, the film respects the important process of how communities investigating the implications of a political identity must come together in negotiation and discussion with each other, and in a sense with their past as well. *The Burning Season* demonstrates that this process is the same with environmentalists. At the start, however, I will say that whether we should put Mendes in the category of "environmentalist" or not is an important question, which I will address below. Even if he is not one, the film challenges self-described environmentalists to think about their own identities and how those identities motivate them to act.

The opening shot of the film focuses on a simple wooden statue, positioned at the corner of a tributary of the Amazon, of the Catholic martyr St. Sebastian. We see boys and men loading rubber, which has been harvested, extracted, and compounded by hand, onto boats that will be taken downstream to market. A voice-over begins: "For generations thousands of men were lured up the Amazon river to harvest precious rubber from the Brazilian rainforest. The barons who traded in this white gold made vast fortunes, the workers who tapped the rubber lived in fear and died in debt. The rubber tappers treasured the forest that sustained them and despised the bosses who enslaved them. Finally, a man was born who would fight back. His name was Chico Mendes." By now it is apparent that a boy in the boat being followed most closely by the camera is the young Mendes, going to sell harvested rubber with his father.

The time is 1951 in the Brazilian province of Cachoeira in the middle of the Amazon rainforest. The first few scenes show us the hard life of the peasants working the rubber trade. Establishment scenes show that they are cheated at every corner and live in debt peonage, beholden to the large companies. A stranger comes to Mendes's village and offers his father reading lessons for the boy in exchange for instruction on how the rubber is tapped. We soon learn that the stranger is a union organizer. He later disappears and eventually the villagers are called together and forced to watch as he is set on fire in front of them by the bosses.

Flash forward to 1983, and we are given aerial views of the rainforest, now on fire. We move to the interior of a church, where Edward James Olmos, as Wilson Pinheiro, an organizer for the Rural Workers Union, is lecturing about how the union will resist the corporations and the state that are burning out the rubber tappers. Here we get the first shots of the adult Mendes, played by Raul Julia, in the audience. Tactics are debated, and as in the central scene in *Matewan* (discussed in chapter 5), some of the workers want armed violence against the forestry companies and cattle ranchers. Pinheiro tries to convince them that the law is on their side: If they can convince the government that the people are making productive use of the land, then it cannot be taken away from them.

From here we move to a scene in the forest where workers with chain saws are cutting into trees; hundreds are falling down around them. The rubber tappers come through the forest toward the site of the clear-cut and Olmos steps forward, announcing that they have a legal claim to this land. The rubber tappers scatter and link arms around the trees, forming a human chain to protect the forest. A crisis builds as the foreman approaches Pinheiro with a powered-up chain saw, threatening to use it on him. Mendes steps out in front of the foreman and speaks as an adult in the film for the first time. He asks one of the workers how much he is getting paid for this job. It is only 20 cruzados a day. Mendes retorts: "You got sold a bag of shit, you know that? . . . This land is no good, once the trees are gone. They didn't tell you that did they? . . . When you've cut down everything then we can all be poor together. And all that for 20 cruzados a day."

From these early scenes the rest of the story unfolds, highlighting several themes demonstrating Mendes's internal and external conflicts over the struggle to save the rainforest and what it means for him to be taking this position. With shots of the statue of St. Sebastian returning in several scenes, and the certain knowledge by viewers in the know that Mendes will be killed in the end, Mendes's struggle with his impending martyrdom is an ever present issue. Shortly after the scenes just described, Pinheiro is killed by agents of the cattle ranchers, and after trying to avoid becoming the leader of the union, Mendes finds that he cannot turn his back on his community and accepts the mantle. But the ghost of Pinheiro is ever present and Mendes knows that, even in victory over the cattle ranchers, he is making enemies who will stop at nothing to eliminate him.

Another theme throughout is the struggle over the use of nonviolent methods. Although Mendes consistently advocates nonviolence throughout the film, many of the members of the union (with one young worker in particular standing in for the pressure of many others) disagree with him. Such a dispute is not uncommon in environmental struggles and continues to the present day in organizations such as Earth First!, the Earth Liberation Front, and the Animal Liberation Front that have carried out acts of "ecotage." But it is clear from the film that the stakes were higher in the Amazon, with human lives constantly on the line. Even in winning these debates in the union, Mendes was still in constant conflict. The film then offers the environmental community an opportunity to debate an important issue of tactics that in turn defined not only the terms of their political position but its very content. Like Martin Luther King, Jr.'s, position on the use of nonviolence in the struggle for civil rights, Mendes argues that defenders of the rainforest cannot stoop to the tactics of the gun thugs of the cattlemen as a principle. The fact that he is challenged in this view throughout the film by vocal elements of the community shows how interpretations of this kind of political position were and are actively in flux.

Still more interesting for my purposes here are two other themes about the meaning of this political position that Mendes struggles with throughout the film. Let us put them in terms of two questions. First, what is the scope of his environmentalism? That is, does it necessarily extend beyond national borders (because environmental problems themselves easily cross political boundaries), or is there another principle that governs how the members of a community, in relationship to the land around them, must look to their own interests in development first, and to the global environment only later? Second, why should one agree not to develop the rainforest? Specifically, what reasons were compatible with Mendes's own identity, history, and community, and, more important, which of those reasons could be used to persuade others, not sharing that identity, that they should cease destruction of the rainforest as well?

Let us take the second question first. In the scene just discussed where the adult Mendes speaks for the first time, he makes a direct appeal to the forestry workers to cease what they are doing for reasons that appeal to their own self-interest. It is not that they should stop what they are doing just because the rubber tappers want them to, but because what they are doing in the end doesn't really make sense from their own point of view. They are all being manipulated by a common foe. In the first protest against the road construction that we see him lead, after he becomes head of the union, Mendes confronts the same foreman clearing the forest that we saw in the earlier scene. His argument again appeals to their interests but also includes a more general appeal, not to the value of the forest itself, but to its importance for future generations: "This is our land for us and for our children. The law says we have a right to it." And speaking to the other workers, he says, "The cattle company has taken the land of a hundred tappers and their families. Would you like them to come to where you live and do this to you?" The point of such scenes should not be lost on us: Mendes does not take the position that his opponents must value the rainforest for the same reason that he values it, or that they must see this issue in the same way he sees it, but appeals to their own worldviews, their own political positions. But more examples are needed to bring out the full force of this point.

Later in the film, a British filmmaker, Steven Kaye (played by Nigel Havers) arrives; he wants to do a story about the fires. Mendes is skeptical but eventually welcomes him. As the film progresses, Kaye becomes an important confidant and contrast to Mendes, representing the international environmental community, which has adopted Mendes as their savior of the Amazon. But throughout the exchanges with Kaye, Mendes continues to argue that the reason for saving the forest has more to do with the needs of the local community, and their future generations, than a universal claim to environmental protection or something like an attached identity with nature.

After Mendes proposes to his future wife in a local pub, he and Kaye are seen alone talking over things. Kaye says, "I know how much you love what you're fighting for." And Mendes corrects him, responding that he is not fighting for any "thing" as such but for the future of his particular community: "I loved my father. He was a simple man, a good man. He loved my mother. He did what he could for us. When I was a boy I saw him let a terrible thing happen because that's what we do. We bend our backs and let them beat us, and we tell each other that everything will be better in the next life. I am not going to do what my father did. No son of mine is going to look at me, the way that I looked at my father."[33]

Later, after Mendes makes a failed run at the federal legislature, Kaye asks him to go to a World Bank conference in Miami to tell the bank directors what their loans to Brazil are actual financing in the Amazon. Upon his arrival, Mendes is immediately swamped by the media. He quickly learns that people all over the world know who he is in part because of a film that Kaye has made about him. Kaye tells him that from Miami they should go to Washington to testify in congressional hearings, and then to New York to receive an award from the UN for Mendes's work. A surprised Mendes says, "For my work with the tappers?" No, replies Kaye, "For saving the rainforest," and he excitedly shows Mendes a T-shirt bearing his picture. It is framed by captions saying "Save the Rainforest" at the top and "Chico Mendes" at the bottom.

Kaye spends the rest of the conference trying to introduce Mendes to important people, but they mostly do not want to talk to him because they see him as antidevelopment, "bad for business," as one delegate puts it. Mendes gets more and more frustrated by the conference and loses faith that any of this is doing any good at all. Kaye finds Mendes in a bathroom and encourages him to continue meeting people. Mendes is dismissive. Kaye tries again saying, "These people can help you." Mendes says:

> Help who? Help my members? You and your friends will beat their chests, and cry about the fate of the planet, and then move on to something else, and we'll still be trying to make a better life for ourselves. . . . You're fighting progress. I'm not fighting progress. We need jobs. We need development. But we want it to happen in a way that doesn't keep us poor. Now, if I can be useful in that, tell me who I can speak to, not on your behalf, not to save the rainforest, [but] because that's what my members pay me to do for them. If not, take me to the airport.

Soon thereafter, we see a shot of Mendes on television at a press conference as he is leaving Miami:

> When I came here I had one thing on my mind. Protecting the trees that gave my members their jobs. The people that brought me here had another thing in theirs, saving the planet. I've come to realize that we're fighting for the same thing. If you help us keep the trees then we have a chance of making good lives for ourselves and for our children. If you help us to do that then the rainforest will be there for you and for your children. . . . Why should you help us? Well, because if you help us defeat the road, you're helping yourselves.

The transition here is important and should be noted. At first Mendes is represented as caring, first and foremost, about the welfare of his fellow workers and their future generations, and only secondarily, if that, about the welfare of the environment as such. But after this conflict with Kaye, he begins arguing in the rest of the film for an extended pluralism: Just as he had appealed to the economic self-interest of the workers in earlier scenes, he now sees that to get the support of the international environmental community he must admit an overlap in the needs of his community and the interests of the broader environmental movement. But Mendes is not here capitulating to the northerners. In highlighting this debate, the film is also suggesting that northern environmentalists should think seriously about the welfare of local workers in environmental hot spots like this rather than only making appeals to the value of the forest itself.[34] The film therefore offers an opportunity for environmentalists holding a detached view of political identity, or even the few attached environmentalists, to think critically about why they hold the views that they do, or at the very least how they should express their views to those who don't hold the same position.

Now, to the first question raised above, concerning the scope of Mendes's environmentalism, two scenes are most important, though the issue comes out throughout the film. Returning to Brazil after the Miami conference, Mendes finds that the international publicity he has brought to their plight has stopped the road project through his province. But the cessation in clearance does not stop for long. A corrupt rancher is given full title to Cachoeira to develop it for ranching. Mendes goes to the rancher's home to tell him that he intends to stop the forest clearance that will start the next day. The rancher thinks that Mendes is threatening him; Mendes approaches him and asks how they can resolve this issue. The rancher rebuffs Mendes, saying: "What right have they [Americans] to send you here to tell me and my sons what we can do and what we cannot do to develop this country? They didn't care too much about who got in their way when they were developing theirs did they? Why don't they clean their own mess before telling us what to do? [*In a cynical tone*] They want to breathe clean air, they should start with their own back yard. . . . We start cutting tomorrow."[35]

Mendes is not presented as having a ready answer to this challenge. Instead, he is apparently speechless, perhaps because he knows that nothing he will say will stop the cattleman from moving forward, or because he doesn't have a reply, or maybe even because Mendes finds himself somewhat sympathetic to the needs of the ranchers to make a living, too. As the film leaves this as an open question, we can imagine that it is an issue that northern environmentalists watching the film need to consider: How do we reconcile the hypocrisy of what we have done to our own natural resources with what we now want the Brazilians to do with their own land?

Later, however, with continuing bad publicity, Mendes is visited by the forestry company president and the legislator who had defeated him in the elections, who are seeking some kind of negotiated settlement. Challenging Mendes, the forestry company president says, "Your American friends, do you know what they are saying now? The Amazon doesn't belong to Brazil. It belongs to the world. . . . What do you think about that Mendes? Are you on their side or ours?" The trio stay up all night and make no progress. Finally, Mendes gives his final offer to them: "Those are my brothers and sisters. No road. No more burning. No more loans unless you ask them what they want the money used for."

As the men emerge from the house they see that the rubber tappers have all gathered around in the night, standing and waiting to hear what has happened. The legislator announces (in what seems a strange turn given that he came to see Chico to try to negotiate a settlement rather than to capitulate to him) that the area is to be designated the next morning as a preserve in trust for all the people of the Amazon, "their children, and their children's children." As we see shots of the police come in and order the evacuation of the land by the ranchers and the cessation of the burnings and clearances, we hear the voice of the legislator: "From this moment forward the forest belongs to all of you and everyone who makes their living in it." It is further announced that the government promises to

step in and investigate the deaths of the rubber tappers killed by the cattlemen: "Chico, we must all forget the past and move together towards the
future."

Success follows, and the film, in portraying these scenes, continually
presses us to think about what it means to be an environmentalist confronted with important local needs and in the face of competing claims
for why we hold the views that we do. The film does not reconcile any of
these questions for us but challenges all watching the film, and in particular the environmental community, to think hard about possible answers.
As in *Do the Right Thing*, we are left with more questions than answers.
But because this is a tragically true story, it must culminate in Mendes's
assassination in 1988, presumably by cattle ranchers who were stopped by
his fight. As we see shots of his funeral procession, we hear voice-overs
from a variety of news reports announcing his death (starting with Scott
Simon in the United States on NPR, but going to European and eventually Asian voices as well).

More reports on the voice-overs tell us that on March 12, 1990, 2.5
million acres around Cachoeira were designated as the "Chico Mendes
Reserve," protected from all cutting, clearing, and burning. Still more
voice-overs offer comparative statistics about how much of the rainforest
continues to disappear and the probable effects of this loss for a variety of
health and environmental issues: Every ten minutes we are losing an area
the size of Central Park; the forest that has been lost contained possible
cancer-fighting plants; the loss promotes global warming and the harmful
consequences of that process; it entails huge losses of endangered species
and drops in biodiversity; the rise of AIDS is connected to the destruction
of the forest; and so on. The final shot shows people singing at the burial
site. One boy, who has been a shadow to Mendes throughout the film, and
who works for the ranchers, enters a frame and is embraced by an elderly
woman who lost her son in a shoot-out with the ranchers. The message is
clear: The next step is yours; we must renounce violence and work together as a community into the future.

If *The Burning Season* is about anything, it is about Mendes's struggle
with his own identity as a rural advocate and environmentalist, and, as I
hope I have shown, about the motivation of environmentalists in general
as tied to their history and their understanding of their present political
predicament. All of this is put in stark relief by the central question of the
film, Why was Chico Mendes motivated to knowingly put his life on the
line in the name of this cause? The film also goes out of its way to show

that Mendes was not simply someone who thought of himself as a "friend of the Earth" in the abstract, but a person motivated by the needs of a particular community.

This is another major point in considering why we should think about how to more responsibly represent political identity, a question I have been alluding to throughout this discussion: because in the end, one of the more interesting things about political identity is how it helps us understand why people make the moral, political, and social choices that they do. As opposed to some other political frameworks, political identities, as explained in the first section of this chapter, have a built-in account of what morally motivates someone who embraces that identity, namely, the object of the identity concern itself and their relation to it. I have argued at length elsewhere in the context of environmental ethics that it fails as a form of philosophy unless it develops some account of moral psychology that will help to motivate people to act more responsibly toward the environment.[36] If the other option is to limit the field to only discussing abstract philosophical questions, such as whether nature has intrinsic value in and of itself that warrants moral recognition, then the field seems like so much intellectual fiddling while the planet literally burns. Such a prospect seems at odds with the point of doing this kind of philosophy in the first place: namely, to make a contribution to the actual resolution of environmental problems. One could extend this approach to any kind of moral, social, or political philosophy that aims to be a practical philosophy (in the sense described in chapter 5).

Thus, to avoid obscurity or worse, any field of philosophy in this vein ought to follow Mendes's lead and be at least partly concerned not only with which arguments most accurately describe what is right and what we ought to do but also with which arguments appeal to the intuitions that people have about why they should set aside their own preferences for other ends. But to make that contribution, we need to know something about why people take certain issues to be important, so important that they set their own desires aside. At minimum, then, a politics of identity gives us a window into a large swath of the political continuum that is more transparent about such motivations than many other explanations for personal action and sacrifice. Knowing these motivations, and the conflicts that go on inside of such communities, will help us to speak to them in terms they will find meaningful, in hopes that they will eventually embrace the concerns that we find important.

As mentioned above, one might still object that Mendes in fact had an attached and not a detached form of identity. His identity is that of a rural worker, perhaps even ethnically distinct from the owners and capitalists. But again, even if this is true, the film still speaks to the conflicts of the environmental community. The film does show, in one very short scene, part of Kaye's film about Mendes. It portrays him talking to indigenous people in the Amazon about the need to stop the forest clear-cuts. He is not the same as the indigenous people, and perhaps he does not share the attached identity to which they could lay claim. But Mendes is a member of many overlapping communities, and in the end that may be the solution to the puzzle of his identity. For while we might be able to distinguish between detached and attached identities, they are both important enough to respect in their representation on film, no matter what combination of motivations produce them.

Conflicts over the meaning and implications of an identity exist for both the detached and attached varieties of political identity, and so both are important for trying to understand this kind of politics. A bad portrayal of any identity, especially one that fails to provide the motivation of characters depicting that identity, is an offense to the political commitment and motivations of actual people who hold these views. Part of the power of film, with its potential for portraying complex characters, is that it can rise above such failings and help us both to grasp the motivations of various political actors and groups and in turn enrich our understanding of our own moral, political, and social motivations. With this power comes responsibility, which, when exercised and balanced with lively and entertaining images, produces something truly beautiful.

Notes

Chapter 1

1. The series of events that got me to actually put pen to paper on these issues is less mysterious. The story, though not typical, may excuse some of the faults that professional film theorists may find with this book. The fact is that I stumbled into writing on film quite by accident. The entry was through an avenue that inspires many people to do many things today: I got a job where I had no choice but to at least temporarily develop this interest. The position was a one-year lectureship at Texas A&M University in 1993, before I had really started my dissertation in environmental ethics. The position was a replacement for Larry Hickman, who was leaving to become director of The Center for Dewey Studies at Southern Illinois University at Carbondale. Larry had a deep and abiding interest in philosophy and film as well and had both written on the topic and regularly taught a course called "Philosophy of Visual Media." So, when I took the job, I inherited Larry's class and with his help developed the course. Two casual acquaintances from the film studies program at UCLA suggested that I develop a professional paper on film while I taught the class and present it at the 1994 meeting of the Society for Cinema Studies. More important about that trip was that I there met Dorit Naaman, a filmmaker and now film theorist at Queen's University in Kingston, Ontario. Dorit and I lived together for five years, and because of her I further developed my interest in film and still teach the subject today. It's not the stuff of a Hollywood summer blockbuster, but it ain't bad.

2. See Richard Rorty, *Contingency, Irony, Solidarity* (Cambridge: Cambridge University Press, 1989), and Martha Nussbaum, *Love's Knowledge: Essays on Philosophy and Literature* (Oxford: Oxford University Press, 1992).

3. Incidentally, I would also side with those who would say the same is true of philosophy itself—it can be taught outside philosophy departments without necessarily having to beg the interaction of philosophers in such discussions. Of course, just as philosophers may criticize others for doing philosophy outside of philosophical circles badly, those philosophers working on film have to be prepared for similar criticisms.

4. Among Carroll's many works on this topic, see *Theorizing the Moving Image* (Cambridge: Cambridge University Press, 1996), and *Interpreting the Moving Image* (Cambridge: Cambridge University Press, 1998).

5. See the contents of the special issue of *Argumentation and Advocacy*, no. 33 (Summer 1996), edited by David S. Birdsell and Leo Groarke.

6. I did, however, discuss the relationship between an account of film as visual argument and Carroll's rejection of reception studies in a philosophical understanding of film in my paper, "Does the Audience Matter?: On Carroll and Visual Argument," *Film and Philosophy* 5–6 (2001), pp. 20–32. Carroll responded to this account in the same volume of the journal.

7. Jan Narveson, "Social Philosophy," in *The Cambridge Dictionary of Philosophy*, general editor, Robert Audi (Cambridge: Cambridge University Press, 1995), p. 747. I do not take dictionary definitions in general, not even those in specialized volumes like this one, to be definitively authoritative, but I do think that this is a good start for an introduction like this one. Though I have many disagreements with Narveson's particular views on an array of topics, and his general approach to social philosophy, I find this to be a helpful overview of the main themes of what is otherwise a very loosely defined philosophical enterprise compared with other fields of philosophy. But I think that social philosophy should be very loosely defined, and I like, for example, how open the North American Society for Social Philosophy is to different people doing different kinds of work. The society has held conferences on the environment, law, and other areas that, quite rightly, overlap considerably with other philosophical subfields.

8. Ibid.

9. The films I like the least are those where I don't care about any of the characters—their welfare is inconsequential to me for good or for bad. That does not mean that a good film from that perspective must make us care about all of the characters, but that it gets better the more characters we come to care about. A good case in point is a comparison between Tim Robbins's *Cradle Will Rock* (1999) and Mike Leigh's *Topsy-Turvey* (1999). Both films are about the creation of artistic productions (musicals), and so both involve large ensemble casts. Both also present a challenge to the filmmaker and the viewer to bring alive a period of history that most of us did not live through: pre-World War II America (*Cradle*) and Victorian England (*Topsy*). But Topsy, to my mind, does a far superior job of bringing us into that world because it creates characters we care about, from the principal leads to the most minor roles. *Cradle* packs in too many stories—not only the story of the musical but also side stories about other important political events of the time, such as the Rockefellers' commission to Diego Rivera to paint a mural for the Rockefeller Center. But even though that is a tale well worth telling, there is too much packed into this film and we wind up not caring much about what happens to any of the characters in any of the stories, no matter how interesting they are, and so fail to appreciate their visions of how we can live in

the world in relation to others. This point would of course require much more argument and analysis of the films in question to make it complete.

10. Those who want a deeper understanding of this connection should see Ray Müller III's *Die Macht der Bilder: Leni Riefenstahl* (1993).

Chapter 2

1. Their interventions on such topics continue to this day, though with more or less attention to current issues of importance rather than purer forms of philosophical argumentation. For a brief history, see Dale Jamieson's "Singer and the Practical Ethics Movement," in Dale Jamieson, ed., *Singer and His Critics* (Oxford: Blackwell, 1999).

2. The point of this chapter is not to survey this work or even critically engage with it (which would be a book-length project in and of itself). Those interested, however, should look at such works as W. Bogard, *The Simulation of Surveillance: Hypercontrol in Telematic Societies* (Cambridge: Cambridge University Press, 1996); C. Boyer, *Cybercities: Visual Perception in the Age of Electronic Communication* (New York: Princeton Architectural Press, 1996); Mike Davis, *City of Quartz* (London: Vintage, 1990); P. Droege, ed., *Intelligent Environments* (Amsterdam: North-Holland, 1997); Derek Gregory, *Geographical Imaginations* (Oxford: Blackwell, 1994); and especially, David Lyon, *The Electronic Eye: The Rise of the Surveillance Society* (Minneapolis: University of Minnesota Press, 1994).

3. Lyons, *The Electronic Eye*, pp. 62–63. The principle source for Foucault's work on the Panopticon is his *Discipline and Punish: The Birth of the Prison* (New York: Vintage, 1977), especially chapter 4.

4. Alison Mitchell, "The Perilous Search for Security at Home," *New York Times*, July 28, 2002, "Week in Review," p. 1.

5. The connection between being watched and effective public or private surveillance is still a challenge. Simply gathering information is fairly inefficient if there is no way of sifting through it for the images and imprints that are useful for some particular purpose. The former East German state security agency had huge vaults full of information on its citizens, much of it gathered by neighbors spying on each other. The problem, however, was that there was so much information that much of it wasn't useful; there was no effective means of sifting through it. But Lyons's nice summary of the power of Bentham's Panopticon—uncertainty breeds subordination—still holds. We're more careful about even the smallest infraction of the law because we know that we could be watched at any given time, and that if someone had the patience and time, they could look through the thousands of hours of tape to find us if they wanted to. Scenes of such efforts have become ubiquitous on the popular *Law and Order* variety of police television shows. Friends who work in the computer industry tell me that

new developments in artificial intelligence will only make this process simpler in the future.

6. See, for example, Jacques Ellul, *The Technological Society*, trans. J. Wilkinson (New York: Vintage, 1964), and Martin Heidegger, *The Question Concerning Technology*, trans. W. Lovitt (New York: Harper and Row, 1977).

7. Very few philosophers of technology hold to such a strong substantive view anymore. The next chapter will look more carefully at two contemporary philosophers of technology, Albert Borgmann and Andrew Feenberg, who both begin with and significantly depart from the arguments of Ellul and Heidegger. For an earlier contrasting view, see, for example, Herbert Marcuse, *One-Dimensional Man* (Boston: Beacon Press, 1964). For a contemporary argument by a philosopher in favor of the neutrality thesis, see Joseph Pitt, *Thinking About Technology* (New York: Seven Bridges Press, 2000).

8. Jean Hillier, "See You in the City," *Arena Magazine*, no. 28 (1997), p. 38.

9. Were these references from the more recent film to the earlier one really intentional? Most likely. My best guess is that many of the shots and casting decisions in this film were inspired by *The Conversation*, which itself was inspired by films before it, but without actually intending to grant any kind of argumentative credibility over the subject of the film. But whether or not these intertextual references, or their implications, were intentional does not really matter for my argument here. Throughout this book I will sometimes make arguments that appeal to the intentions of a director, but there are good reasons, established not only in the annals of film scholarship but also in the theory of argumentation, not to base the interpretation of a text (be it a film, novel, play, or something that can be "read" as a text such as a painting or sculpture) on the intentions of the author. Where intentions are identified, I think that they can only serve as additional support for an interpretation of a text, rather than as a definitive reason for agreeing with it, and in most cases will never serve as the final word over the issue of whether one interpretation of a film is better than another. One need not embrace a wholesale form of postmodernism about texts (where we might say that they exist independently of their authors) to hold such a view in the case of film. For even though most of the films I will discuss in these chapters are auteur films, or films that can be more reasonably interpreted as the vision of a strong director (who may also serve as the film's writer and editor), all films involve a plethora of "authors" beyond simply the screenwriter or director. A reading of a film as simply the text of the script is in most cases too limiting for an adequate appreciation of it. In addition to screenwriters and directors, editors, directors of photography, production designers, producers, and many others all play vital and significant roles in determining what winds up on a finished film product. (For this reason I am tempted to take the position that the current fashion of producing "director's cuts" of films, usually amounting to recovering scenes from the cutting-room floor that never made it into the finished product, or eliminating soundtracks or

voice-overs, actually produces a different film that needs to be analyzed differently.) In addition, many things happen in films for no intentional reason at all: Shots are set up in a certain way because of a lack of resources or equipment, and scenes get cut because of time constraints. My assumption in these chapters, then, which certainly would need a more adequate defense than I will offer here, is that a film, as a finished and coherent whole, can be read as taking positions independent of any of its authors' intentions and can be interpreted and criticized as such. This claim should not, however, be interpreted as a strong substantive view that films actively do things by themselves.

10. Some film theorists would interpret this last series of suggestions as an exercise in "gap filling." When we watch films we are called upon through many visual and audio cues to fill in information that is not explicitly offered to us. For example, it is usually only experimental or avant-garde film that shows us events in real time where we experience much of what a character is portrayed as experiencing. More conventional films take place over days, weeks, months, years, even decades without depicting events using a one-to-one temporal format, where the time we spend in the theater is equivalent to the time frame we observe on the screen. But to make these narratives coherent, films must provide cues, some obvious, some less so, which help us follow the story of the film despite such temporal gaps. There are ample shots and bits of dialogue in The Conversation to lead us to conclude that Caul is going through much torment in his work in this plot and that it is connected to his past, even though we don't need flashbacks or other on-screen footage to make this connection clearer. But in Enemy there are no scenes, not even minor digressions in the plot, to lead us to the conclusion that the techno-geeks suffer through any similar worries. Often, filmmakers play with these moments of gap filling to mislead the viewer so as to build suspense and surprise endings. But such work is highly crafted and aesthetically quite rich. Films aimed more at stimulating our cognitive abilities than at just filling our need for unreflective entertainment often make the gaps ambiguous so that multiple interpretations of a film are possible. See Dorit Naaman, *Sensing Film: A Cognitive Approach to Film*, Unpublished Dissertation, University of Alberta, Canada, 2000. One of my favorite examples of gap filling is in Lars Von Trier's 1996 film *Breaking the Waves*, which ends with a supernatural shot of church bells magically appearing over an oil platform in the Scottish North Sea. Are the bells really supposed to be there? It's unclear since the characters who see them are roused by the bells from their beds. Are they really awake, or is this just a dream? The answer to that question is important for an understanding of the film but never really answered. My thanks to Bruce Milem for pointing out this ambiguity in the ending of this film.

11. This is not to say that films cannot be fun, titillating, or exciting, and also be critically interesting. My favorite example in the genre of warfare is Paul Verhoeven's 1997 sci-fi blockbuster *Starship Troopers*. This film combines rivet-

ing action sequences, sensuous love scenes, and military bravado with a fairly scathing critique of militarism, jingoism, and xenophobia. The film is also, so far as I know, one of the more interesting portrayals of what a more gender-equitable military would actually look like. Despite many lapses into schlocky machismo, the film has some incredibly strong female characters who are, more or less, accepted as equals among men in combat training and battle roles. A viewer of this film who doesn't appreciate these more nuanced elements, and only focuses on the sex and violence, is missing much of what makes this a good movie.

12. Let me be clear, though, that I do not think the older technology of *The Conversation* poses an inherent limitation of the argument of the film. Human surveillance is as old as language itself, and though it has been augmented and expanded by computer technology, it is not creating a new social phenomenon as such. But still, it is understandable that contemporary viewers may come to see *The Conversation* as antiquated, and ineffectual as a persuasive warning against the problems that may be inherent to surveillance technology.

13. Interestingly, Byrne has a very small part in *Enemy* as the fake Brill sent by the NSA to intercept Smith when he is going to meet the real Brill.

14. In the next chapter I will more fully unpack the possible significance of the representation of democratic alternatives, or, as the philosopher Andrew Feenberg put it, "subversive rationalizations" to dominant forms of technology.

15. Another interesting twist on this more balanced portrayal of different relationships to technology is that the Pullman character winds up going underground to escape detection by the surveillance network by living with a family of Mexican-American gardeners. This family is represented as relatively secure from the network because they are out of the loop it is meant to benefit, though there are ample indicators throughout the film that they are familiar with the latest in personal computer technology.

16. A more extreme version of this paradox may be at work in Steven Spielberg's summer 2002 blockbuster *Minority Report*. There, at least in the case of murder, surveillance is taken to its ultimate height as the plot pivots off of the creation of genetically modified humans who can see acts of violence before they occur, and even in some cases before they are known by the perpetrators. Though I haven't thought enough about this film yet, I suspect that there might even be a similar Hestonite message going on with it: The fall of this technical system ultimately is due to its corruption, in this case by its original creators. Everyone in the film seems to agree that without this level of corruption, the world would be a better and safer place. There appears to be nothing intrinsically wrong with the system or intrinsically worrisome about the development or use of this kind of technology, except for minor qualms expressed throughout the film, which ultimately do not count as the reason for dismantling the system.

17. Summary of the details of the decision and all quotes concerning it are taken from Linda Greenhouse, "Justices Say Warrant Is Required in High-Tech

Searches of Homes," *New York Times*, June 12, 2001, pp. A1, A29. The article also includes excerpts from the decision by Justice Scalia and the dissent by Justice Stevens.

18. Ibid.

Chapter 3

1. Wim Wenders, *The Logic of Images*, trans. Michael Hofmann (London: Faber and Faber, 1991), p. 8.

2. See, for example, Allen Carlson, *Aesthetics and the Environment: The Appreciation of Nature, Art, and Architecture* (New York: Routledge, 2000).

3. See, for example, Richard Shusterman, *Pragmatist Aesthetics: Living Beauty, Rethinking Art*, 2nd ed. (Lanham, Md.: Rowman and Littlefield, 2000), and *Practicing Philosophy: Pragmatism and the Philosophical Life* (New York: Routledge, 1997). See also Andrew Light and Jonathan M. Smith, eds., *The Aesthetics of Everyday Life* (New York: Seven Bridges Press, 2002).

4. Again, this field of philosophy is primarily concerned with understanding the social implications of modern technologies on the way we live. For general background surveys of this field, see Federick Ferre, *Philosophy of Technology* (Athens, Ga.: The University of Georgia Press, 1995), and Don Ihde, *Philosophy of Technology: An Introduction* (New York: Paragon House, 1993).

5. See Stanley Cavell, *Themes Out of School* (San Francisco: North Point Press, 1984).

6. Whether philosophy of technology should have such a strong focus on social questions is a matter of some debate. For views critical of the claim that it should, see, for example, Joseph Pitt, *Thinking About Technology* (New York: Seven Bridges Press, 2000), and Andrew Light and David Roberts, "Toward New Foundations in Philosophy of Technology: Mitcham and Wittgenstein on Descriptions," *Research in Philosophy and Technology* 19 (2000), pp. 125–147.

7. Albert Borgmann, *Technology and the Character of Contemporary Life* (Chicago: University of Chicago Press, 1984), p. 42. For more background on Borgmann's views and critical discussions of them, see Eric Higgs, Andrew Light, and David Strong, eds., Technology and the Good Life? (Chicago: University of Chicago Press, 2000).

8. Ibid.

9. Ibid.

10. See, for example, Kevin Lynch, *The Image of the City* (Cambridge, Mass.: MIT Press, 1960), and Michal de Certau, *The Practice of Everyday Life* (Berkeley and Los Angeles: University of California Press, 1984).

11. Given the intuitive plausibility of this sort of argument, it is no surprise that many philosophers of technology have also been theoreticians of social space, in particular, cities and suburbs. Diverse theorists such as Murray Bookchin, John

McDermott, and especially Lewis Mumford not only have written on both topics but also have often used the same theoretical base for their criticism of certain types of artifacts and spaces. See, for example, Murray Bookchin, "Toward a Liberatory Technology," in *Post-Scarcity Anarchism* (Montreal: Black Rose Books, 1986), and *Urbanization Without Cities* (Montreal: Black Rose Books, 1992); John McDermott, "The Aesthetic Drama of the Ordinary," and "Glass Without Feet: Dimensions of Urban Aesthetics," in *Streams of Experience* (Amherst: University of Massachusetts Press, 1986); and Lewis Mumford, *Technics and Civilization* (New York: Harcourt, Brace and Company, 1934), and *The Culture of Cities* (New York: Harcourt, Brace and Company, 1938).

12. Henri Lefebvre, *Critique of Everyday Life*, vol. 1, trans. John Moore (London: Verso, 1992).

13. See Michel Trebitsch's preface to Lefebvre, *Critique of Everyday Life*, p. xxiv.

14. Ibid., p. xvii. Lefebvre put the point somewhat extravagantly: "In so far as a science of man exists, it finds its material in the 'trivial,' the everyday." Ibid., p. 133.

15. Not surprisingly, Borgmann has made an attempt to extend the device paradigm to spaces, particularly cities. He argued that cities need to be preserved as bastions of what I am calling thick spaces and that their "energetically chaotic qualities" need to be preserved. See Albert Borgmann, *Crossing the Postmodern Divide* (Chicago: University of Chicago Press, 1992), especially chapter 5. I have some reservations about this application of the device paradigm because Borgmann introduced a wholly new distinction to talk about spaces and artifacts in this book—conglomerations of artifacts are either "real" or "hyperreal." I have questioned this change in Borgmann's argument in part because I think that the real-hyperreal distinction does not appear to do any work that the device paradigm does not. One can argue that the older device-thing distinction could have been applied more straightforwardly to spaces. I am also worried that the effect of this shift may be to open up the possibility of a wholesale critique of city space using Borgmann's new distinction. See Andrew Light, "Three Questions on Hyperreality," *Research in Philosophy and Technology* 15 (1995), pp. 211–222.

16. See Andrew Feenberg, *Alternative Modernity: The Technical Turn in Philosophy and Social Theory* (Berkeley and Los Angeles: University of California Press, 1995), p. 3. For more on this argument also see Feenberg, *Critical Theory of Technology* (Oxford: Oxford University Press, 1992), as well as his "Subversive Rationalization: Technology, Power and Democracy," *Inquiry* 35 (1992), pp. 301–322, and, more recently, *Questioning Technology* (London: Routledge, 1999).

17. See Feenberg, *Alternative Modernity*, chapter 7.

18. This gap in Borgmann's account may be due to the fact that his argument is not structured so that such a transformative view is needed. It is not the case

that Borgmann does not have a theory of social transformation. His claims are coherent without the sort of argument made by Feenberg. My argument is simply that Borgmann's and Feenberg's views would do better to incorporate part of the structure of each other's accounts.

19. See Feenberg, *Critical Theory of Technology*, chapter 1.

20. These themes are familiar for anyone who has followed Wenders's career and can be picked up in many of his films—*Kings of the Road* (1976), *The State of Things* (1982), *Wings of Desire* (1987), and others. Elements of this aesthetic appreciation could also be found in a reading of *The End of Violence*, discussed in chapter 2.

21. Wim Wenders, *The Logic of Images*, p. 1, my emphasis. I am not suggesting that Wenders (or Balázs) is using "things" in Borgmann's philosophically substantive sense. There is, however, a striking resemblance between the two uses, no doubt inspired by the substantive use of the term "thing" in German art, cultural criticism, and philosophy.

22. Ibid., p. 2.

23. Ibid., p. 8.

24. Of course, I realize the problems with basing any substantive claim on the intentions of the artist. As mentioned in the notes in chapter 2, nothing hangs on the correlation I have identified here to the substance of my argument about the film's narrative, so we might think of this point as only providing a supportive correlation between my reading of Wenders's film and his understanding of his own project.

25. Wenders would admit his focus on such themes is primarily true of only some of his films, specifically what he calls the "A" films—those that are in black and white, which originate in his own ideas and impressions (rather than from someone else's script): "In these films, I saw my task as bringing in as much as possible of what (already) existed." Wenders, *The Logic of Images*, p. 56. Ed Dimendberg reminded me that Wenders is a great admirer of Siegfried Kracauer's *Theory of Film: The Redemption of Physical Reality* (Oxford: Oxford University Press, 1960), which is an explicitly Benjaminian theory of film. On that evidence we have at least one reason to think seriously about the A films as locations of a thick account of space, technology, and place.

26. While I hope it is clear that *Alice* demonstrates the potential of Wenders's films to serve as a commentary on the philosophical issue previously discussed, I realize that it is not the most accessible film in Wenders's filmography. The film has been out of print for over ten years and is not available in many video rental stores. But the themes covered in the film that I find of interest are common in much of Wenders's work. In a series of endnotes I have pointed out some common themes in this piece with other films that may be more readily available.

27. Robert Philip Kolker and Peter Beicken, *The Films of Wim Wenders* (Cambridge: Cambridge University Press, 1993), p. 36. This volume is an excel-

lent book-length introduction to Wenders in English. Other titles in French and German include: Michel Boujut, *Wim Wenders* (Paris: Edilig, 1986); Uwe Küntzel, *Wim Wenders: Ein Filmbuch* (Freiburg: Dreisam, 1989); and Reinhold Rauh, *Wim Wenders und seine Filme* (Munich: Heyene, 1990). Also, several books on the New German Cinema in English contain significant sections on Wenders: Thomas Elsaesser, *New German Cinema: A History* (Piscataway, N.J.: Rutgers University Press, 1989); James Franklin, *New German Cinema: From Oberhausen to Hamburg* (Boston: Twayne, 1983); John Sandford, *The New German Cinema* (New York: Da Capo, 1980).

28. I would expect that Kolker and Beicken would take these scenes as evidence for their claim that photographic images in Wenders's films are signs of angst and rootlessness. The artifact of the camera and of the produced image is directly connected to the aimless wanderings of the male characters: "The images made by the Polaroid camera or the five-and-dime photo booth become, for Wenders's characters, signs of their insecurity and a mark of their creator's interest in the problems of representing individual experience." *The Films of Wim Wenders*, p. 42. But I reject such a narrow interpretation of the photographs in this film. The role of image making in identity problems shows up more directly in other Wenders films. It is particularly evident in *Until the End of the World* (1991), which warns us of the potentially hazardous connections between image production and self-identity. In this film several characters get addicted to watching the technically produced representations of their own dreams.

29. Again, contra Kolker and Beicken's interpretation of Wenders's searches as movement without reason, here a search is undertaken for a definite place. The purposeful searching of this part of the film also does not fit well with Kolker and Beicken's claim that Wenders's films, in their search mode, "attempt to establish a transnational space, unstable and full of longing for someplace else." *The Films of Wim Wenders*, p. 36. In *Alice*, the continuation of the second search, after Wuppertal, is not simply for any place, but for a particular place. There is a longing for someplace else, but it isn't just any place.

30. Walter Benjamin, "The Work of Art in the Age of Mechanical Reproduction," reprinted in Gerald Mast, Marshall Cohen, and Leo Braudy, eds., *Film Theory and Criticism* (Oxford: Oxford University Press, 1992), p. 669.

31. See Doug Kellner and Michael Ryan, *Camera Politica: The Politics and Ideology of Contemporary Hollywood Film* (Bloomington: Indiana University Press, 1990).

32. Benjamin, "The Work of Art," p. 672.

33. This theme of the deadening of the audience, and consequently of the social sphere of films and filmmaking, shows up in several ways in Wenders's *Kings of the Road*. There, we follow a film projector repairman traveling through Germany. Among other themes in the film, we discover with him the corruption

and loss of local cinema, in part caused by the disappearance of critical viewers. In one scene he attends a pornographic movie and notices that the image is marred by something obstructing the projector's lens. No one else in the theater seems to notice anything. The repairman walks up to the projection booth to complain and finds that the projectionist has hung a small mirror in front of the camera's lens so that it projects a reverse image onto the back wall of the projection booth. When the repairman walks in, the projectionist is masturbating to the image on the wall that is the source of the obstruction of the image on the screen. One may interpret this scene to fit nicely into my analysis here: Participation in the film is reduced to the most uncritical level of enjoyment, and in such an atmosphere the quality of the image becomes unimportant in the delivery of the needed stimulation. Of course, a good counter argument is that not every film is best appreciated through a critical viewing!

34. Wenders, *The Logic of Images*, p. 24.

35. Other, more recent films of Wenders also speak to this worry about the relationship between film and TV or video. In his documentary *A Notebook on Cities and Clothes* (1989), Wenders experiments by shooting portions of the film with a video camera or an old film camera. He talks about the differences between the two and experiments with interviews depicting the subject on film alongside a delayed representation of the subject on a video screen. This is a hard film and requires a lot of skill on the part of the viewer, but it is clear by the end that there is at least an issue concerning the difference between the two media that must eventually be addressed by a critical audience.

Chapter 4

1. Throughout this chapter I will refer to the events in Los Angeles as the "King riots" or just "the riots." By doing this, however, I am not taking a position on whether what happened was a riot, an uprising, an insurrection, a rebellion, or something else. In a response to an interviewer's question on this issue, Mike Davis, to be discussed shortly, suggested that while "riot" does not necessarily have a negative connotation for him as a labor historian, he tries to respect the wishes of inner-city residents, making reference to a meeting of Crips and Bloods gang members in Inglewood in May 1992, where the riots were called a "slave rebellion." Still, as he went on to say, what happened in L.A. cannot be easily reduced to a single essence, characteristic, or identity. I agree, but for the sake of convenience only I will still refer to these events as the King riots. See "Uprising and Repression in L.A.: An Interview with Mike Davis by the Covert Action Information Bulletin," reprinted in Robert Gooding-Williams, ed. *Reading Rodney King/Reading Urban Uprising* (New York: Routledge, 1993), p. 142.

2. Mike Davis, *City of Quartz* (New York: Vintage Books, 1992). For another very fine treatment of the politics of spatial division in another city, see Neil

Smith, *The New Urban Frontier: Gentrification and the Revanchist City* (New York: Routledge, 1996).

3. See William Cronon, ed., *Uncommon Ground: Toward Reinventing Nature* (New York: W. W. Norton & Co., 1995).

4. The two original papers written after the riots were Andrew Light, "Urban Wilderness," in David Rothenberg, ed., *Wild Ideas* (Minneapolis: University of Minnesota Press, 1995), pp. 195–211, and "The Metaphorical Drift of Classical Wilderness," *Geography Research Forum* 15 (1995), pp. 14–32. Since that time I have expanded my work on urban environmental ethics along more traditional lines in environmental ethics, though attention to urban issues is still severely lacking in the field. See Andrew Light, "Elegy for a Garden: Thoughts on an Urban Environmental Ethic," *Philosophical Writings* 14 (2000), pp. 41–47, "The Urban Blind Spot in Environmental Ethics," *Environmental Politics* 10, no. 1 (2001), pp. 7–35, and "Urban Ecological Citizenship," *Journal of Social Philosophy*, forthcoming, 2003. Through my reading of Davis's book, I also, as mentioned above, began reading more extensively in the field of geography. This literature, plus work and conversations with the geographer Jonathan Smith at Texas A&M in my first full-time job, led me to an understanding of how much more advanced geographers were on philosophical questions of space and place than philosophers. This experience led me and Smith to found the Society for *Philosophy and Geography* and later the journal Philosophy and Geography, which we continue to edit.

5. See the essays in Gooding-Williams, *Reading Rodney King/Reading Urban Uprising*, especially those by Houston Baker, Patricia Williams, and Gooding-Williams.

6. John Rennie Short, *Imagined Country: Environment, Culture and Society* (New York: Routledge, 1991), p. 6.

7. Ibid. For a history of this argument see Roderick Nash, *Wilderness and the American Mind* (New Haven, Conn.: Yale University Press, 1982).

8. Such a view has been popular in many circles in the environmental movement for some time as well as in my field of environmental ethics. "Deep ecologists," for example, have long tried to justify and better articulate such a view. They are not alone though, and even more theoretically modest elements of the environmental movement often take such a sentiment as gospel. I have long been skeptical of such an account, as well as the corollary view that lack of exposure to wilderness, or even some approximation, distances people from nature. Such claims strike me as the worst form of irresponsible folk psychology. For a partial argument against such views, see my "Restoring Ecological Citizenship," in Ben Minteer and Bob Pepperman Taylor, eds., *Democracy and the Claims of Nature* (Lanham, Md.: Rowman & Littlefield, 2002), pp. 153–172.

9. I mean by "cognitive" here only that reasoning is involved, as opposed to only direct perception itself or physical description. I do not mean to invoke the more complex understandings of the term "cognitive" from fields such as cognitive science, though I'm sure work on metaphor in that field by thinkers such as George Lakoff and Mark Johnson would be very helpful in more fully fleshing out the metaphorical sense of "wilderness" that I will highlight below.

10. The classical view of wilderness is certainly not the only form of environmental determinism that has ever been espoused. There have been numerous other accounts in the long history of environmental history, mostly questionable ones—for example, the notion that one's physical location generates a certain kind of character, or that particular places generate specific kinds of attitudes or traits, with urbanites, say, being greedy and selfish because of their surroundings, and the like.

11. Short, *Imagined Country*, p. 9.

12. See Ronald Takaki, *Iron Cages* (Oxford: Oxford University Press, 1988).

13. Short, *Imagined Country*, p. 9.

14. See, for example, Max Oelschlaeger, *The Idea of Wilderness: From Prehistory to the Age of Ecology* (New Haven, Conn.: Yale University Press, 1991), for an excellent genealogy of the idea of wilderness, especially his account of the evolution of the idea in the Western Middle Ages.

15. For more on the idea of wilderness, see J. Baird Callicott and Michael P. Nelson, eds., *The Great New Wilderness Debate* (Athens, Ga.: University of Georgia Press, 1998). In my earlier papers on this topic, rather than concluding with a call to abandon the term "wilderness," as some in this debate have done, I chose to adopt what I referred to, loosely and somewhat tongue-in-cheek, as an "indexical" account of wilderness and, as much as possible, an ideologically empty conception of wilderness. "Wilderness" should just be the term we use to specify particular places for special protective status. That status is dependent upon some kind of legislatively adopted convention for distinguishing one place from another, which certainly should refer to some distinguishing range of biological and ecological properties. See the conclusion of Light, "Urban Wilderness."

16. Others have noted this shift as well. Roderick Nash briefly mentioned such a transition of reference for the term "wilderness" to cities in *Wilderness and the American Mind* (especially pp. 143–144), but it is not clear whether he would share my views on the cognitive context of classical wilderness. Short also argued that big cities are "now the modern equivalent of the medieval forest populated by demons." Short, *Imagined Country*, p. 26. From now on when I use the phrase "urban wilderness" I will mean the metaphorical use of classical wilderness as applied to cities. I know of no use of a romantic notion of wilderness applied to cities, but I can imagine it would be possible. After all, one who recognized the

metaphorical, or at least cognitive, content of romantic notions of wilderness (which could be spelled out in the same way that I have done with classical wilderness) might recognize the seemingly organic jumble of some cities as a wild quality that could improve people.

17. See Light, "Urban Wilderness," for more detail on this account.

18. Mike Davis, "Who Killed Los Angeles? Part Two: The Verdict Is Given," *New Left Review*, no. 199 (1993).

19. Davis, City of Quartz, p. 223.

20. Davis, "Who Killed Los Angeles?" p. 47. In his more recent research Davis has argued that nature itself has also become demonized in Los Angeles. See Mike Davis, *Ecology of Fear: Los Angeles and the Imagination of Disaster* (New York: Metropolitan Books, 1998).

21. I attempted some preliminary conclusions on the effects of the urban wilderness imagery on inner-city residents in "The Metaphorical Drift of Classical Wilderness." A full analysis, however, would require more rigorous psychological and sociological research.

22. Robert Gooding-Williams, "Look, A Negro!" in Gooding-Williams, *Reading Rodney King/Reading Urban Uprising*, p. 166. Gooding-Williams in part drew the record of the trial from the *Los Angeles Times*, April 3, 1992; April 21, 1992; and April 22, 1992. My emphasis.

23. It seems noteworthy that Caine in Menace is also depicted as planning to escape L.A. by moving to Atlanta. Both depictions of a reverse migration of African-Americans back to the South offer a positive suggestion that not all cities are bad for black people (or people in general). Though Atlanta is a racially divided city as well, and certainly violent in many respects, it has a more successful black power structure than Los Angeles. This is no doubt a legacy of its history as one of the central cities of the civil-rights movement, as well as a byproduct of its demographics. Having grown up in and around Atlanta, I have often remarked that in some respects it is a less racist city than L.A. That an event like the riots could be explained without appeal to its racial elements as mass opportunistic looting, which I said at the start was the far Right response in L.A., would never get any serious consideration in Atlanta. The reason is that the city's and region's history of racial oppression is so blatant, and so clearly an important factor shaping the area, that no one would seriously consider an explanation of any social problem that did not take race into account. Of course, I make this claim, perhaps naively, as a white person.

Chapter 5

1. For very helpful historical background to this period, see David Alan Corbin, *Life, Work, and Rebellion in the Coal Fields: The Southern West Virginia Miners, 1880–1922* (Urbana and Chicago: University of Illinois Press, 1981).

2. John Sayles, *Thinking in Pictures: The Making of the Movie* Matewan (Boston: Houghton Mifflin Company, 1987), pp. 4–5. This book includes the full script for Matewan as well, which is numbered separately from the first half of the book where Sayles discusses why and how he made the film. When I quote from the script below, I will indicate this different pagination.

3. Corbin, *Life, Work, and Rebellion*, p. 202.

4. Sayles, *Thinking in Pictures*, p. 11. This chapter draws from the published thoughts of a filmmaker about a film more than others in this book. Still, as I stated in earlier chapters, I realize that there are good reasons not to appeal to the author's intentions in the interpretation of a text, especially in a film. Again, though, my critical reading of this film does not depend on my understanding of Sayles's intentions in making the film. The view I am assuming in this book is that such testimony, especially by a strong auteur director, can count as confirming evidence for an interpretation, though it is not sufficient to make that interpretation right or even plausible.

5. Ernesto Laclau and Chantal Mouffe, *Hegemony and Socialist Strategy: Towards a Radical Democratic Politics* (London: Verso, 1985). For those interested, Laclau and Mouffe have since published several monographs and anthologies that further clarify their views, including one that Laclau edited, *The Making of Political Identities* (London: Verso, 1994), and his *Emancipation(S)* (London: Verso, 1996); *New Reflections on the Revolution of Our Time* (London: Verso, 1997); *The Populist Reason* (London: Verso, forthcoming); and Mouffe, ed., *Dimensions of Radical Democracy: Pluralism, Citizenship, Community* (London: Verso, 1996); as well as her *The Return of the Political* (London: Verso, 1996); *The Challenge of Carl Schmitt* (London: Verso, 1999); and *The Democratic Paradox* (London: Verso, 2000). Together they also wrote a second edition of *Hegemony and Socialist Strategy* (London: Verso, 2001). Also see Anna Marie Smith, Laclau, and Mouffe: *The Radical Democratic Imaginary* (London: Routledge, 1998). Those steeped in this literature should note that my mention of this work is not meant to even approach a full critique or assessment of it. I leave that up to others.

6. See Ellen Meiksins Wood, *The Retreat from Class: The New "True" Socialism* (London: Verso, 1999, reprint from 1986 ed.), and especially Norman Geras, *Discourses of Extremity: Radical Ethics and Post-Marxist Extravagances* (London: Verso, 1990), for the full versions of these arguments and many others directed at the post-Marxists. I am not endorsing these critiques here, though I am very sympathetic to them, especially those offered by Geras. Again, interested readers should dive into these debates and see what they find for themselves.

7. For a good overview of the field of environmental ethics and selections of many of the important papers in the field thus far, see Andrew Light and Holmes Rolston III, eds., *Environmental Ethics: An Anthology* (Malden, Mass.: Blackwell, 2002). This book includes a short section on "environmental prag-

matism" with contributions by Bob Manning, Ben Minteer, and Anthony Weston, as well as several other essays in which Norton and I apply a pragmatist view in environmental ethics to both theoretical and practical issues in philosophy and policy.

8. The central reason that I reject the focus in environmental ethics on finding a nonhuman-centered value of nature is that, even if philosophically successful, the terms of such a theory of value would have little to do with the arenas of environmental policy and politics, which are oriented toward human understandings of the value of nature. For more detail on this position, see Andrew Light, "Contemporary Environmental Ethics: From Metaethics to Public Philosophy," *Metaphilosophy* 33, no. 4 (2002), pp. 426–449.

9. Bryan Norton, "Why I Am Not a Nonanthropocentrist," *Environmental Ethics* 17, no. 4 (1995), p. 344.

10. See Andrew Light, "Taking Environmental Ethics Public," in David Schmidtz and Elizabeth Willott, eds., *Environmental Ethics: What Really Matters? What Really Works?* (Oxford: Oxford University Press, 2002), pp. 556–566.

11. I realize that some may now wish to accuse me of doing an applied philosophy of film throughout this book—taking philosophical debates and distinctions and then applying them from the top to interpret films. It's a fair criticism. But first, I would want to know what the practical warrant is in the case of a philosophy of film (though I must admit that some would want to say that I'm really doing social philosophy here instead), and second, I would respond that it actually is the case that I got the idea for a number of these chapters first by watching a film and then by going back and thinking about what philosophical issues were stimulated for me by the film.

12. See Douglas Kellner's reading of Slacker in *Media Culture: Cultural Studies, Identity and Politics Between the Modern and the Postmodern* (New York: Routledge, 1995), especially pp. 139–143. Kellner was keen to point out the media and cultural politics at work in the film, noting, for example, the scene where a young black man sells "Free Mandela" T-shirts and pamphlets while giving a political rap "delivered from media clichés." Since there is ample evidence in the film for how the slackers subvert traditional media, we can read into this scene and others a subversion of the relationship between political identity and media. I will discuss *Media Culture* in more detail in the next chapter.

13. Ibid.

14. Kellner claimed that one of the students is reading Hal Foster's collection on postmodern culture, The *Anti-Aesthetic*. After watching the scene several times, however, I could not identify the titles of any of the books on the students' table.

15. We may question, though, the complicated relationship that the film may have with older socialist texts. Kellner pointed out, for example, that the closing sequence of the film contains clear intertextual references to Godard's *One Plus One*. Kellner, Media Culture, p. 141.

16. For an excellent history of the life and death of the IWW, see Michael Dubofsky, *We Shall Be All: A History of the IWW* (New York: Quadrangle Books, 1969). It is well known that many members of overtly socialist, communist, and anarcho-syndicalist organizations turned to labor organizing between the world wars in the United States and largely abandoned their independent political activities. See Stanley Aronowitz, "Remaking the American Left. Part One: Currents in American Radicalism," *Socialist Review* 13, no. 1 (January-February 1983), p. 11.

17. See, for example, Ronald Takaki, *Iron Cages* (Oxford: Oxford University Press, 1988), especially chapters 4 and 9.

18. See David Roediger, *The Wages of Whiteness: Race and the Making of the American Working Class* (London: Verso, 1992).

19. Sayles, *Thinking in Pictures*, p. 34 (of script). Emphasis in original in all quotations from the script.

20. Ibid., p. 35 (of script).

21. Ibid., p. 33 (of script).

22. Sayles used an early synopsis of what would become the screenplay for *Matewan* in his novel *Union Dues* (New York: HarperCollins, 1977), pp. 209–218. The story is told by an adolescent from West Virginia one evening during a party at a socialist-feminist collective in Boston in the early 1970s. In the novel it seems clear that the purpose of the story is to help to establish some sort of link between the Old Left and the New Left. But notably, when the story is told in the novel, there is absolutely no mention of the racial and ethnic themes that eventually play such an important role in the later film. So, we know that this particular story could be told without the racial elements.

23. Sayles, *Thinking in Pictures*, p. 35 (of script).

24. We can see these themes most clearly in films like *Passion Fish*, and *City of Hope*, as well as in the novels *Pride of the Bimbos* and *Los Gusanos*.

25. That the story of *Matewan* is not supposed to be locked in the past is fairly clear from its portrayal in *Union Dues*, as mentioned in note 22 of this chapter. Sayles also uses a voice-over in the film of an old man, named "Pappy," whom we never see, but he turns out to be someone who, as we later learn, was a young man at the time of the events and has taken the lessons of Kenehan with him to the end of his life (the character, Danny Radner, is played by Will Oldham). As with Ken Loach's explicitly political films, we are encouraged to take lessons from the past and apply them to the present. Loach encourages this view in *Land and*

Freedom by using the narrative device of a granddaughter discovering her grand-father's letters and clippings from his service in the international brigades to tell a story about the Spanish Civil War. Loach also encourages us to understand situations in the present through the lens of the past (as in his 2000 film *Bread and Roses*).

26. Sayles, *Thinking in Pictures*, p. 86.

Chapter 6

1. There are many possible titles to cite in this literature. As with all the chapters in this book, however, it is not my intention here to provide a thorough overview of the areas of philosophy under discussion. A good summary, though, of the rise of identity politics in the U.S. Left can be found in Stanley Aronowitz, "The Situation of the Left in the United States," *Socialist Review* 23, no. 3 (1994), pp. 5–79. One of the most important titles by a philosopher in this area is Iris Marion Young, *Justice and the Politics of Difference* (Princeton: Princeton University Press, 1990).

2. See, for example, Cornel West, *Race Matters* (New York: Vintage Books, 1994); Joan Tronto, *Moral Boundaries: A Political Argument for an Ethic of Care* (New York: Routledge, 1993); and Will Kymlicka, *Liberalism, Community and Culture* (Oxford: Oxford University Press, 1991). There are many more recent titles in this vein by these authors and others, but these particular books were very influential during the heyday of this literature.

3. These papers include the two mentioned in the Acknowledgments as foundations of this chapter, Andrew Light, "Media, Identity, and Politics: A Critique of Kellner," *Research in Philosophy and Technology* 17 (1998), pp. 187–200, and "What Is an Ecological Identity?" *Environmental Politics* 9, no. 4 (2000), pp. 59–81. These papers are joined principally by Andrew Light and William Chaloupka, "Angry White Men: Right Nationalism and Left Identity Politics," in Tamar Mayer, ed., *Gender Ironies of Nationalism: Sexing the Nation* (London: Routledge, 1999), pp. 329–350, and Andrew Light, "What Is a Pragmatic Philosophy?" *Journal of Speculative Philosophy*, forthcoming, which is a critique of Iris Young's *Intersecting Voices: Dilemmas of Gender, Political Philosophy and Policy* (Princeton: Princeton University Press, 1997).

4. See Andrew Light, "Restoring Ecological Citizenship," in Ben Minteer and Bob Pepperman Taylor, eds., *Democracy and the Claims of Nature* (Lanham, Md.: Rowman & Littlefield, 2002), pp. 153–172, and Andrew Light, "Urban Ecological Citizenship," *Journal of Social Philosophy*, forthcoming.

5. Perhaps the most famous exchange on such worries to make its way into the popular media was Martha Nussbaum's critique of Judith Butler in "The Professor of Parody: The Hip Defeatism of Judith Butler," *The New Republic*, February 22, 1999, pp. 37–45. Nussbaum's criticisms were aimed at what she took

to be the disastrous influence that Butler's work was having on feminism, especially because it prioritized abstract and arcane theory over concern for practical issues (such as Nussbaum's own work on women and development). The piece by Nussbaum garnered a firestorm of protest from other feminists, bringing strong letters in defense of Butler from Gayatri Spivak, Seyla Benhabib, Nancy Fraser, Linda Nicholson, Joan Scott, Drucilla Cornell, and Sara Murphy, published as "Martha C. Nussbaum and Her Critics: An Exchange," *The New Republic*, April 19, 1999, pp. 43–45. I'm sure that some would want to correct me on the characterization of Butler's work as part of the literature on "identity politics," though I think that broadly speaking it is at least inclusive of that literature, and has certainly been very influential on it.

6. A counterexample could be a person who thought of herself as a feminist (to choose just one political identity) but then went on to do nothing based on that feminism. Let's say she simply went off to the top of a mountain and meditated on the nature of the universe for the rest of her life, never again seeing or speaking to another human. Two answers to such a case: (1) If a feminist were to isolate herself in that way, then she could reasonably be described as a bad feminist, insofar as one could make the claim that embracing a political identity such as feminism entails the necessity of even minimally supporting the improvement of the equality of women; and (2) If this objection fails, or if one could not make an argument that a feminist actually would of necessity be something like an active feminist, then the counterexample still does not disprove the basic point about the constitutive profiles of political identities like this one and their link to moral or political motivation. The reason is that the absence of having any motivation to examine the object of one's identity concerns does not mean that if such an agent were to act, we could not use their identity position in part to explain why they acted as they did.

7. See Aronowitz, "The Situation of the Left in the United States," and his earlier "Remaking the American Left. Part One: Currents in American Radicalism," *Socialist Review* 13, no. 1 (1983), pp. 9–51.

8. See Catriona Sandilands, "From Natural Identity to Radical Democracy," *Environmental Ethics* 17, no. 1 (1995), pp. 75–91. Sandilands argued that an ecological identity should embrace the radical democratic theory of the new social movements as expressed by Laclau and Mouffe (referenced in chapter 5). For an update of her argument, see Sandilands, *The Good-Natured Feminist: Ecofeminism and the Quest for Democracy* (Minneapolis: University of Minnesota Press, 1999).

9. In my paper "What Is an Ecological Identity?" I more fully fleshed out this claim by looking at Iris Young's description of environmentalism as a kind of identity politics in *Justice and the Politics of Difference* (especially p. 83). I find this discussion illuminating but still incomplete. Young made an excellent point there that environmentalism can best be thought of as a position opposing the power

of the consumer culture. She wanted to distinguish such a position from a movement like feminism, which is for her a more robust "cultural identity." But opposition to consumer culture can be a cultural stance, so the question is again begged whether environmentalism is a political identity like feminism.

10. For example, as Bill Devall and George Sessions have suggested, "Most people in Deep Ecology have had the feelings—usually, but not always in nature—that they are connected with something greater than their ego, greater than their home, their family, their special attributions as an individual—a feeling that is often called oceanic because many have it on the ocean. Without that identification, one is not easily drawn to become involved in Deep Ecology." Bill Devall and George Sessions, *Deep Ecology: Living As If Nature Mattered* (Salt Lake City: Peregrine Smith Books, 1985), p. 76. Anyone wanting to learn more about deep ecology should start with Arne Naess, *Ecology, Community and Lifestyle*, translated by David Rothenberg (Cambridge: Cambridge University Press, 1989). For critical discussions of deep ecology, see the essays in Eric Katz, Andrew Light, and David Rothenberg, eds., *Beneath the Surface: Critical Essays in the Philosophy of Deep Ecology* (Cambridge, Mass.: MIT Press, 2000).

11. A sympathetic summary of the basis for some of these views by both deep ecologists and ecofeminists can be found in Sandilands, "From Natural Identity to Radical Democracy." More detail on essentialist, or as she put it, "classical" ecofeminist arguments is available in Judy Evans, "Ecofeminism and the Politics of the Gendered Self," in Andrew Dobson and Paul Lucardie, eds., *The Politics of Nature: Explorations in Green Political Theory* (London: Routledge, 1995), pp. 177–189.

12. See Andrew Light, "What Is an Ecological Identity?" section 2, "Defending a Detached Ecological Identity," for some arguments against deep ecology and essentialist ecofeminism.

13. More detail on the argument for why an identity politics must be embraced is offered in Andrew Light and William Chaloupka, "Angry White Men."

14. So, too, those who can hold an attached identity may easily reject it. Just as all women are not necessarily feminists (nor are all women who would endorse one or another of a range of feminist political issues necessarily feminists, nor do all feminists conceive of their feminism as an identity politics), all environmentalists are not by definition holders of an ecological identity. And although I find the position incoherent for reasons discussed in "What Is an Ecological Identity?" it is certainly possible for some environmentalists to insist that they are "closer to the Earth" than the rest of us and so hold an attached ecological identity. Identities are chosen, as suggested above, so all of these different combinations are possible. Additionally, as one might expect, we can be certain that this detached-attached distinction exists on a continuum. It is plausible that new information (e.g., empirical psychological studies) could change our views of whether

an identity is attached or detached, and given a more careful analysis, we might see different identities as constituted somewhere in between. Several readers of this original distinction pointed out that this could be the case with the politics of sexual orientation. This point seems reasonable to me and not a challenge to my distinction.

15. One criticism of the attached-detached distinction offered by one of the original reviewers of "What Is an Ecological Identity?" was that it emptied identity politics (and on my account, most ecological identities) of any particular meaning. As I have described it, one could argue that a detached identity is so thin that it does not really refer to anything. In the original paper (toward the end of section one), I offered a more thorough answer to this criticism, but given the way I have set up the issues here, it doesn't really matter that much. I'm not actually claiming that my description of attached or detached identities adequately captures the categories of a formal identity politics, but merely that it provides a good way to understand a more general politics of personal identity. I do think this distinction is helpful for understanding a more robust sense of identity politics, although those interested in this issue should look to the original paper. In general, I think that such a criticism can only be maintained if one is willing to import into a description of identity politics a view that it can only be explained as evidence of a strong psychological drive to politicize something about one's self, or by some other reasoning that would build in an essential component of ontological attachment to any conceivable political identity. This would either make identity politics very limiting as a phenomenon, or give more credence to the distinction I am using in this chapter between identity politics and a politics of identity.

16. Douglas Kellner, *Media Culture: Cultural Studies, Identity and Politics Between the Modern and the Postmodern* (New York: Routledge, 1995). For background to this work, see Kellner's two previous books on television, *Television and the Crisis of Democracy* (Boulder, Colo.: Westview Press, 1990), and *The Persian Gulf TV War* (Boulder, Colo.: Westview Press, 1992), as well as a book he coauthored with Michael Ryan on film, *Camera Politica: The Politics and Ideology of Contemporary Hollywood Film* (Bloomington: Indiana University Press, 1990).

17. See, for example, Steven Best and Douglas Kellner, *Postmodern Theory* (New York: Guilford Press, 1991), and *The Postmodern Adventure* (New York: Guilford Press, 2001).

18. Douglas Kellner, *Media Culture*, p. 40.

19. Ibid., p. 41.

20. Another point that Kellner made is that identity politics can become fragmentary when one single determinant of identity is fetishized over others. He is certainly right. Though I have intentionally set aside the issue of mixed identities, I did not intend to discourage those investing in a politics of identity from em-

bracing multiple identities. It seems reasonable that most people would, and that identifying with multiple groups is a good way, as Kellner put it, to encourage coalitions among more discernible groups.

21. Kellner's disagreements with my original reading of *Media Culture* (previously published as "Media, Identity and Politics: A Critique of Kellner") are published as "Media Culture, Social Theory, and Cultural Studies," *Research in Philosophy and Technology* 17 (1998), especially pp. 210–214. There (on p. 210), Kellner made a point of stating that he does not reject all identity politics as such, by which he meant the more modest politics of identity that I have distinguished in this chapter. But the problem is that in his particular criticisms of Spike Lee, Kellner still conflated what I take to be a representation of a politics of identity with a representation of a fragmentary identity politics. Therefore, we need to look at the particular examples that Kellner employed in his criticisms of Lee to settle the issue of which kind of politics of identity is endorsed by Lee. I do this below. As I have stated, though, I do not dispute the claim that a culturalist, fragmentary identity politics is something to be avoided and that should be criticized. In a few notes that follow I will point out where Kellner disagreed with specific arguments I made in my original piece, which I am retaining for this chapter, and offer some replies to those responses. I have intentionally dropped the last section of that original paper, in part because I no longer wish to defend the particular criticisms offered there about Kellner's positive project in *Media Culture* advocating a democratic media.

22. Kellner, *Media Culture*, p. 173.

23. Ibid., p. 172.

24. Ibid., p. 173.

25. Ibid., p. 162.

26. Ibid., p. 161.

27. This is not the only problem with the misrepresentation of identities, to be sure, though it is the one I will focus on here. More simply, representations of identities can be offensive and crude, even if their point is to be funny. Kellner, interestingly, argued that this is part of what he found objectionable in Lee's work: "I have indeed become increasingly disturbed by the derogatory representations of Jews, Hispanics, gays and other social groups in Lee's films which often deploy prejudicial stereotypes for cheap laughs; the depictions of Jews in *'Mo Better Blues* was sharply criticized and I found the representation of Jews, Hispanics, and gays extremely disturbing in *Crooklyn*." Kellner, "Media Culture, Social Theory, and Cultural Studies," p. 213. I do not wish to dispute Kellner's protestations against Lee's representations of these groups here. I think he has a point, though I do think (and I'm sure Kellner would agree) that parody is not always offensive. My favorite example in this regard is Christopher Best's *Waiting*

for Guffman (1996), which, as Guest's homosexual friend once remarked to me, is brilliant despite having "very questionable gay politics." Anecdotally, many other gay friends also told me how much they liked this film, though of course the fact that any of them are gay does not excuse what other complaints some may justifiably have of this film. At minimum, though, those holding this identity, and those who do not, can have a healthy disagreement about this film as it is not easily described as offering an offensive representation of gay men. But the more important point I wish to make on Kellner's specific critique of Lee just cited is that even if we could criticize Lee for bad representations of any identity group, for whatever reason, this does not necessarily mean that we couldn't praise him for the good and complex representations he offers of other groups. The only question would be whether the positive portrayals depended on the bad ones. I don't think that they do in this case, but if Kellner or someone else can or has demonstrated this point then it would be a valid criticism that I would have to be prepared to answer.

28. In his earlier exchange with me on this film, Kellner did indeed admit to the political importance of Lee's status as a black filmmaker in this regard. Ibid., p. 212.

29. Though I will not go into detail here, I think a strong case can be made that the characters played by Ruby Dee and Ossie Davis in *Do the Right Thing* embody the historical dimension of this conversation in the community. Particular scenes would have to be analyzed to make this point salient, such as the reaction of Dee's character during the riot when firefighters, trying to put out the blaze at the pizzeria, turn their hoses on the black community who are outraged over the death of Radio Raheem, who was killed by the police during the riot. The image is startling and a clear reference to the images of fire hoses being turned on civil-rights demonstrators in Alabama, which Dee's character no doubt would have seen, if not experienced directly.

30. For excellent arguments on the metaphysics of race, see Charles Mills, *The Racial Contract* (Ithaca, N.Y.: Cornell University Press, 1999), and Lawrence Blum, *"I'm Not a Racist, But . . . "*: The Moral Quandary of Race (Ithaca, N.Y.: Cornell University Press, 2001).

31. Kellner said in response to my original claim in this regard: "And while I agree with Light that we should allow [this deference] . . . I think it is appropriate to have critical dialogue about those grounds." Kellner, "Media Culture, Social Theory, and Cultural Studies," p. 213. I believe my "process-product" distinction, however, mitigates this reply. It is certainly fine to have a critical dialogue with other identity groups, especially when the representation of the historical process of identity negotiation takes the form of a publicly consumable piece of mass art like a popular film. But I still think that the point about respecting the

process goes some way toward not sweating the consumer references in Lee's films so long as we have good reason to believe that a good process is being encouraged in the representation. Note, however, that I am not arguing that what Kellner was doing in criticizing Lee was ethically wrong in any sense—he can criticize whomever he wants—but that it is more charitable to refrain from such criticisms in some cases.

32. I've not been able to find any such prior film to explain the origins of Jack Taggart, so he remains a mystery. Seagal did make an earlier film, *On Deadly Ground* (1994) where he plays Forrest Taft, a disgruntled employee of an oil company in Alaska who is chosen by an Eskimo chief as the savior of his people. Seagal's mission in this case was to prevent a new oil refinery from going online before the land rights were returned to the Eskimos. Since Seagal actually directed this film, and coproduced *Fire Down Below*, I imagine that he must have personal environmental commitments himself that have played some role in his participation in and support of these projects. One could argue that *On Deadly Ground* offers a more coherent explanation for Seagal's identity as an environmentalist, but unfortunately it is tied in this case to an occult connection with the Eskimos as a kind of transferred attached identity. We are left with the question then of whether Forrest Taft would have gotten involved in this fight if it were not for his spiritual adoption by Native Americans, stereotypically played here as necessarily having a closer connection to the Earth than white folks.

33. The view expressed here of obligations to future generations is strikingly similar to that advocated by Avner de-Shalit in his *Why Posterity Matters: Environmental Policies and Future Generations* (London: Routledge, 1995): We should care about the future in part because we exist in a community that extends into the future and we care about how those in the future will perceive us.

34. See my "Contemporary Environmental Ethics: From Metaethics to Public Philosophy," *Metaphilosophy* 33, no. 4 (2002), pp. 426–449. In the second section of this paper I explicitly critiqued the dominant view in environmental ethics (summarized in chapter 5), which would focus on the value of the Brazilian rainforest in and of itself rather than recognizing the important value of the forest to the people actually living there. In this paper Mendes is used as my principal example of a figure who was sufficiently motivated to protect the forest primarily for reasons that are considered insufficient as grounds for environmental protection by most environmental ethicists. While I will not go into detail on the matter here, too many environmental ethicists, and some environmentalists, take the position that we should not make human-centered arguments about preservation of the environment. For more background on this problem, see my "The Case for a Practical Pluralism," in Andrew Light and Holmes Rolston III, eds., *Environmental Ethics: An Anthology* (Malden, Mass.: Blackwell, 2002).

35. One thing I didn't like in *The Burning Season* was the portrayal of the lead cattleman as almost uniformly bad. Even assuming it was the cattlemen who ac-

tually killed Mendes (we are told in the film that the family assumed responsible for Mendes's murder fled the area, thus implying their guilt), we never really see them as human. They are more the dupes of the land clearing company, easily bribed by prostitutes and liquor. Although certainly this characterization is not as bad as the portrayal of Kris Kristofferson in *Fire Down Below*, they are still extraordinarily underdeveloped.

36. See Andrew Light, "Taking Environmental Ethics Pubic," in David Schmidtz and Elizabeth Willott, eds., *Environmental Ethics: What Really Matters? What Really Works?* (Oxford: Oxford University Press, 2002), pp. 556–566.

Index